The
Reference Shelf®

Representative American Speeches
2023–2024

The Reference Shelf
Volume 96 • Number 6
H.W. Wilson
a division of EBSCO Information Services, Inc.

Published by
GREY HOUSE PUBLISHING
Amenia, New York
2024

The Reference Shelf

Cover photo: Getty Images/Andrew Harnik

The Reference Shelf: Representative American Speeches 2023–2024, published by Grey House Publishing, Inc., Amenia, NY, under exclusive license from EBSCO Information Services, Inc.

The books in this series contain reprints of articles, excerpts from books, addresses on current issues, and studies of social trends in the United States and other countries. There are six separately bound numbers in each volume, all of which are usually published in the same calendar year. Numbers one through five are each devoted to a single subject, providing background information and discussion from various points of view and concluding with an index and comprehensive bibliography that lists books, pamphlets, and articles on the subject. The final number of each volume is a collection of recent speeches. Books in the series may be purchased individually or on subscription.

Copyright © 2024 by Grey House Publishing, Inc. All rights reserved. No part of this work may be used or reproduced in any manner whatsoever or transmitted in any form or by any means, electronic or mechanical, including photocopying, recording, or any information storage and retrieval system, without written permission from the copyright owner. For subscription information and permissions requests, contact Grey House Publishing, 4919 Route 22, PO Box 56, Amenia, NY 12501.

∞ The paper used in these volumes conforms to the American National Standard for Permanence of Paper for Printed Library Materials, Z39.48 1992 (R2009).

Publisher's Cataloging-in-Publication Data
(Prepared by The Donohue Group, Inc.)

Names: Grey House Publishing, Inc., publisher.
Title: Representative American speeches.
Other Titles: Representative American speeches (2015)
Description: Amenia, N.Y. : Grey House Publishing, 2015- | Series: The reference shelf / H.W. Wilson
Identifiers: ISSN 2639-9016 | ISBN 9781637008997 (v. 96, no. 6) | ISBN 9781637008935 (volume set)
Subjects: LCSH: Speeches, addresses, etc., American—21st century—Periodicals. | LCGFT: Speeches. | Serial publications.
Classification: LCC PS668 .B3 | DDC 815—dc23

Printed in Canada

Contents

Preface   ix

1

The Democratic Campaign

The Best Way Forward Is to Pass the Torch to a New Generation   3
Joe Biden

Reproductive Freedom Is on the Ballot: We Trust Women to Know What
Is in Their Own Best Interests   7
Kamala Harris

Remarks during the Nationwide "Fight for Reproductive Freedoms" Tour   11
Kamala Harris and Sarah Traxler

Acceptance Speech for President   18
Kamala Harris

Acceptance Speech for Vice President   26
Tim Walz

Hope Is Making a Comeback   30
Michelle Obama

It's Up to All of Us to Fight for the America We Believe In   35
Barack Obama

I See a Leader with a Real Commitment to Working Families   42
Alexandria Ocasio-Cortez

Values and Character Matter Most of All in Leadership and in Life   44
Oprah Winfrey

Democracy Must Be Preserved   47
Joe Biden

2

The Republican Campaign

Acceptance Speech for President   59
Donald Trump

Address at the National Rifle Association's Annual Meeting   80
Donald Trump

vi Contents

Hulk Hogan Says Donald Trump Is the Toughest of Them All 93
Terry Bollea

We Must Elect Leaders Who Will Preserve the Bill of Rights 96
Robert F. Kennedy Jr.

Elect Trump President Again and America Will Be Unstoppable 106
Matt Gaetz

Presidential Candidate Suspends His Campaign and Endorses
Donald Trump 108
Robert F. Kennedy Jr.

Vice Presidential Nominee's Remarks on the Economy, Inflation,
and Manufacturing 120
J.D. Vance

3

U.S. Issues

Texas Governor Speaks to Republican Governors at the US-Mexico Border 129
Greg Abbott

Former President Speaks at the Southern Border 138
Donald Trump

President Unveils New Border Plans 148
Joe Biden

Remarks on the CHIPS and Science Act 151
Joe Biden

Remarks on the Third Anniversary of the January 6th Attack and on
Defending the Sacred Cause of American Democracy 157
Joe Biden

When Labor Unions Are Strong, America Is Strong 165
Kamala Harris

4

International Issues

An Update on the Crisis in the Middle East 171
Joe Biden

Contents **vii**

Remarks Following a Meeting with Prime Minister Benjamin
Netanyahu of Israel 175
Kamala Harris

We Must Summon the Courage to Stand Up to Wealth and Power
and Deliver Justice for People at Home and Abroad 178
Bernie Sanders

Address to the United Nations: On the Cusp of an Historic Saudi-
Israel Peace 181
Benjamin Netanyahu

Speech to the European Parliament on the Houthi Attacks in the
Red Sea 188
Josep Borrell

NATO Secretary Warns China That It Must Stop Financially
Supporting Russia's Invasion of Ukraine 191
Jens Stoltenberg

Statement on Russia's Aerial Assault on Ukraine's Energy Grid 195
Joe Biden

Address on Attempted Assassination of Trump: We Cannot Go
Down This Road 197
Joe Biden

5

2024 Commencement Speeches

Commencement Speech to the Morehouse College Class of 2024 203
Joe Biden

What "Follow Your Dreams" Misses 210
Grant Sanderson

Our World Is on Fire: Welcome to the Battlefield 217
Maria Ressa

I Cannot Wait to See How You Will Harness the Power of Love 223
John Legend

Index 233

Preface

Election Years and Electoral Fears

In 2024, President Joe Biden, despite a strong record in a number of key areas, including economic growth and a successful recovery from COVID-19 destabilization, chose not to seek reelection, instead passing the torch to his vice president Kamala Harris, who became the second woman in history to win the nomination of one of the major parties. This historic development shook up the political field on both sides of the aisle and set up a historic race that would either see the United States elect their first female president or would see the return of traditionalist conservativism under Trump. With the election looming, much of the attention was shifted onto Kamala Harris's campaign and efforts to credit or discredit her featured prominently in many of the most impactful speeches of the year, while less attention was placed on the outgoing Biden administration and on Joe Biden's legacy.

Deciding to voluntarily surrender power places Biden in the company of a very small number of men who decided the same in the past. Some of the former presidents who chose not to seek reelection did so to preserve what they had accomplished, or because they had only planned to serve a single term, and others, perhaps, to hide from their failures.

James K. Polk was one of the former and is often considered one of the most successful presidents of all time, despite his single term. Polk was a surprise "dark horse" candidate for the office and not expected to win, but he won by popular demand. In his single term he accomplished feats that, for better or worse, redefined the boundaries and nature of America. During this fractious time, when the Civil War was looming, it was popular for many candidates to promise to hold only a single term in office, essentially relieving voters by saying "If I don't do well, you can replace me sooner rather than later." Polk was popular and likely would have won a second term, but he promised he would only serve one term and he kept his word, becoming the first incumbent president to refuse to campaign for a second term. This decision likely spared Polk his legacy, as the years that followed saw Civil War tensions growing ever more intense.[1]

James Buchanan also, like Polk, promised to serve only a single term, but, unlike Polk, was so unpopular that it was virtually guaranteed he would have lost if he had run. Ranked as one of the worst presidents in history, stepping away from the race was a way for Buchanan to cut his losses. He virtually ran from the White House before he would be blamed for the Civil War, which was by this time inevitable. His departure did not spare him the shame of his failed presidency. Rutherford Hayes entered the White House in 1877 in controversy, having failed to win the popular vote and he, like Polk, also pledged to serve only a single term and followed through by declining the nomination, though it is likely he would have been easily defeated had he chosen to run.

The next man to decline a second term was, more like Polk, seen as highly successful. Calvin Coolidge entered office to finish the term of Warren Harding, after Harding's unexpected death. He nonetheless won the 1925 election by a wide margin and served during a time of what was, for white Americans, relative prosperity. Coolidge did very little, but he was extremely well liked and seemed to avoid major mistakes. It is believed that he would've coasted to an easy reelection if he'd chosen to do so, but instead he chose to step away, simply stating, "I do not choose to run for reelection in 1928." The decision was a shock to many and it is even rumored that he had not even discussed the issue at any length with his own wife. A man of few words, Coolidge never saw fit to explain the decision much further than that and it was only in his autobiography that he shed some light on the matter stating that he had never been comfortable with power or fame and had been more than ready to be "relieved of the pretentions and delusions of public life."[2]

Harry S. Truman chose to step away more in disgrace than triumph, though his presidency was not generally considered a failure and his legacy on some issues was preserved. Truman served during a difficult time and the transformations of the nation and a turn of opinion on the Democratic Party. The next president to voluntarily step away from the office was Lyndon Baines Johnson, another president who came to power at first only through the assassination of John F. Kennedy. Despite this start and lack of popular mandate, Johnson accomplished more than most presidents can in two terms with his single turn in the office. Much of the legislation that was passed under Johnson dealt with protecting natural resources, with significant achievements in the realm of air quality, water, and the preservation of wilderness. His administration oversaw a significant increase in funding to education and the establishment of the Medicare and Medicaid programs that made a major impact on the lives of Americans living with various challenges. In many ways, the Johnson years saw major progressive achievements in many areas, including federal support for the arts, the environment, poverty reduction and, perhaps most importantly, racial justice. This made him an enemy of the conservative elite and the corporate leaders whose interests they serve. In their campaign against him, conservatives enflamed the racial fears of white voters, claiming that Johnson only served the interest of minorities, and they intensified economic fears by propagandizing Johnson's "Great Society" program as a tax burden. Meanwhile, Johnson's effort to avoid a losing quagmire in Vietnam brought him the ire of the political left.

On March 31, 1968, facing division from both sides, Johnson announced that he would leave the office behind:

> Throughout my entire public career I have followed the personal philosophy that I am a free man, an American, a public servant, and a member of my party, in that order always and only.

Works Used

Greenberg, David. "Calvin Coolidge: Life After the Presidency." *UVA Miller Center*, millercenter.org/president/coolidge/life-after-the-presidency.

Johnson, Lyndon B. "The President's Address to the Nation Announcing Steps to Limit the War in Vietnam and Reporting His Decision Not to Seek Reelection." *The American Presidency Project*, Mar. 31, 1968, www.presidency.ucsb.edu/documents/the-presidents-address-the-nation-announcing-steps-limit-the-war-vietnam-and-reporting-his.

Zeitz, Joshua. "The President Who Did It All in One Term—and What Biden Could Learn from Him." *Politico*, Dec. 2, 2022, www.politico.com/news/magazine/2022/12/02/biden-president-james-k-polk-reelection-00071709.

Notes

1. Zeitz, "The President Who Did It All in One Term-and What Biden Could Learn from Him."
2. Greenberg, "Calvin Coolidge: Life After the Presidency."
3. Johnson, "The President's Address to the Nation Announcing Steps to Limit the War in Vietnam and Reporting His Decision Not to Seek Reelection."

1
The Democratic Campaign

An August 2024 campaign rally in Arizona for Kamala Harris and Tim Walz. Photo by Gage Skidmore, CC BY-SA 2.0, via Wikimedia.

The Best Way Forward Is to Pass the Torch to a New Generation

By Joe Biden

"I revere this office, but I love my country more." President Joe Biden, in a historic act, stepped down from his candidacy as the incumbent Democratic Party nominee for the presidency. Elected in 2020 in a decisive victory marred by misinformation and false claims, Biden withdrew from the race over questions about his age and capability to serve another term. In this speech he highlighted his successes in addressing the pandemic, inflation, and instituting infrastructure reform.

My fellow Americans, I'm speaking to you tonight from behind the Resolute Desk in the Oval Office.

In this sacred space, I'm surrounded by portraits of extraordinary American presidents. Thomas Jefferson, who wrote the immortal words that guide this nation. George Washington, who showed us presidents are not kings. Abraham Lincoln, who implored us to reject malice. Franklin Roosevelt, who inspired us to reject fear.

I revere this office, but I love my country more.

It's been the honor of my life to serve as your president. But in the defense of democracy, which is at stake, I think it's more important than any title.

I draw strength and I find joy in working for the American people. But this sacred task of perfecting our Union—it's not about me. It's about you, your families, your futures. It's about "We the People." We can never forget that, and I never have.

I've made it clear that I believe America is at an inflection point, one of those rare moments in history when the decisions we make now will determine our fate of our nation and the world for decades to come. America is going to have to choose between moving forward or backward, between hope and hate, between unity and division.

We have to decide: Do we still believe in honesty, decency, and respect; freedom, justice, and democracy?

In this moment, we can see those we disagree with not as enemies or—as fellow Americans. Can we do that? Does character in public life still matter?

I believe I know the answer to these questions, because I know you, the American people.

And I know this: We are a great nation because we are a good people.

Delivered on July 24, 2024 at the White House, Washington, DC.

When you elected me to this office, I promised to always level with you, to tell you the truth. And the truth, the sacred cause of this country is larger than any one of us.

And those of us who cheri[sh] that cause—cherish it so much—the cause of American democracy itself—must unite to protect it.

You know, in recent weeks, it's become clear to me that I needed to unite my party in this critical endeavor. I believe my record as president, my leadership in the world, my vision for America's future all merited a second term, but nothing—nothing—can come in the way of saving our democracy. That includes personal ambition.

So, I've decided the best way forward is to pass the torch to a new generation. That's the best way to unite our nation.

I know there is a time and a place for long years of experience in public life. But there is also a time and place for new voices, fresh voices—yes, younger voices. And that time and place is now.

Over the next six months, I'll be focused on doing my job as president. That means I will continue to lower costs for hardworking families, grow our economy. I'll keep defending our personal freedoms and our civil rights, from the right to vote to the right to choose. And I'll keep calling out hate and extremism and make it clear there is no place—no place in America for political violence or any violence ever, period.

I'm going to keep—keep speaking out to protect our kids from gun violence, our planet from the climate crisis. It is the existential threat.

And I will keep fighting my—for my Cancer Moonshot so we can end cancer as we know it, because we can do it.

And I'm going to call for Supreme Court reform because this is critical to our democracy—Supreme Court reform.

You know, I will keep working to ensure America remains strong and secure and the leader of the free world.

I'm the first president in this century to report to the American people that the United States is not at war anywhere in the world.

I will keep rallying a coalition of proud nations to stop Putin from taking over Ukraine and doing more damage.

I will keep NATO stronger, and I'll make it more powerful and more united than any time in all of our history. And I'll keep doing the same for our allies in the Pacific.

You know, when I came to office, the conventional wisdom was that China would inevitably—would inevitably pass the United—surpass the United States. That's not the case anymore.

And I'm going to keep working to end the war in Gaza, bring home all the hostages, and bring peace and security to the Middle East and end this war.

We're also working around the clock to bring home Americans being unjustly detained all around the world.

You know, we have come so far since my inauguration. On that day, I told you as I stood in that winter—we stood in a winter of peril and a winter of possibilities—peril and possibilities.

We were in the grip of the worst pandemic in a century, the worst economic crisis since the Great Depression, the worst attack on our democracy since the Civil War. But we came together as Americans and we got through it.

We emerged stronger, more prosperous, and more secure.

And today, we have the strongest economy in the world, creating nearly 16 million new jobs—a record. Wages are up. Inflation continues to come down. The racial wealth gap is the lowest it's been in 20 years.

We're literally rebuilding our entire nation—urban, suburban, rural, and Tribal communities.

Manufacturing has come back to America. We're leading the world again in chips and science and innovation.

And we finally beat Big Pharma after all these years to lower the cost of prescription drugs for seniors. And I'm going to keep fighting to make sure we lower the costs for everyone, not just seniors.

More people have health care today in America than ever before. And I signed one of the most significant laws helping millions of veterans and their families who were exposed to toxic materials.

You know, the most significant climate law ever—ever in the history of the world. The first major gun safety law in 30 years. And today, the violent crime rate is at a 50-year low.

We're also securing our border. Border crossings are lower today than when the previous administration left office.

And I kept my commitment to appoint the first Black woman to the Supreme Court of the United States of America. I also kept my commitment to have an administration that looks like America and to be a president for all Americans. That's what I've done.

I ran for president four years ago because I believed and still do that the soul of America was at stake. The very nature of who we are was at stake. And that's still the case.

America is an idea—an idea stronger than any army, bigger than any ocean, more powerful than any dictator or tyrant. It's the most powerful idea in the history of the world.

That idea is that we hold these truths to be self-evident. We're all created equal, endowed by our Creator with certain unalienable rights: life, liberty, the pursuit of happiness.

We've never fully lived up to it—to this sacred idea, but we've never walked away from it either. And I do not believe the American people will walk away from it now.

In just a few months, the American people will choose the course of America's future.

I made my choice. I have made my views known.

6 The Democratic Campaign

I would like to thank our great vice president, Kamala Harris. She's experienced. She's tough. She's capable. She has been an incredible partner to me and a leader for our country.

Now the choice is up to you, the American people.

When you make that choice, remember the words of Benjamin Franklin, who's hanging on my wall here in the Oval Office alongside the busts of Dr. King and Rosa Parks and Cesar Chavez.

When Ben Franklin was asked as he emerged from the convention going on whether the Founders had given America a monarchy or a republic, Franklin's response was, "A republic, if you can keep it." "A republic, if you can keep it." Whether we keep our republic is now in your hands.

My fellow Americans, it's been the privilege of my life to serve this nation for over 50 years. Nowhere else on Earth could a kid with a stutter from modest beginnings in Scranton, Pennsylvania, and Claymont, Delaware, one day sit behind the Resolute Desk in the Oval Office as president of the United States. But here I am.

That's what's so special about America. We are a nation of promise and possibilities, of dreamers and doers, of ordinary Americans doing extraordinary things.

I have given my heart and my soul to our nation, like so many others. And I have been blessed a million times in return with the love and support of the American people.

I hope you have some idea how grateful I am to all of you. The great thing about America is here kings and dictators do not rule. The people do.

History is in your hands. The power is in your hands. The idea of America lies in your hands.

We just have to keep faith—keep the faith and remember who we are. We are the United States of America, and there is simply nothing—nothing beyond our capacity when we do it together. So, let's act together, preserve our democracy.

God bless you all. And may God protect our troops.

Thank you.

Print Citations

CMS: Biden, Joe. "The Best Way Forward Is to Pass the Torch." Speech at the White House, Washington, DC, July 24, 2024. In *The Reference Shelf: Representative American Speeches, 2023–2024,* edited by Micah L. Issitt, 3–6. Amenia, NY: Grey House Publishing, 2024.

MLA: Biden, Joe. "The Best Way Forward Is to Pass the Torch." The White House, 24 July 2024, Washington, DC. Speech. *The Reference Shelf: Representative American Speeches, 2023–2024,* edited by Micah L. Issitt, Grey House Publishing, 2024, pp. 3–6.

APA: Biden, J. (2024). The best way forward is to pass the torch [Speech]. The White House, Washington, DC. In Micah L. Issitt (Ed.), *The reference shelf: Representative American speeches, 2023–2024* (pp. 3–6). Grey House Publishing. (Original work published 2024)

Reproductive Freedom Is on the Ballot: We Trust Women to Know What Is in Their Own Best Interests

By Kamala Harris

"This is a fight for freedom—the fundamental freedom to make decisions about one's own body and not have their government tell them what they're supposed to do." Vice President Kamala Harris spoke in Jacksonville, Florida, on the anniversary of the US Supreme Court's Dobbs decision, allowing states to ban all abortion services. Harris discussed the threat to physicians, the threat to patients, and the risk of a Donald Trump presidency to women's rights and reproductive freedoms.

Hi, everyone. Hello. Hello. Good afternoon, everyone. Can we please give it up for Dr. Tien? Where is she?

I had the chance to spend some time with her this afternoon, and I thanked her for her courage and for the work that she and her colleagues are doing at this critical time in our country in the midst of this critical healthcare crisis. She has been an extraordinary leader. So, thank you, Dr. Tien, for all that you are.

And thank you to all the leaders who are with us today—Leader Driskell, Leader Davis, Mayor Deegan—and Democratic State Party Chair Nikki Fried. And a special thank you to all the organizers and advocates and elected leaders who have been on the forefront of this fight for so long.

So, listen, I think we all know this is a fight for freedom. This is a fight for freedom—the fundamental freedom to make decisions about one's own body and not have their government tell them what they're supposed to do.

And as we know, almost two years ago, the highest court in our land—the court of Thurgood and RBG—took a constitutional right that had been recognized from the people of America, from the women of America. And now, in states across our nation, extremists have proposed and passed laws that criminalize doctors, punish women; laws that threaten doctors and nurses with prison time, even for life, simply for providing reproductive care; laws that make no exception for rape or incest, even reviving laws from the 1800s.

Across our nation, we witnessed a full-on assault state by state on reproductive freedom.

And understand who is to blame. Former President Donald Trump did this. Donald Trump handpicked three members of the United States Supreme Court because he intended for them to overturn *Roe*. And as he intended, they did.

Delivered on May 1, 2024 at the Prime F. Osborne III Convention Center, Jacksonville, FL.

The Democratic Campaign

Now, many of you here may recall I served on the Judiciary Committee as a United States senator, and I questioned two of those nominees. To one of them I asked, quote—I will quote myself—"Can you think of any law that give the government the power to make decisions about the male body?" And it will come as no shock to everyone here, he had no good answer. And that day, we all knew what was about to come, and it happened just as Donald Trump intended.

Now, present day, because of Donald Trump, more than 20 states have abortion bans, more than 20 Trump abortion bans. And today, this very day, at the stroke of midnight, another Trump abortion ban went into effect here in Florida. As of this morning, 4 million women in this state woke up with fewer reproductive freedoms than they had last night. This is the new reality under a Trump abortion ban.

Starting this morning, medical professionals like Dr. Tien could be sent to prison for up to five years for providing reproductive care even earlier in pregnancy—reality under a Trump abortion ban.

Starting this morning, women in Florida became subject to an abortion ban so extreme it applies before many women even know they are pregnant—which, by the way, tells us the extremists who wrote this ban either don't know how a woman's body works or they simply don't care.

Trump says he wants to leave abortion up to the states. He says "up to the states."

All right. So, here's how that works out. Today, one in three women of reproductive age live in a state with a Trump abortion ban, many with no exception for rape or incest.

Now, on that topic, as many of you know, I started my career as a prosecutor specializing in crimes against women and children. What many of you may not know is why.

So, when I was in high school, I learned that my best friend was being molested by her stepfather. And I said to her, "Well, you've got to come and live with us." I called my mother, and my mother said, "Of course, she does." And so, she did.

So, the idea that someone who survives a crime of violence to their body, a violation of their body would not have the authority to make a decision about what happens to their body next, that's immoral. That's immoral.

And one does not have to abandon their faith or deeply held beliefs to agree the government should not be telling her what to do.

And let us understand—let us understand the impact of these bans, the horrific reality that women face every single day. Folks, since *Roe* was overturned, I have met women who were refused care during a miscarriage. I met a woman who was turned away from an emergency room, and it was only when she developed sepsis that she received care.

Now, I'm proud to be the first president or vice president in history to visit a reproductive health clinic. But around our country, since that decision came down, clinics have been forced to close. Think about it: Clinics that provide breast cancer screenings, contraceptive care, Paps, lifesaving care.

And I have seen firsthand, then, that this truly is a healthcare crisis. And Donald Trump is the architect.

And, by the way, that is not a fact he hides. In fact, he brags about it. He has said the collection of abortion bans in the state is, quote, "working the way it's supposed to." Just this week, in an interview, he said states have the right to monitor pregnant women to enforce these bans and states have the right to punish pregnant women for seeking out abortion care.

So, Florida, the contrast in this election could not be more clear. Basically, under Donald Trump, it would be fair game for women to be monitored and punished by the government, whereas Joe Biden and I have a different view.

We believe the government should never come between a woman and her doctor. Never.

And as much harm as he has already caused, a second Trump term would be even worse. Donald Trump's friends in the United States Congress are trying to pass a national ban. And understand: A national ban would outlaw abortion in every single state, even in states like New York and California.

And now Trump wants us to believe he will not sign a national ban. Well, I say, enough with the gaslighting. Enough with the gaslighting. Because we all know if Donald Trump gets the chance, he will sign a national abortion ban.

And how do we know? Well, let's take a look at the evidence and follow the facts. Maybe as a former prosecutor, I like to say: We should really look at the evidence and follow the facts.

Okay. Congress tried to pass a national abortion ban in 2017. And the then-President, Trump, endorsed it—2017—and promised to sign it if it got to his desk.

And in that same interview he gave this week, he seemed perfectly fine signing a national ban that would make it illegal to receive IVF treatment.

Well, the great Maya Angelou once said, "When someone tells you who they are, believe them the first time." And Donald Trump has told us who he is.

So, here's what a second Trump term looks like: more bans, more suffering, less freedom. But we are not going to let that happen.

Because, you see, we trust women. We trust women to know what is in their own best interests. And women trust all of us to fight to protect their most fundamental freedoms.

And this November, up and down the ballot, reproductive freedom is on the ballot. And you, the leaders—you, the people, have the power to protect it with your vote.

Donald Trump may think he can take Florida for granted. It is your power that will send Joe Biden and me back to the White House.

And when Congress passes a law that restores the reproductive freedoms of *Roe*, our President, Joe Biden, will sign it. Donald Trump was the president who took away the protections of *Roe*. Joe Biden will be the president who puts the protections of *Roe* back in place.

And it's going to take all of us to get there. And, by the way, momentum—momentum is on our side. Just think about it. Since *Roe* was overturned, every time reproductive freedom has been on the ballot, the people of America voted for freedom.

From Kansas to California to Kentucky, in Michigan, Montana, Vermont, and Ohio, the people of America voted for freedom—and not by little but often by overwhelming margins, proving also that this is not a partisan issue—it's not a partisan issue—and proving that the voice of the people has been heard and will be heard.

So, today, I ask: Florida, are you ready to make your voices heard?

Do we trust women?

Do we believe in reproductive freedom?

Do we believe in the promise of America?

Are we ready to fight for it?

And when we fight, we win.

God bless you and God bless the United States of America. Thank you all.

Print Citations

CMS: Harris, Kamala. "Reproductive Freedom Is on the Ballot: We Trust Women to Know What Is in Their Own Best Interests." Speech at the Prime F. Osborne III Convention Center, Jacksonville, FL, May 1, 2024. In *The Reference Shelf: Representative American Speeches, 2023–2024*, edited by Micah L. Issitt, 7–10. Amenia, NY: Grey House Publishing, 2024.

MLA: Harris, Kamala. "Reproductive Freedom Is on the Ballot: We Trust Women to Know What Is in Their Own Best Interests." The Prime F. Osborne III Convention Center, 1 May 2024, Jacksonville, FL. Speech. *The Reference Shelf: Representative American Speeches, 2023–2024*, edited by Micah L. Issitt, Grey House Publishing, 2024, pp. 7–10.

APA: Harris, K. (2024). Reproductive freedom is on the ballot: We trust women to know what is in their own best interests [Speech]. The Prime F. Osborne III Convention Center, Jacksonville, FL. In Micah L. Issitt (Ed.), *The reference shelf: Representative American speeches, 2023–2024* (pp. 7–10). Grey House Publishing. (Original work published 2024)

Remarks during the Nationwide "Fight for Reproductive Freedoms" Tour

By Kamala Harris and Sarah Traxler

"How dare these elected leaders believe they are in a better position to tell women what they need, to tell women what is in their best interest. We have to be a nation that trusts women." Vice President Kamala Harris spoke at a Planned Parenthood clinic in St. Paul, Minnesota, addressing the ongoing fight for reproductive rights and freedoms, and the many peripheral impacts to women from the loss of clinics and reproductive care facilities around the country.

The Vice President: Good afternoon, everyone. I first want to thank the governor, Tim Walz, for your leadership both for this beautiful state, but nationally you've been a great friend and advisor to the President and me. And thank you for all of that.

Governor Walz: Thank you.

The Vice President: Congresswoman—I mean, just an extraordinary leader. She is strong, she is powerful, she is committed, and always working on behalf of the people of the state. And I thank you, and thank you for traveling with me to be here today.

Representative McCollum: It was an honor.

The Vice President: And, Mayor, thank you, as well. We shared a lot of stories about your leadership. And I know that you have a lot of support here in the city for the work that you have done. Thank you for that.

So, many of you have asked why am I here at this at—this facility, in particular. And I will tell you, it is because, right now in our country, we are facing a very serious health crisis. And the crisis is affecting many, many people in our country, most of whom are, frankly, silently suffering after the United States Supreme Court took a constitutional right that had been recognized from the people of America, from the women of America.

In states around our country, extremists have proposed and passed laws that have denied women access to reproductive healthcare. And the stories abound.

I have heard stories of—and have met with women who had miscarriages in—in toilets. Women who were being denied emergency care because the

---

Delivered on March 14, 2024 at Planned Parenthood, St. Paul, MN.

healthcare providers there, at an emergency room, were afraid that because of the laws in their state, that they could be criminalized, sent to prison for providing healthcare.

So, I'm here at this healthcare clinic to uplift the work that is happening in Minnesota as an example of what true leadership looks like, which is to understand it is only right and fair that people have access to the healthcare they need and that they have access to healthcare in an environment where they are treated with dignity and respect.

And please do understand that when we talk about a clinic such as this, it is absolutely about healthcare and reproductive healthcare. So, everyone get ready for the language: uterus. That part of the body needs a lot of medical care from time to time. Issues like fibroids—we can handle this—breast cancer screenings, contraceptive care—that is the kind of work that happens here, in addition, of course, to abortion care.

So, to have laws in states that have caused clinics like this to shut down so that women have no access within any reasonable distance of where they live to get this vital care that is necessary to address their health needs and concerns.

So, again, I say thank you to the governor, the congresswoman, the mayor, and the doctor and all those who work here, and the staff.

This work includes having people here who go out and talk to young people—our young people in high schools. And sadly, in so many places around our country, Sex Ed is a thing of the past, which leaves our young people to learn about their bodies and reproductive systems on social media—often with a profound amount of misinformation, which leaves them confused about what is happening to their own bodies.

The work that happens here is about providing assistance to women who do not live in the state of Minnesota, because, sadly, this state exists in a neighborhood where laws have been passed to deny people reproductive healthcare. And so, women have to travel here.

You know, the majority of women who receive an abortion are mothers. God help her that she's got affordable childcare. If she is working, God help her she's got paid family leave so she can figure out how is she going to get to the place that will provide her the care she needs.

Well, the work that happens in a clinic like this includes answering those questions for someone who might be in great distress, letting her know what is available to her in terms of transportation, in terms of housing or a hotel, what is available to her in terms of assistance for her childcare needs.

So, I'll close with this. In this environment, these attacks against an individual's right to make decisions about their own body are outrageous and, in many instances, just plain old immoral.

How dare these elected leaders believe they are in a better position to tell women what they need, to tell women what is in their best interest. We have to be a nation that trusts women.

And with that, I will introduce this extraordinary healthcare provider. And, Doctor, please.

Dr. Traxler: Thank you. Thank you so much. I have to use my notes, folks. I'm not used to doing this. So, good afternoon, everyone.

The Vice President: Good afternoon.

Dr. Traxler: I'm Sarah Traxler. I'm the Chief Medical Officer here at Planned Parenthood North Central States. I'm a board-certified obstetrician-gynecologist with a subspecialty in complex family planning, and I also have my masters of science in health policy.

I am a proud abortion provider. And I'm honored that Vice President Kamala Harris has visited our clinic today. It's a historic moment and one that demonstrates how critically important access to reproductive healthcare is to people and their families across the country.

So, thank you so much—

The Vice President: Thank you.

Dr. Traxler: —for being here today.

The Vice President: Thank you.

Dr. Traxler: Thank you.

After the *Dobbs* decision a year and a half ago, Minnesota has become a bastion of access for abortion care. But abortion rights are not only a Minnesota issue; it is a national issue.

Our Planned Parenthood has seen a 25 percent increase in abortions here in Minnesota since *Roe* was overturned. We've seen nearly 100 percent increase in patients coming here from outside of our state.

This is not by accident. Surrounding states have been limiting and banning abortion, while Minnesota, with the help of our governor, has been increasing access.

Since *Roe* was overturned, I've cared for patients from everywhere, from nearby states like South Dakota and North Dakota and Wisconsin, but from far-away states like Texas, Alabama, Wyoming, Florida, Oklahoma, Missouri, and the list goes on.

I've seen patients who've flown from places like Louisiana only to have me tell her that her complex pregnancy condition would keep her from having her abortion here with me, forcing her to continue a dangerous pregnancy because hospital-based care was not available to her in her home state.

Traveling to access essential healthcare can be intimidating and overwhelming. It is not an easy thing to do, as we have all pretended that it is.

Like the experience of our patient who traveled from a small rural town and became lost in downtown Minneapolis with a dead cell phone after her flight landed. We were able to get her a Lyft driver, our patient navigators, and she described that Lyft driver as a savior for her. And like our patient who drove hundreds and hundreds of miles through blizzard conditions just to get her abortion.

Our new abortion landscape is difficult, it is dangerous, and it is putting my patients and healthcare providers at severe risk. I've talked to my colleagues practicing in states where abortion is now illegal, and they are unnecessarily struggling with decisions around providing ethical, proper medical care and conflicting with the law. This should never happen.

Thankfully, providing abortion care has gotten less complicated in Minnesota. Here, I'm trusted as a provider and an expert to work with my patients to provide the best care possible.

To know that I'm trusted to do my job is a comfort to me, but it should be the standard everywhere. Private medical decisions should be made between patients and their doctors without interference from politicians or the protesters standing outside on the street in front of our clinic today.

You know, I didn't always feel this way. I came to understand bodily autonomy after a long history of being anti-abortion and having a very distorted point of view about abortion care. It wasn't until a friend told me her abortion story that I came to see the light.

After hearing her, knowing her history, I knew that an abortion was the right choice for her, for her life, for her future and nobody else's. And it dawned on me. If she is making the right decision for her life, then there are countless other people who are making the right decision for their lives. And no one should be interfering in that.

From my—from that point on, my awakening into understanding bodily autonomy and freedom grew to the point that I am today.

Everyone should have the right to access healthcare. Your ZIP Code shouldn't dictate the care that you can access. Your race, your socioeconomic status—none of that should determine it.

So, in 2024 and beyond, we will keep fighting, we will keep working until we live in a world where everyone can access the care they decide is best for their futures and their bodies and in their own community.

Thank you.

Aide: We're going to take a couple of questions, and we're—we're going to start with Rochelle from the Star Tribune.

Q: Hi, Madam Vice President. Why do you think it took so long for a sitting president or vice president to visit an abortion provider? And, also, how concerned are you about the 20 percent who voted uncommitted in the Minnesota presidential primary?

The Vice President: Well, I'll tell you, the reason I'm here is because this is a healthcare crisis. And I think that of the many stories that we can tell—

Of the many stories that we need to tell about what has happened after the *Dobbs* decision, one of them is that part of this healthcare crisis is the clinics like this that have had to shut down and what that has meant to leave no options with any reasonable geographic area for so many women who need this essential care.

And, again, it runs the gamut of reproductive healthcare. So, yes, it is abortion care. It is also, as I mentioned earlier, essential and critical reproductive healthcare like paps, like breast cancer screenings, things of that nature.

So, I'm here to highlight that of the many, I believe, potentially intended consequences of the *Dobbs* decision, one of them has been for healthcare providers such as this in the states that have banned or outlawed access to reproductive care—clinics like this to shut down. And it's a travesty. It's a travesty.

Q: Madam Vice President, can I—

Aide: We're going to go to our next question, Madam Vice President. Darlene, right to your left, with the AP.

Q: Hi. Thank you. We were not able to go with you on the tour, obviously. Can you give us a sense of what you saw back there—

The Vice President: Yeah.

Q: —and also what you learned by coming here today?

The Vice President: Well, what I saw were, I don't know, maybe two dozen healthcare workers who really care—really care about their patients and who understand that in the healthcare delivery system, regardless of your gender or your healthcare need, I think we should all expect and certainly we all desire that you will be treated with dignity and you'll be treated in an environment where you feel safe. And by that, I mean safe to be free from judgment, to be in an environment where you are actually and really listened to, where your needs and your expression of your needs are taken seriously.

And walking through this clinic, that's what I saw are people who have dedicated their lives to the profession of providing healthcare in a safe place that gives people dignity.

And I think we should all want that for each other.

Aide: Thank you, Vice President. We'll going to Nick at the *New York Times*.

Q: Madam Vice President, what do you see as your role on this issue, given that the administration has run up to the limit of what it can do to protect abortion rights and Congress is unlikely to pass a bill codifying them?

The Vice President: Well, Congress will pass that bill when we win back the House. And so, I am sure of that.

And I think that the—the point—one of the points that must be made on this issue, as we attempt to uplift the real stories and the real consequences of the *Dobbs* decision is to remind people elections matter. Elections matter.

What happened here in Minnesota, with the reelection of the governor and the turning of the state legislature is what has led to ensuring that these fundamental rights are intact and are protected. Elections matter.

And let me be very clear about this. When it comes to national elections and who sits in the United States Congress on this, there's a fundamental point on this issue that I think most people agree with, which is that one does not have to abandon their faith or deeply held beliefs to agree the government should not be telling women what to do with their body. If she chooses, she will consult with—with her priest, her pastor, her rabbi, her imam. But it's not for the government to tell her what she can and cannot do with her own body.

Q: And so, what do you see as your role on this issue?

The Vice President: My role is to do what I just did, which is to articulate exactly these points and to continue to articulate them and to organize folks around what I know is an issue that is impacting more people than you'll ever really know, who, as I said earlier, are silently suffering.

And so, we who have the ability to have a bouquet of microphones in front of us, as I do, I take on then the responsibility of uplifting these stories and reminding people—with some belief, by the way, when I do it, that the vast majority of Americans do have empathy and that, even if they don't agree that this would be the best decision for them, would agree that other people should not be suffering the way they are.

Aide: Thank you, Vice President. We have one more question right here from Patricia—

The Vice President: Yes.

Aide: —at *Bloomberg*.

The Vice President: Yes. Hi.

Q: Madam Vice President, *Roe* was always an imperfect vessel. What exactly would you like to see replace it? What form should it take? What should the scope of it be?

The Vice President: What we want is to put back in place the protections that the Supreme Court took away, which is to codify, put into law the protections of *Roe v. Wade*. That's what we want.

Aide: Madam Vice President, thank you so much.

Print Citations

CMS: Harris, Kamala, and Sarah Traxler. "Remarks during the Nationwide 'Fight for Reproductive Freedoms' Tour." Speech at Planned Parenthood, St. Paul, MN, March 14, 2024. In *The Reference Shelf: Representative American Speeches, 2023–2024,* edited by Micah L. Issitt, 11–17. Amenia, NY: Grey House Publishing, 2024.

MLA: Harris, Kamala, and Sarah Traxler. "Remarks during the Nationwide 'Fight for Reproductive Freedoms' Tour." Planned Parenthood, 14 March 2024, St. Paul, MN. Speech. *The Reference Shelf: Representative American Speeches, 2023–2024,* edited by Micah L. Issitt, Grey House Publishing, 2024, pp. 11–17.

APA: Harris, K., & Traxler, S. (2024). Remarks during the nationwide "Fight for Reproductive Freedoms" tour [Speech]. Planned Parenthood, St. Paul, MN. In Micah L. Issitt (Ed.), *The reference shelf: Representative American speeches, 2023–2024* (pp. 11–17). Grey House Publishing. (Original work published 2024)

Acceptance Speech for President

By Kamala Harris

"With this election, our nation has a precious, fleeting opportunity to move past the bitterness, cynicism, and divisive battles of the past." Vice President Kamala Harris spoke at the Democratic National Convention, officially accepting the nomination for the presidency. Harris talked about her history, as the child of immigrants, growing up in the East Bay, pursuing her education, and her work as a prosecutor.

Good evening. To my husband, Doug, thank you for being an incredible partner to me and father to Cole and Ella. And happy anniversary. I love you so very much.

To Joe Biden—Mr. President. When I think about the path we have traveled together, I am filled with gratitude. Your record is extraordinary, as history will show. And your character is inspiring. Doug and I love you and Jill. And I am forever thankful to you both.

And to Coach Tim Walz, you are going to be an incredible Vice President.

And to the delegates and everyone who has put your faith in our campaign—your support is humbling.

America, the path that led me here in recent weeks, was no doubt... unexpected. But I'm no stranger to unlikely journeys.

My mother Shyamala Harris had one of her own. I miss her every day. Especially now. And I know she's looking down tonight. And smiling.

My mother was 19 when she crossed the world alone. Traveling from India to California. With an unshakeable dream to be the scientist who would cure breast cancer.

When she finished school, she was supposed to return home to a traditional arranged marriage. But, as fate would have it, she met my father, Donald Harris. A student from Jamaica. They fell in love and got married. And that act of self-determination made my sister Maya and me.

Growing up, we moved a lot. I will always remember that big Mayflower truck packed with all our belongings, ready to go: to Illinois, to Wisconsin, and wherever our parents' jobs took us.

My early memories of my parents together are joyful ones. A home filled with laughter and music. Aretha. Coltrane. And Miles.

At the park, my mother would tell us to stay close. But my father would just smile, and say, "Run, Kamala. Run. Don't be afraid. Don't let anything stop you."

Delivered on August 22, 2024 at the Democratic National Convention, Chicago, IL.

From my earliest years, he taught me to be fearless. But the harmony between my parents did not last. When I was in elementary school, they split up. And it was mostly my mother who raised us.

Before she could finally afford to buy a home, she rented a small apartment in the East Bay. In the Bay, you either live in the hills or the flatlands. We, lived in the flats. A beautiful working-class neighborhood of firefighters, nurses and construction workers. All, who tended their lawns with pride.

My mother worked long hours. And, like many working parents, she leaned on a trusted circle to help raise us. Mrs. Shelton, who ran the daycare below us and became a second mother. Uncle Sherman. Aunt Mary. Uncle Freddy. And Auntie Chris. None of them, family by blood. And all of them, family by love.

Family who taught us how to make gumbo. How to play chess. And sometimes even let us win. Family who loved us. Believed in us. And told us we could be anything. Do anything.

They instilled in us the values they personified. Community. Faith. And the importance of treating others as you would want to be treated. With kindness. Respect. And compassion.

My mother was a brilliant, five-foot-tall, brown woman with an accent. And, as the eldest child, I saw how the world would sometimes treat her.

But she never lost her cool. She was tough. Courageous. A trailblazer in the fight for women's health.

And she taught Maya and me a lesson that Michelle mentioned the other night—she taught us to never complain about injustice. But...do something about it.

She also taught us—never do anything half-assed. That's, a direct quote.

I grew up immersed in the ideals of the Civil Rights Movement. My parents had met at a civil rights gathering. And they made sure we learned about civil rights leaders, including lawyers like Thurgood Marshall and Constance Baker Motley.

Those who battled in the courtroom to make real the Promise of America.

So, at a young age, I decided I wanted to do that work. I wanted to be a lawyer. And when it came time to choose—the type, of law I would pursue—I reflected on a pivotal moment in my life.

When I was in high school, I started to notice something about my best friend Wanda.

She was sad at school. And there were times she didn't want to go home.

So, one day, I asked if everything was alright and she confided in me that she was being sexually abused by her stepfather. And I immediately told her she had to come stay with us.

And she did. That is one of the reasons I became a prosecutor.

To protect people like Wanda. Because I believe everyone has a right to safety. To dignity. And to justice.

As a prosecutor, when I had a case, I charged it not in the name of the victim. But in the name of "The People."

For a simple reason. In our system of justice, a harm against any one of us is a harm against all of us.

I would often explain this, to console survivors of crime. To remind them no one should be made to fight alone. We are all in this together.

Every day in the courtroom, I stood proudly before a judge and said five words: "Kamala Harris, for the People."

And to be clear, my entire career, I have only had one client. The People. And so, on behalf of The People, on behalf of every American. Regardless of party, race or gender. Or the language your grandmother speaks.

On behalf of my mother and everyone who has ever set out on their own unlikely journey. On behalf of Americans like the people I grew up with. People who work hard. Chase their dreams and look out for one another.

On behalf of everyone whose story could only be written in the greatest nation on Earth. I accept your nomination for President of the United States of America.

With this election, our nation has a precious, fleeting opportunity to move past the bitterness, cynicism and divisive battles of the past.

A chance to chart a New Way Forward. Not as members of any one party or faction But as Americans.

I know there are people of various political view watching tonight. And I want you to know: I promise to be a President for all Americans.

You can always trust me to put country above party and self. To hold sacred America's fundamental principles. From the rule of law. To free and fair elections. To the peaceful transfer of power.

I will be a President who unites us around our highest aspirations. A President who leads and listens. Who is realistic. Practical. And has common sense and always fights for the American people.

From the courthouse to the White House, that has been my life's work.

As a young courtroom prosecutor in Oakland, I stood up for women and children against predators who abused them.

As Attorney General of California, I took on the Big Banks. Delivered $20 billion for middle-class families who faced foreclosure. And helped pass a homeowner Bill of Rights—one of the first of its kind.

I stood up for veterans and students being scammed by big for-profit colleges. For workers who were being cheated out of the wages they were due. For seniors facing elder abuse. I fought against cartels who traffic in guns, drugs, and human beings. Who threaten the security of our border and the safety of our communities.

Those fights were not easy. And neither were the elections that put me in those offices. We were underestimated at every turn. But we never gave up. Because the future is always worth fighting for. And that's the fight we are in right now. A fight for America's future.

Fellow Americans, this election is not only the most important of our lives. It is one of the most important in the life of our nation. In many ways, Donald

Trump is an unserious man. But the consequences of putting Donald Trump back in the White House are extremely serious.

Consider not only the chaos and calamity when he was in office, but also the gravity of what has happened since he lost the last election. Donald Trump tried to throw away your votes.

When he failed, he sent an armed mob into the U.S. Capitol, where they assaulted law enforcement officers.

When politicians in his own party begged him to call off the mob and send help, he did the opposite. He fanned the flames.

And now, for an entirely different set of crimes, he was found guilty of fraud by a jury of everyday Americans. And separately, found liable for committing sexual abuse.

And consider what he intends to do if we give him power again. Consider his explicit intent to set free the violent extremists who assaulted those law enforcement officers at the Capitol.

His explicit intent to jail journalists. Political opponents. Anyone he sees as the enemy.

His explicit intent to deploy our active-duty military against our own citizens.

Consider the power he will have—especially after the United States Supreme Court just ruled he would be immune from criminal prosecution.

Just imagine Donald Trump with no guardrails. How he would use the immense powers of the presidency of the United States. Not to improve your life. Not to strengthen our national security. But to serve the only client he has ever had: Himself.

And we know what a second Trump term would look like. It's all laid out in "Project 2025." Written by his closest advisors. And its sum total is to pull our country back into the past.

But America, we are not going back.

We are not going back to when Donald Trump tried to cut Social Security and Medicare. We are not going back to when he tried to get rid of the Affordable Care Act. When insurance companies could deny people with pre-existing conditions.

We are not going to let him eliminate the Department of Education that funds our public schools. We are not going to let him end programs like Head Start, that provide preschool and child care.

America, we are not going back. We are charting a new way forward. Forward—to a future with a strong and growing middle class.

Because we know a strong middle class has always been critical to America's success. And building that middle class will be a defining goal of my presidency.

This is personal for me. The middle class is where I come from. My mother kept a strict budget. We lived within our means. Yet, we wanted for little.

And she expected us to make the most of the opportunities that were available to us. And to be grateful for them. Because opportunity is not available to everyone.

That's why we will create what I call an Opportunity economy. An Opportunity economy where everyone has a chance to compete and a chance to succeed.

Whether you live in a rural area, small town, or big city. As President, I will bring together: Labor and workers, small business owners and entrepreneurs and American companies to create jobs. Grow our economy. And lower the cost of everyday needs. Like health care, housing, and groceries.

We will provide access to capital for small business owners, entrepreneurs and founders. We will end America's housing shortage and protect Social Security and Medicare.

Compare that to Donald Trump. He doesn't actually fight for the middle class. Instead, he fights for himself and his billionaire friends. He will give them another round of tax breaks that will add $5 trillion to the national debt.

All while, he intends to enact what, in effect, is a national sales tax—call it, a Trump tax—that would raise prices on middle-class families by almost $4,000 a year. Well, instead of a Trump tax hike, we will pass a middle class tax cut that will benefit more than 100 million Americans.

Friends, I believe America cannot truly be prosperous unless Americans are fully able to make their own decisions about their own lives. Especially on matters of heart and home.

But tonight, too many women in America are not able to make those decisions. Let's be clear about how we got here: Donald Trump hand-picked members of the United States Supreme Court to take away reproductive freedom. And now he brags about it. His words: Quote—"I did it, and I'm proud to have done it." End quote.

Over the past two years, I have traveled across our country. And women have told me their stories. Husbands and fathers have shared theirs. Stories of women miscarrying in a parking lot, getting sepsis, losing the ability to ever have children again, all because doctors are afraid of going to jail for caring for their patients. Couples just trying to grow their family, cut off in the middle of IVF treatments. Children who have survived sexual assault, potentially forced to carry the pregnancy to term.

This is what is happening in our country. Because of Donald Trump. And understand, he is not done.

As a part of his agenda, he and his allies would limit access to birth control, ban medication abortion and enact a nation-wide abortion ban with or without Congress.

And, get this, he plans to create a National anti-abortion coordinator, and force states to report on women's miscarriages and abortions. Simply put: They are out of their minds.

And one must ask: Why exactly is it that they don't trust women? Well. We trust women.

And when Congress passes a bill to restore reproductive freedom, as President of the United States, I will proudly sign it into law.

In this election, many other fundamental freedoms are at stake. The freedom to live safe from gun violence—in our schools, communities and places of worship. And the freedom to love who you love openly and with pride. The freedom to breathe clean air, drink clean water and live free from the pollution that fuels the climate crisis. And the freedom that unlocks all the others: The freedom to vote.

With this election, we finally have the opportunity to pass the John Lewis Voting Rights Act and the Freedom to Vote Act. And let me be clear. After decades in law enforcement, I know the importance of safety and security, especially at our border.

Last year, Joe and I brought together Democrats and conservative Republicans to write the strongest border bill in decades. The Border Patrol endorsed it.

But Donald Trump believes a border deal would hurt his campaign. So he ordered his allies in Congress to kill the deal.

Well, I refuse to play politics with our security. Here is my pledge to you: As President, I will bring back the bipartisan border security bill that he killed. And I will sign it into law.

I know we can live up to our proud heritage as a nation of immigrants—and reform our broken immigration system. We can create an earned pathway to citizenship—and secure our border.

America, we must also be steadfast in advancing our security and our values abroad.

As Vice President, I have confronted threats to our security, negotiated with foreign leaders, strengthened our alliances and engaged with our brave troops overseas.

As Commander-in-Chief, I will ensure America always has the strongest, most lethal fighting force in the world. I will fulfill our sacred obligation to care for our troops and their families. And I will always honor, and never disparage, their service and their sacrifice.

I will make sure that we lead the world into the future on space and Artificial Intelligence. That America—not China—wins the competition for the 21st century. And that we strengthen—not abdicate—our global leadership.

Trump, on the other hand, threatened to abandon NATO. He encouraged Putin to invade our allies. Said Russia could—quote—"do whatever the hell they want."

Five days before Russia attacked Ukraine, I met with President Zelensky to warn him about Russia's plan to invade. I helped mobilize a global response—over 50 countries—to defend against Putin's aggression. And as President, I will stand strong with Ukraine and our NATO allies.

With respect to the war in Gaza, President Biden and I are working around the clock. Because now is the time to get a hostage deal and ceasefire done.

Let me be clear: I will always stand up for Israel's right to defend itself, and I will always ensure Israel has the ability to defend itself. Because the people of Israel must never again face the horror that the terrorist organization Hamas

24 The Democratic Campaign

caused on October 7th. Including unspeakable sexual violence and the massacre of young people at a music festival.

At the same time, what has happened in Gaza over the past 10 months is devastating. So many innocent lives lost. Desperate, hungry people fleeing for safety, over and over again. The scale of suffering is heartbreaking.

President Biden and I are working to end this war such that Israel is secure, the hostages are released, the suffering in Gaza ends and the Palestinian people can realize their right to dignity, security, freedom and self-determination.

And know this: I will never hesitate to take whatever action is necessary to defend our forces and our interests against Iran and Iran-backed terrorists. And I will not cozy up to tyrants and dictators like Kim-Jong-Un, who are rooting for Trump because they know he is easy to manipulate with flattery and favors. They know Trump won't hold autocrats accountable—because he wants to be an autocrat.

As President, I will never waver in defense of America's security and ideals. Because, in the enduring struggle between democracy and tyranny, I know where I stand—and where the United States of America belongs.

Fellow Americans, I love our country with all my heart. Everywhere I go—n everyone I meet—I see a nation ready to move forward. Ready for the next step in the incredible journey that is America.

I see an America where we hold fast to the fearless belief that built our nation. That inspired the world. That here, in this country, anything is possible. Nothing is out of reach.

An America, where we care for one another, look out for one another, and recognize that we have so much more in common than what separates us. That none of us has to fail for all of us to succeed. And that, in unity, there is strength.

Our opponents in this race are out there, every day, denigrating America. Talking about how terrible everything is. Well, my mother had another lesson she used to teach: Never let anyone tell you who you are. You show them who you are.

America, let us show each other—and the world—who we are and what we stand for: Freedom, opportunity, compassion, dignity, fairness and endless possibilities.

We are the heirs to the greatest democracy in the history of the world. And on behalf of our children and grandchildren and all those who sacrificed so dearly for our freedom and liberty, we must be worthy of this moment. It is now our turn to do what generations before us have done. Guided by optimism and faith, to fight for this country we love.

To fight for the ideals we cherish. And to uphold the awesome responsibility that comes with the greatest privilege on Earth. The privilege and pride of being an American.

So, let's get out there and let's fight for it. Let's get out there and let's vote for it.

And together, let us write the next great chapter in the most extraordinary story ever told.

Thank you. God bless you. May God bless the United States of America.

Print Citations

CMS: Harris, Kamala. "Acceptance Speech for President." Speech at the Democratic National Convention, Chicago, IL, August 22, 2024. In *The Reference Shelf: Representative American Speeches, 2023–2024,* edited by Micah L. Issitt, 18–25. Amenia, NY: Grey House Publishing, 2024.

MLA: Harris, Kamala. "Acceptance Speech for President." Democratic National Convention, 22 August 2024, Chicago, IL. Speech. *The Reference Shelf: Representative American Speeches, 2023–2024,* edited by Micah L. Issitt, Grey House Publishing, 2024, pp. 18–25.

APA: Harris, K. (2024). Acceptance speech for president [Speech]. Democratic National Convention, Chicago, IL. In Micah L. Issitt (Ed.), *The reference shelf: Representative American speeches, 2023–2024* (pp. 18–25). Grey House Publishing. (Original work published 2024)

Acceptance Speech for Vice President

By Tim Walz

"Let me just say this—even if you've never experienced the hell of infertility, I guarantee you know somebody who has." Minnesota Governor and Vice Presidential Candidate Tim Walz spoke at the Democratic National Convention, formally accepting the role as Harris's running mate for the 2024 election. Walz discussed his history in politics and education, his family's struggles with fertility, and the importance of healthcare and reproductive health for Americans.

Thank you! Thank you, Vice President Kamala Harris, for putting your trust in me and for inviting me to be part of this incredible campaign. Thank you to President Joe Biden for four years of strong, historic leadership. And it is the honor of my life to accept your nomination for vice president of the United States.

We're all here tonight for one beautiful, simple reason—we love this country! So thanks to all of you here in Chicago and watching at home tonight—for your passion, for your determination, for the joy that you're bringing to this fight.

I grew up in the small town of Butte, Nebraska, population 400. I had 24 kids in my high school class and none of 'em went to Yale. Growing up in a small town like that, you learn to take care of each other. The family down the road—they may not think like you do, they may not pray like you do, they may not love like you do, but they're your neighbors. And you look out for them, just like they do for you.

Everybody belongs, and everybody has a responsibility to contribute. For me, it was serving in the Army National Guard. I joined up two days after my 17th birthday and I proudly wore our country's uniform for 24 years. My dad, a Korean War-era veteran, died of lung cancer a couple years later and left behind a mountain of medical debt. Thank God for Social Security survivor benefits. And thank God for the GI Bill that allowed both my dad and me to go to college—just like it has for millions of Americans.

Eventually, I fell in love with teaching, just like the rest of my family. Heck, three out of four of us even married teachers. I wound up teaching social studies and coaching football at Mankato West High School. Go Scarlets! We ran a 4-4 defense, played through the whistle every single down, and even won a state championship. Never close that yearbook, people.

It was my students who first inspired me to run for Congress. They saw in me what I hoped to instill in them—a commitment to the common good. An

---

Delivered on August 21, 2024 at the Democratic National Convention, Chicago, IL.

Acceptance Speech for Vice President **27**

understanding that we're all in this together. And a true belief that one person can make a real difference for their neighbors.

So there I was, a 40-something high school teacher with young kids, zero political experience, no money, and running in a deep-red district. But you know what? Never underestimate a public school teacher.

I represented my neighbors in Congress for 12 years and I learned an awful lot. I learned how to work across the aisle on issues like growing rural economies and taking care of our veterans. And I learned how to compromise without compromising my values.

Then I came back home to serve as governor and we got right to work making a difference in our neighbors' lives. We cut taxes for middle-class families. We passed paid family and medical leave. We invested in fighting crime and affordable housing. We cut the cost of prescription drugs and helped people escape the kind of medical debt that nearly sank my family. And we made sure that every kid in our state got breakfast and lunch at school. So while other states were banning books from their schools, we were banishing hunger from ours.

We also protected reproductive freedom because, in Minnesota, we respect our neighbors and the personal choices they make. And even if we wouldn't make the same choices for ourselves, we've got a Golden Rule—mind your own damn business.

That includes IVF and fertility treatments. This is personal for Gwen and me. Let me just say this—even if you've never experienced the hell of infertility, I guarantee you know somebody who has. I remember praying each night for a call with good news, the pit in my stomach when the phone would ring, and the agony when we heard the treatments hadn't worked. It took me and Gwen years.

But we had access to fertility treatments and when our daughter was finally born, we named her Hope. Hope, Gus, Gwen—you are my whole world. I love you all so much.

I'm letting you in on how we started our family because that's a big part of what this election is about—freedom. When Republicans use that word, they mean that the government should be free to invade your doctor's office. Corporations free to pollute the air and water. Banks free to take advantage of customers. But when we Democrats talk about freedom, we mean your freedom to make a better life for yourself and the people you love. The freedom to make your own health care decisions. And, yeah, your kids' freedom to go to school without worrying they'll be shot dead in the halls.

Look, I know guns. I'm a veteran. I'm a hunter. I was a better shot than most Republicans in Congress and I have the trophies to prove it. But I'm also a dad. I believe in the Second Amendment. But I also believe that our first responsibility is to keep our kids safe. That's what this is all about. The responsibility we have to our kids, to each other, and to the future we're building together—a future in which everyone is free to build the kind of life they want.

But not everyone feels the same sense of responsibility. Some folks just don't understand what it means to be a good neighbor. Take Donald Trump and JD

28   The Democratic Campaign

Vance—their Project 2025 will make things much, much harder for people who are just trying to live their lives. They've spent a lot of time pretending they know nothing about it. But look, I coached high school football long enough, I promise you this—when somebody takes the time to draw up a playbook, they plan on using it.

We know what they'll do if they get back in the White House. They'll jack up costs on middle-class families. They'll repeal the Affordable Care Act. They'll gut Social Security and Medicare. They'll ban abortion across America, with or without Congress.

It's an agenda that nobody asked for. It's an agenda that serves nobody but the richest people and the most extreme voices in our country. An agenda that does nothing for our neighbors in need. Is it weird? Absolutely. But it's also wrong. And it's dangerous. It's not just me saying so. It's Trump's own people. They were with him for four years. And they're warning us that the next four years would be much, much worse.

When I was teaching, we would always elect a student body president. And you know what? Those teenagers could teach Donald Trump a lesson about what it means to be a leader. Leaders don't spend all day insulting people and blaming people. Leaders do the work. I don't know about you all, but I'm ready to turn the page on these guys. So say it with me: "We're not going back."

We've got something better to offer the American people. It starts with our candidate, Kamala Harris. From her first day as a prosecutor, as a district attorney, as an attorney general, as a U.S. senator, and then, as our vice president, she's fought on the side of the American people. She's taken on predators and fraudsters. She's taken down transnational gangs. She's stood up to powerful corporate interests. She's never hesitated to reach across the aisle if it meant improving lives. And she's always done it with energy, passion, and joy.

Folks, we have a chance to make Kamala Harris the next president of the United States. But I think we owe it to the American people to tell them exactly what she'd do as president before we ask for their votes. So here's the part you clip and save and send to that undecided relative.

If you're a middle-class family or a family trying to get into the middle class, Kamala Harris is gonna cut your taxes. If you're getting squeezed by the price of your prescription drugs, Kamala Harris is gonna take on Big Pharma. If you're hoping to buy a home, Kamala Harris is gonna help make it more affordable. And no matter who you are, Kamala Harris is gonna stand up and fight for your freedom to live the life you want to lead. Because that's what we want for ourselves. And that's what we want for our neighbors.

You know, I haven't given a lot of big speeches like this one in my life. But I've given a lot of pep talks. So let me finish with this, team. It's the fourth quarter. We're down a field goal. But we're on offense. We're driving down the field. And, boy, do we have the right team to win this. Kamala Harris is tough. She's experienced. And she's ready. Our job is to get in the trenches and do the blocking and tackling. One inch at a time, one yard at a time, one phone call at a time, one door knock at a time, one $5 donation at a time. We've only got 76 days to go. That's nothing. We'll sleep when we're dead. And we're gonna leave it all on the field.

That's how we'll keep moving forward. That's how we'll turn the page on Donald Trump. That's how we'll build a country where workers come first, health care and housing are human rights, and the government stays the hell out of our bedrooms. That's how we make America a place where no child is left hungry. Where no community is left behind. Where nobody gets told they don't belong.

That's how we're gonna fight. And as the next president of the United States says, "When we fight, we win!" When we fight, we win! When we fight, we win!

Thank you, and God bless America!

Print Citations

CMS: Walz, Tim. "Acceptance Speech for Vice President." Speech at the Democratic National Convention, Chicago, IL, August 21, 2024. In *The Reference Shelf: Representative American Speeches, 2023–2024,* edited by Micah L. Issitt, 26–29. Amenia, NY: Grey House Publishing, 2024.

MLA: Walz, Tim. "Acceptance Speech for Vice President." Democratic National Convention, 21 August 2024, Chicago, IL. Speech. *The Reference Shelf: Representative American Speeches, 2023–2024,* edited by Micah L. Issitt, Grey House Publishing, 2024, pp. 26–29.

APA: Walz, T. (2024). Acceptance speech for vice president [Speech]. Democratic National Convention, Chicago, IL. In Micah L. Issitt (Ed.), *The reference shelf: Representative American speeches, 2023–2024* (pp. 26–29). Grey House Publishing. (Original work published 2024)

Hope Is Making a Comeback

By Michelle Obama

In what was widely described as one of the best speeches of the night, former First Lady Michelle Obama addressed the Democratic National Convention in Chicago, Illinois. She spoke about multigenerational families, the "unseen labor" that drives American industry and growth, and highlighted Kamala Harris's qualifications for the presidency, claiming that Harris is "more than ready" for the job.

Thank you guys. OK. We got a big night ahead. Thank you all so much. Thank you. Hello, Chicago!

Something, something wonderfully magical is in the air, isn't it? Yeah.

You know, we're feeling it here in this arena, but it's spreading all across this country we love. A familiar feeling that's been buried too deep for far too long. You know what I'm talking about. It's the contagious power of hope, the anticipation, the energy, the exhilaration of once again being on the cusp of a brighter day. The chance to vanquish the demons of fear, division, and hate that have consumed us and continue pursuing the unfinished promise of this great nation. The dream that our parents and grandparents fought and died and sacrificed for. America, hope is making a comeback.

But, to be honest, I am realizing that until recently, I have mourned the dimming of that hope. And maybe you've experienced the same feelings—it's that deep pit in my stomach, a palpable sense of dread about the future. And for me, that mourning has also been mixed with my own personal grief. The last time I was here in my hometown was to memorialize my mother, the woman who showed me the meaning of hard work and humility and decency. The woman who set my moral compass high and showed me the power of my own voice. Folks, I still feel her loss so profoundly. I wasn't even sure if I'd be steady enough to stand before you tonight, but my heart compelled me to be here because of the sense of duty that I feel to honor her memory and to remind us all not to squander the sacrifices our elders made to give us a better future.

You see, my mom in her steady quiet way, lived out that striving sense of hope every single day of her life. She believed that all children, all people have value. That anyone can succeed if given the opportunity. She and my father didn't aspire to be wealthy—in fact, they were suspicious of folks who took more than they needed. They understood that it wasn't enough for their kids to thrive if everyone else around us was drowning. So my mother volunteered at the local school. She always looked out for the other kids on the block. She was glad to do

---

Delivered on August 20, 2024 at the Democratic National Convention, Chicago, IL.

the thankless, unglamorous work that, for generations, has strengthened the fabric of this nation. The belief that if you do unto others, if you love thy neighbor, if you work and scrape and sacrifice, it will pay off—if not for you, then maybe for your children or your grandchildren.

You see, those values have been passed on through family farms and factory towns, through tree-lined streets and crowded tenements, through prayer groups and national guard units and social studies classrooms. Those were the values my mother poured into me until her very last breath.

Kamala Harris and I built our lives on those same foundational values. Even though our mothers grew up an ocean apart, they shared the same belief in the promise of this country. That's why her mother moved here from India at 19. It's why she taught Kamala about justice, about the obligation to lift others up, about our responsibility to give more than we take. She'd often tell her daughter: "Don't sit around and complain about things. Do something."

So, with that voice in her head, Kamala went out and she worked hard in school, graduating from an HBCU, earning her law degree at a state school. And then she went on to work for the people fighting to hold law breakers accountable, strengthening the rule of law, fighting to get folks better wages, cheaper prescription drugs, a good education, decent healthcare, childcare, elder care. From a middle class household, Kamala worked her way up to become Vice President of the United States of America.

My girl, Kamala Harris, is more than ready for this moment. She is one of the most qualified people ever to seek the office of the presidency. And she is one of the most dignified—a tribute to her mother, to my mother, and to your mother too. The embodiment of the stories we tell ourselves about this country. Her story is your story. It's my story. It's the story of the vast majority of Americans trying to build a better life.

Look, Kamala knows, like we do, that regardless of where you come from, what you look like, who you love, how you worship, or what's in your bank account, we all deserve the opportunity to build a decent life. All of our contributions deserve to be accepted and valued. Because no one has a monopoly on what it means to be an American. No one.

Kamala has shown her allegiance to this nation, not by spewing anger and bitterness, but by living a life of service and always pushing the doors of opportunity open to others. She understands that most of us will never be afforded the grace of failing forward. We will never benefit from the affirmative action of generational wealth. If we bankrupt the business or choke in a crisis, we don't get a second, third, or fourth chance. If things don't go our way, we don't have the luxury of whining or cheating others to get further ahead. No. We don't get to change the rules, so we always win. If we see a mountain in front of us, we don't expect there to be an escalator waiting to take us to the top. No. We put our heads down. We get to work. In America, we do something.

The Democratic Campaign

And throughout her entire life, that's what we've seen from Kamala Harris, the steel of her spine, the steadiness of her upbringing, the honesty of her example, and yes, the joy of her laughter and her light.

It couldn't be more obvious: Of the two major candidates in this race, only Kamala Harris truly understands the unseen labor and unwavering commitment that has always made America great.

Now, unfortunately, we know what comes next. We know folks are going to do everything they can to distort her truth. My husband and I, sadly, know a little something about this. For years, Donald Trump did everything in his power to try to make people fear us. See, his limited, narrow view of the world made him feel threatened by the existence of two hardworking, highly educated, successful people who happen to be Black.

Wait, I want to know: Who's going to tell him that the job he's currently seeking might just be one of those "Black jobs"?

Look, it's his same old con: doubling down on ugly, misogynistic, racist lies as a substitute for real ideas and solutions that will actually make people's lives better. Look, because cutting our healthcare, taking away our freedom to control our bodies, the freedom to become a mother through IVF like I did—those things are not going to improve the health outcomes of our wives, mothers, and daughters. Shutting down the Department of Education, banning our books—none of that will prepare our kids for the future. Demonizing our children for being who they are and loving who they love—look, that doesn't make anybody's life better.

Instead, it only makes us small. And let me tell you this: Going small is never the answer. Going small is the opposite of what we teach our kids. Going small is petty, it's unhealthy, and quite frankly, it's unpresidential.

So, why would any of us accept this from anyone seeking our highest office? Why would we normalize that type of backward leadership? Doing so only demeans and cheapens our politics. It only serves to further discourage good, big-hearted people from wanting to get involved at all. America, our parents taught us better than that, and we deserve so much better than that.

That's why we must do everything in our power to elect two of those good, big-hearted people. There is no other choice than Kamala Harris and Tim Walz. No other choice.

But, as we embrace this renewed sense of hope, let us not forget the despair we have felt. Let us not forget what we are up against. Yes, Kamala and Tim are doing great now. We're loving it. They're packing arenas across the country. Folks are energized. We are feeling good. But, remember there are still so many people who are desperate for a different outcome, who are ready to question and criticize every move Kamala makes, who are eager to spread those lies, who don't want to vote for a woman, who will continue to prioritize building their wealth over ensuring that everyone has enough.

So no matter how good we feel tonight or tomorrow or the next day, this is going to be an uphill battle. So folks, we cannot be our own worst enemies. No. See, because the minute something goes wrong, the minute a lie takes hold, folks, we cannot start wringing our hands. We cannot get a Goldilocks complex about whether everything is just right. And we cannot indulge our anxieties about whether this country will elect someone like Kamala instead of doing everything we can to get someone like Kamala elected.

Kamala and Tim, they have lived amazing lives and I am confident that they will lead with compassion, inclusion, and grace. But they are still only human. They are not perfect. And like all of us, they will make mistakes. But luckily y'all, this is not just on them. No, uh-uh. This is up to us, all of us, to be the solution that we seek. It's up to all of us to be the antidote to the darkness and division. Look, I don't care how you identify politically—whether you're a Democrat, Republican, Independent, or none of the above. This is our time to stand up for what we know in our hearts is right. To stand up, not just for our basic freedoms but for decency and humanity; for basic respect, dignity, and empathy; for the values at the very foundation of this democracy.

It's up to us to remember what Kamala's mother told her: "Don't just sit around and complain. Do something." So if they lie about her—and they will—we've got to do something. If we see a bad poll—and we will—we've got to put down that phone and do something. If we start feeling tired, if we start feeling that dread creeping back in, we gotta pick ourselves up, throw water on our face, and what?

We only have two and a half months, y'all, to get this done. Only 11 weeks to make sure every single person we know is registered and has a voting plan. So we cannot afford for anyone, anyone, anyone, America, to sit on their hands and wait to be called. Don't complain if no one from the campaign has specifically reached out to you to ask you for your support. There is simply no time for that kind of foolishness. You know what you need to do.

So, consider this to be your official ask: Michelle Obama is asking you—no, I'm telling y'all—to do something.

Because, y'all, this election is gonna be close. In some states, just a handful—listen to me—a handful of votes in every precinct could decide the winner. So we need to vote in numbers that erase any doubt. We need to overwhelm any effort to suppress us. Our fate is in our hands. In 77 days, we have the power to turn our country away from the fear, division, and smallness of the past. We have the power to marry our hope with our action. We have the power to pay forward the love, sweat, and sacrifice of our mothers and fathers and all those who came before us.

We did it before, y'all, and we sure can do it again. Let us work like our lives depend on it, and let us keep moving our country forward and go higher—yes, always higher—than we've ever gone before, as we elect the next President and Vice President of the United States, Kamala Harris and Tim Walz.

Thank you all. God bless.

Now, before I go, I have one more job tonight. Yeah, one more job. You all, thank you for all the love, but it is now my honor to introduce somebody who knows a whole lot about hope, someone who has spent his life strengthening our democracy—and let me tell you, as someone who lives with him, he wakes up every day, every day, and thinks about what's best for this country. Please welcome America's 44th President and the love of my life, Barack Obama.

Print Citations

CMS: Obama, Michelle. "Hope Is Making a Comeback." Speech at the Democratic National Convention, Chicago, IL, August 20, 2024. In *The Reference Shelf: Representative American Speeches, 2023–2024,* edited by Micah L. Issitt, 30–34. Amenia, NY: Grey House Publishing, 2024.

MLA: Obama, Michelle. "Hope Is Making a Comeback." Democratic National Convention, 20 August 2024, Chicago, IL. Speech. *The Reference Shelf: Representative American Speeches, 2023–2024,* edited by Micah L. Issitt, Grey House Publishing, 2023, pp. 30–34.

APA: Obama, M. (2024). Hope is making a comeback [Speech]. Democratic National Convention, Chicago, IL. In Micah L. Issitt (Ed.), *The reference shelf: Representative American speeches, 2023–2024* (pp. 30–34). Grey House Publishing. (Original work published 2024)

It's Up to All of Us to Fight for the America We Believe In

By Barack Obama

Former President Barack Obama delivered a speech at the Democratic National Convention in Chicago, Illinois. He spoke about his own experience as president working alongside Joe Biden, the threat of another Trump presidency, and Kamala Harris's qualifications for the presidency.

Hello, Chicago! Hello! Thank you, thank you! Thank you everybody, thank you!

Alright, alright, alright that's enough. Thank you. Chicago! It is good to be home!

It is good to be home and I don't know about you, but I'm feeling fired up! I'm feeling ready to go—even if, even if I'm the only person stupid enough to speak after Michelle Obama...

I'm feeling hopeful because this convention has always been pretty good to kids with funny names who believe in a country where anything is possible. Because we have the chance to elect someone who's spent her entire life trying to give people the same chances America gave her. Someone who sees you and hears you and will get up every single day and fight for you: the next President of the United States of America, Kamala Harris.

It's been sixteen years since I had the honor of accepting this party's nomination for president. I know it's hard to believe since I haven't aged a bit, but it's true. And looking back, I can say without question that my first big decision as your nominee turned out to be one of my best—and that was asking Joe Biden to serve by my side as Vice President.

Now, other than some common Irish blood, Joe and I come from different backgrounds. But we became brothers. And as we worked together for eight sometimes pretty tough years, what I came to admire most about Joe wasn't just his smarts, his experience, it was his empathy and his decency and his hard-earned resiliency, his unshakable belief that everyone in this country deserves a fair shot.

And over the last four years, those are the values America has needed most.

At a time when millions of our fellow citizens were sick and dying, we needed a leader with the character to put politics aside and do what was right. At a time when our economy was reeling, we needed a leader with the determination to drive what would become the world's strongest recovery—15 million jobs, higher

---

Delivered August 20, 2024 at the Democratic National Convention, Chicago, IL.

wages, lower health care costs. And at a time when the other party had turned into a cult of personality, we needed a leader who was steady, and brought people together, and was selfless enough to do the rarest thing there is in politics: putting his own ambition aside for the sake of the country.

History will remember Joe Biden as an outstanding president who defended democracy at a moment of great danger. I am proud to call him my president, but I am even prouder to call him my friend.

Now the torch has been passed. Now it's up to all of us to fight for the America we believe in. And make no mistake: it will be a fight. For all the incredible energy we've been able to generate over the last few weeks, for all the rallies and the memes, this will still be a tight race in a closely divided country—a country where too many Americans are still struggling. Where a lot of Americans don't believe government can help.

And as we gather here tonight, the people who will decide this election are asking a very simple question:

Who will fight for me? Who's thinking about my future; about my children's future—about our future together?

One thing is for certain: Donald Trump is not losing sleep over these questions. Here's a 78-year-old billionaire who hasn't stopped whining about his problems since he rode down his golden escalator nine years ago. It's been a constant stream of gripes and grievances that's actually been getting worse now that he's afraid of losing to Kamala. There's the childish nicknames, the crazy conspiracy theories, this weird obsession with crowd sizes. It just goes on and on and on. The other day, I heard someone compare Trump to the neighbor who keeps running his leaf blower outside your window every minute of every day.

From a neighbor, that's exhausting. From a president, it's just dangerous. The truth is, Donald Trump sees power as nothing more than a means to his ends. He wants the middle class to pay the price for another huge tax cut that would mostly help him and his rich friends. He killed a bipartisan immigration deal written by some of the most conservative Republicans in Congress that would've helped secure our southern border because he thought trying to actually solve the problem would hurt his campaign.

Do not boo! Vote.

He doesn't seem to care if more women lose their reproductive freedoms since it won't affect his life. Most of all, Donald Trump wants us to think that this country is hopelessly divided between us and them; between the real Americans who of course support him and the outsiders who don't. And he wants you to think that you'll be richer and safer if you just give him the power to put those "other" people back in their place.

It is one of the oldest tricks in politics—from a guy whose act has, let's face it, gotten pretty stale. We don't need four more years of bluster and bumbling and chaos. We have seen that movie—and we all know that the sequel is usually worse. America is ready for a new chapter. America's ready for a better story.

We are ready for a President Kamala Harris.

And Kamala Harris is ready for the job. This is a person who has spent her life fighting on behalf of people who need a voice and a champion. As you heard from Michelle, Kamala wasn't born into privilege. She had to work for what she's got, and she actually cares about what other people are going through. She's not the neighbor running the leaf blower—she's the neighbor rushing over to help when you need a hand.

As a prosecutor, Kamala stood up for children who had been victims of sexual abuse. As Attorney General of the most populous state in the country, she fought big banks and for-profit colleges, securing billions of dollars for the people they had scammed. After the home mortgage crisis, she pushed me and my administration hard to make sure homeowners got a fair settlement. Didn't matter that I was a Democrat. Didn't matter that she had knocked on doors for my campaign in Iowa—she was going to fight to get as much relief as possible for the families who deserved it.

As Vice President, she helped take on the drug companies to cap the cost of insulin, lower the cost of health care, and give families with kids a tax cut. And she's running for president with real plans to lower costs even more, protect Medicare and Social Security, and sign a law to guarantee every woman's right to make her own health care decisions.

In other words, Kamala Harris won't be focused on her problems—she'll be focused on yours. As president, she won't just cater to her own supporters, punish those who refuse to kiss the ring or bend the knee. She'll work on behalf of every American.

That's who Kamala is. And in the White House, she will have an outstanding partner in Governor Tim Walz.

Lemme tell you something: I love this guy. Tim's the kind of person who should be in politics—born in a small town, served his country, taught kids, coached football, took care of his neighbors. He knows who he is and what's important. You can tell those flannel shirts he wears don't come from some consultant, they come from his closet, and they've been through some stuff.

Together, Kamala and Tim have kept faith with America's central story—a story that says we're all created equal, that everyone deserves a chance, and that, even when we don't agree with each other, we can find a way to live with each other.

That's Kamala's vision. That's Tim's vision. That's the Democratic Party's vision. And our job over the next eleven weeks is to convince as many people as possible to vote for that vision.

It won't be easy. The other side knows it's easier to play on people's fears and cynicism. They'll tell you that government is corrupt; that sacrifice and generosity are for suckers; and that since the game is rigged, it's ok to take what you want and look after your own.

That's the easy path. We have a different task. Our job is to convince people that democracy can actually deliver. And we can't just point to what we've already accomplished. We can't just rely on the ideas of the past. We need to chart a new way forward to meet the challenges of today.

And Kamala understands this. She knows, for example, that if we want to make it easier for more young people to buy a home, we need to build more units, and clear away some of the outdated laws and regulations that have made it harder to build homes for working people in this country. And she's put out a bold new plan to do just that.

On health care, we should all be proud of the enormous progress we've made through the Affordable Care Act—providing millions of people access to affordable coverage and protecting millions more from unscrupulous insurance practices. And I've notice, by the way, that since it's become popular they don't call it Obamacare no more. But Kamala knows we can't stop there, which is why she'll keep working to limit out of pocket costs.

Kamala knows that if we want to help people get ahead, we need to put a college degree within reach of more Americans. But she also knows college shouldn't be the only ticket to the middle class. We need to follow the lead of governors like Tim Walz who've said, if you've got the skills and the drive, you shouldn't need a degree to work for state government. And in this new economy, we need a president who actually cares about the millions of people all across this country who wake up every single day to do the essential, often thankless work to care for our sick, to clean our streets, to deliver our packages. We need a president to stand up for their right to bargain for better wages and working conditions.

And Kamala will be that president. Yes she can.

A Harris-Walz administration can help us move past some of the tired old debates that keep stifling progress, because at their core, Kamala and Tim understand that when everybody gets a fair shot, we're all better off. They understand that when every child gets a good education, the whole economy gets stronger. When women are paid the same as men for doing the same job, all families benefit. They understand that we can secure our border without tearing kids away from their parents, just like we can keep our streets safe while also building trust between law enforcement and the communities they serve and eliminating bias. That will make it better for everybody.

Donald Trump and his well-heeled donors don't see the world that way. For them, one group's gains is necessarily another group's loss. For them, freedom means that the powerful can do pretty much what they please, whether its fire workers trying to organize a union or poisoning our rivers or avoid paying taxes like everybody else has to do.

We have a broader idea of freedom. We believe in the freedom to provide for your family if you're willing to work hard; the freedom to breathe clean air and drink clean water and send your kids to school without worrying if they'll come home. We believe that true freedom gives each of us the right to make decisions about our own life—how we worship, what our family looks like, how many kids we have, who we marry. And we believe that freedom requires us to recognize that other people have the freedom to make choices that are different than ours. That's OK!

That's the America Kamala Harris and Tim Walz believe in. An America where "We the People" includes everyone. Because that's the only way this American experiment works. And despite what our politics might suggest, I think most Americans understand that. Democracy isn't just a bunch of abstract principles and dusty laws in some book somewhere. It's the values we live by, and the way we treat each other—including those who don't look like us or pray like us or see the world exactly like we do.

That sense of mutual respect has to be part of our message. Our politics has become so polarized these days that all of us, across the political spectrum, seem so quick to assume the worst in others unless they agree with us on every single issue. We start thinking that the only way to win is to scold and shame and out yell the other side. And after a while, regular folks just tune out, or don't bother to vote at all.

That approach may work for the politicians who just want attention and thrive on division. But it won't work for us. To make progress on the things we care about, the things that really affect people's lives, we need to remember that we've all got our blind spots and contradictions and prejudices; and that if we want to win over those who aren't yet ready to support our candidate, we need to listen to their concerns—and maybe learn something in the process.

After all, if a parent or grandparent occasionally says something that makes us cringe, we don't automatically assume they're bad people. We recognize the world is moving fast, and that they need time and maybe a little encouragement to catch up. Our fellow citizens deserve the same grace we hope they'll extend to us.

That's how we can build a true Democratic majority. And by the way, that doesn't just matter to people in this country. The rest of the world is watching to see if we can actually pull this off.

No nation, no society, has ever tried to build a democracy as big and as diverse as ours before. One that includes people who over decades have come from every corner of the globe. One where our allegiances and our community are defined not by race or blood, but by a common creed. That's why when we uphold our values, the world's a little brighter. When we don't, the world's a little dimmer. And dictators and autocrats feel emboldened, and over time we become less safe. We shouldn't be the world's policeman, and we can't eradicate every cruelty and injustice in the world. But America can be and must be, a force for good—discouraging conflict, fighting disease, promoting human rights, protecting the planet from climate change, defending freedom, promoting peace. That's what Kamala Harris believes—and so do most Americans.

I know these ideas can feel pretty naïve right now. We live in a time of such confusion and rancor, with a culture that puts a premium on things that don't last—money, fame, status, likes. We chase the approval of strangers on our phones; we build all manner of walls and fences around ourselves and then wonder why we feel so alone. We don't trust each other as much because we don't take the time know each other—and in that space between us, politicians and algorithms teach us to caricature each other and troll each other and fear each other.

But here's the good news, Chicago. All across America, in big cities and small towns, away from all the noise, the ties that bind us together are still there. We still coach Little League and look out for our elderly neighbors. We still feed the hungry, in churches and mosques and synagogues and temples. We still share the same pride when our Olympic athletes compete for the gold. Because the vast majority of us don't want to live in a country that's bitter and divided. We want something better. We want to be better. And the joy and excitement we're seeing around this campaign tells us we're not alone.

I've spent a lot of time thinking about this these past few months because, as Michelle mentioned, this summer we lost her mom, Ms. Marion Robinson.

I don't know that anybody has ever loved their mother-in-law any more than I loved mine. Mostly it's because she was funny and wise and the least pretentious person I knew. That and she always defended me with Michelle when I messed up. I'd hide behind her.

But I also think one of the reasons we became so close was she reminded me of my grandmother, the woman who raised me as a child. On the surface, the two of them didn't have a lot in common — one was a Black woman from right here, South Side of Chicago, right down the way, went to Englewood High School. The other a rural white woman born in a tiny town called Peru, Kansas. And yet, they shared a basic outlook on life—strong, smart, resourceful women, full of common sense, who, regardless of the barriers they encountered, and women growing up in the 40s, 50s and 60s, they encountered barriers, they still went about their business without fuss or complaint and provided an unshakable foundation of love for their children and grandchildren.

In that sense, they both represented an entire generation of working people who, through war and depression, discrimination and limited opportunity, helped build this country. A lot of them toiled every day at jobs that were often too small for them and didn't pay a lot. They willingly went without just to give their children something better. But they knew what was true. They knew what mattered. Things like honesty and integrity, kindness and hard work. They weren't impressed with braggarts or bullies. They didn't think putting other people down lifted you up or made you strong. they didn't spend a lot of time obsessing about what they didn't have. Instead, they ?? on what they did. They found pleasure in simple things—a card game with friends, a good meal and laughter around the kitchen table, helping others and seeing their children do things and go places that they would have never imagined for themselves.

Whether you're a Democrat or a Republican or somewhere in between, we've all had people like that in our lives. People like Kamala's parents, who crossed oceans because they believed in the promise of America. People like Tim's parents, who taught him about the importance of service. Good, hardworking people who weren't famous or powerful, but who managed, in countless ways, to leave this country just a little better than they found it.

As much as any policy or program, I believe that's what we yearn for—a return to an America where we work together and look out for each other. A restoration of what Lincoln called, on the eve of civil war, "our bonds of affection." An America that taps what he called "the better angels of our nature." That's what this election is about. And I believe that's why, if we each do our part over the next 77 days—if we knock on doors, if we make phone calls, if we talk to our friends, if we listen to our neighbors—if we work like we've never worked before, if we hold firm to our convictions—we will elect Kamala Harris as the next President of the United States, and Tim Walz as the next Vice President of the United States. We'll elect leaders up and down the ballot who will fight for the hopeful, forward-looking America we all believe in. And together, we too will build a country that is more secure and more just, more equal and more free.

So let's get to work. God bless you, and God bless the United States of America.

Print Citations

CMS: Obama, Barack. "It's Up to Us to Fight for the America We Believe In." Speech at the Democratic National Convention, Chicago, IL, August 20, 2024. In *The Reference Shelf: Representative American Speeches, 2023–2024,* edited by Micah L. Issitt, 35–41. Amenia, NY: Grey House Publishing, 2024.

MLA: Obama, Barack. "It's Up to Us to Fight for the America We Believe In." Democratic National Convention, 20 August 2024, Chicago, IL. Speech. *The Reference Shelf: Representative American Speeches, 2023–2024,* edited by Micah L. Issitt, Grey House Publishing, 2024, pp. 35–41.

APA: Obama, B. (2024). It's up to us to fight for the America we believe in [Speech]. Democratic National Convention, Chicago IL. In Micah L. Issitt (Ed.), *The reference shelf: Representative American speeches, 2023–2024* (pp. 35–41). Grey House Publishing. (Original work published 2024)

I See a Leader with a Real Commitment to Working Families

By Alexandria Ocasio-Cortez

"I am here tonight because America has before us a rare and precious opportunity." New York Representative Alexandria Ocasio-Cortez spoke at the Democratic National Convention in Chicago, Illinois. She talked about the political value of having lived the middle-class and working-class experience and claimed that Kamala Harris has the knowledge and history to represent all Americans, calling this election cycle an opportunity for America to begin a new chapter.

Thank you Chicago for your energy. Thank you Kamala Harris and Tim Walz for your vision. Thank you. Thank you. Thank you. Thank you, Chicago for your energy. Thank you, Kamala Harris and Tim Walz for your vision. And thank you, Joe Biden for your leadership.

Six years ago I was taking omelet orders as a waitress in New York City. I didn't have health insurance. My family was fighting off foreclosure and we were struggling with bills after my dad passed away unexpectedly from cancer.

Like millions of Americans, we were just looking for an honest shake and we were tired of a cynical politics that seem blind to the realities of working people. It was then only through the miracles of democracy and community that the good people of the Bronx and Queens chose someone like me to elect them in Congress.

And America, in my heart, I know from that same cloth of hope and aspiration, we will also elect Kamala Harris and Tim Walz as presidents and vice presidents of the United States of America. I am here tonight because America has before us a rare and precious opportunity. In Kamala Harris have a chance to elect a president who is for the middle class because she is from the middle class. She understands the urgency of rent checks and groceries and prescriptions. She is as committed to our reproductive and civil rights as she is to taking on corporate greed. And she is working tirelessly to secure a ceasefire in Gaza and bringing hostages home.

In Kamala Harris, I see a leader who understands. I see a leader with a real commitment to a better future for working families. And Chicago, we have to help her win because we know that Donald Trump would sell this country for a dollar if it meant lining his own pockets and greasing the palms of his Wall Street friends. And I, for one am tired about of hearing about how a two-bit union

---

Delivered on August 19, 2024 at the Democratic National Convention, Chicago, IL.

buster thinks of himself as more of a patriot than the woman who fights every single day to lift working people out from under the boots of greed trampling on our way of life.

The truth is done. You cannot love this country if you only fight for the wealthy and big business. To love this country is to fight for its people, all people, working people, every day Americans like bartenders and factory workers, and fast food cashiers who punch a clock and are on their feet all day in some of the toughest jobs out there.

Ever since I got elected, Republicans have attacked me by saying that I should go back to bartending. But let me tell you, I'm happy to, any day of the week because there is nothing wrong with working for a living. Imagine having leaders in the White House who understand that, leaders like Kamala and Tim. But Chicago, just because the choice is clear to us does not mean that the path will be easy.

Over the next 78 days, we will have to pour every ounce, every minute, every moment into making history on November 5th. But we cannot send Kamala and Tim to the White House alone. Together, we must also elect strong democratic majorities in the House and in the Senate so that we can deliver on an ambitious agenda for the people. Because if you are a working parent trying to afford rent and childcare, Kamala is for you. If you are a senior who had to go back to work because your retirement didn't stretch far enough, Kamala is for you. If you're an immigrant family, just starting your American story, Kamala is for you.

America, when we knock on our neighbor's door, organize our communities and elect Kamala Harris to the presidency on November 5th, we will send a loud message that the people of this nation will not go back. We choose a new path and open the door to a new day, one that is for the people and by the people. Thank you. Thank you very much. God bless. God bless you all.

Print Citations

CMS: Ocasio-Cortez, Alexandria. "I See a Leader with a Real Commitment to Working Families." Speech at the Democratic National Convention, Chicago, IL, August 19, 2024. In *The Reference Shelf: Representative American Speeches, 2023–2024,* edited by Micah L. Issitt, 42–43. Amenia, NY: Grey House Publishing, 2024.

MLA: Ocasio-Cortez, Alexandria. "I See a Leader with a Real Commitment to Working Families." Democratic National Convention, 19 August 2024, Chicago, IL. Speech. *The Reference Shelf: Representative American Speeches, 2023–2024,* edited by Micah L. Issitt, Grey House Publishing, 2024, pp. 42–43.

APA: Ocasio-Cortez, A. (2024). I see a leader with a real commitment to working families [Speech]. Democratic National Convention, Chicago, IL. In Micah L. Issitt (Ed.), *The reference shelf: Representative American speeches, 2023–2024* (pp. 42–43). Grey House Publishing. (Original work published 2024)

Values and Character Matter Most of All in Leadership and in Life

By Oprah Winfrey

"The work will never be done because freedom isn't free. America is an ongoing project. It requires commitment." Academy Award–nominated actress, author, and entrepreneur Oprah Winfrey spoke at the Democratic National Convention in Chicago, Illinois. She discussed the ongoing need to continue committing to the effort to make the nation better and the power of organization in helping to overcome difficult odds.

Good evening, everybody. Who says you can't go home again? After watching the Obamas last night, that was some epic fire, wasn't it? Some epic fire. We're now so fired up, we can't wait to leave here and do something. And what we're going to do is elect Kamala Harris as the next President of the United States.

I am so honored to have been asked to speak on tonight's theme about what matters most to me, to you, and all of us Americans: freedom. There are people who want you to see our country as a nation of us against them, people who want to scare you, who want to rule you. People who'd have you believe that books are dangerous and assault rifles are safe, that there's a right way to worship and a wrong way to love. People who seek first to divide and then to conquer.

But here's the thing. When we stand together, it is impossible to conquer us. In the words of an extraordinary American, the late Congressman John Lewis, he said, "No matter what ship our ancestors arrived on, we are all in the same boat now." Congressman Lewis knew very well how far this country has come because he was one of the brilliant Americans who helped to get us where we are. But he also knew that the work is not done. The work will never be done because freedom isn't free. America is an ongoing project. It requires commitment. It requires being open to the hard work and the heart work of democracy. And every now and then, it requires standing up to life's bullies.

I know this. I've lived in Mississippi, in Tennessee, in Wisconsin, Maryland, Indiana, Florida, Hawaii, Colorado, California and California and sweet home, Chicago, Illinois. I have actually traveled this country from the redwood forest, love those redwoods, to the Gulf Stream waters. I've seen racism and sexism and income inequality and division. I've not only seen it. At times, I've been on the receiving end of it.

But more often than not, what I've witnessed and experienced are human beings, both conservative and liberal, who may not agree with each other, but who'd still help you in a heartbeat if you were in trouble. These are the people

---

Delivered on August 21, 2024 at the Democratic National Convention, Chicago, IL.

Values and Character Matter Most of All in Leadership and in Life   **45**

who make me proud to say that I am an American. They are the best of America. And despite what some would have you think, we are not so different from our neighbors. When a house is on fire, we don't ask about the homeowner's race or religion. We don't wonder who their partner is or how they voted. No. We just try to do the best we can to save them. And if the place happens to belong to a childless cat lady, well, we try to get that cat out too.

Because we are a country of people who work hard for the money. We wish our brothers and sisters well, and we pray for peace. We know all the old tricks and tropes that are designed to distract us from what actually matters. But we are beyond ridiculous tweets and lies and foolery. These are complicated times, people, and they require adult conversation. And I welcome those conversations because civilized debate is vital to democracy and it is the best of America.

Now, over the last couple of nights, we have all seen brave people walk onto the stage and share their most private pain. Amanda and Josh, Kaitlyn, Hadley, they told us their stories of rape and incest and near death experiences from having the state deny them the abortion that their doctor explained was medically necessary. And they've told us these things for one reason and that is to keep what happened to them from happening to anybody else.

Because if you do not have autonomy over this, over this, if you cannot control when and how you choose to bring your children into this world and how they are raised and supported, there is no American dream. The women and men who are battling to keep us from going back to a time of desperation and then shame and stone coal fear, they are the new freedom fighters. And make no mistake, they are the best of America.

I want to talk now about somebody who's not with us tonight. Tessie Prevost Williams was born in New Orleans not long after the Supreme Court ruled that segregated public schools were unconstitutional. That was in 1954, same year I was born. But I didn't have to head to first grade at the all white McDonough 19 School with a US marshal by my side like Tessie did. And when I got to school, the building wasn't empty like it was for Tessie. You see, rather than allowing McDonough to be integrated, parents pulled their kids out of the school, leaving only Tessie and two other little Black girls, Gail Etienne and Leona Tate, to sit in a classroom with the windows papered over to block snipers from attacking their six year old bodies.

Tessie passed away six weeks ago, and I tell this story to honor her tonight because she, like Ruby Bridges and her friends, Leona and Gail, the New Orleans Four, they were called. They broke barriers and they paid dearly for it. But it was the grace and guts and courage of women like Tessie Prevost Williams that paved the way for another young girl who nine years later became part of the second class to integrate the public schools in Berkeley, California.

And it seems to me that at school and at home, somebody did a beautiful job of showing this young girl how to challenge the people at the top and empower the people at the bottom. They showed her how to look at the world and see not just what is, but what can be. They instilled in her a passion for justice and freedom and the glorious fighting spirit necessary to pursue that passion. And soon and very soon, soon and very soon, we're going to be teaching our daughters and sons about how this child of an Indian mother and a Jamaican father, two idealistic, energetic immigrants, immigrants, how this child grew up to become the 47th president of the United States. That is the best of America.

Let me tell you this. This election isn't about us and them. It's about you and me and what we want our futures to look like. There are choices to be made when we cast our ballot. Now, there's a certain candidate says, "If we just go to the polls this one time that we'll never have to do it again." Well, you know what? You're looking at a registered Independent who's proud to vote again and again and again because I'm an American and that's what Americans do. Voting is the best of America. And I have always, since I was eligible to vote, I've always voted my values and that is what is needed in this election now more than ever.

So I'm calling on all you Independents and all you undecideds. You know this is true. You know I'm telling you the truth, that values and character matter most of all in leadership and in life. And more than anything, you know this is true, that decency and respect are on the ballot in 2024. And just plain common sense. Common sense tells you that Kamala Harris and Tim Walz can give us decency and respect. They're the ones that give it to us.

So we are Americans. We are Americans. Let us choose loyalty to the Constitution over loyalty to any individual because that's the best of America. And let us choose optimism over cynicism because that's the best of America. And let us choose inclusion over retribution. Let us choose common sense over nonsense because that's the best of America. And let us choose the sweet promise of tomorrow over the bitter return to yesterday. We won't go back. We won't be set back, pushed back, bullied back, kicked back. We're not going back. Not going back. We're not going back.

So let us choose. Let us choose truth. Let us choose honor, and let us choose joy because that's the best of America. But more than anything else, let us choose freedom. Why? Because that's the best of America. We're all Americans and together, let's all choose Kamala Harris. Thank you, Chicago.

Print Citations

CMS: Winfrey, Oprah. "Values and Character Matter Most of All in Leadership and Life." Speech at the Democratic National Convention, Chicago, IL, August 21, 2024. In *The Reference Shelf: Representative American Speeches, 2023–2024,* edited by Micah L. Issitt, 44–46. Amenia, NY: Grey House Publishing, 2024.

MLA: Winfrey, Oprah. "Values and Character Matter Most of All in Leadership and Life." Democratic National Convention, 21 August 2024, Chicago, IL. Speech. *The Reference Shelf: Representative American Speeches, 2023–2024,* edited by Micah L. Issitt, Grey House Publishing, 2024, pp. 44–46.

APA: Winfrey, O. (2024). Values and character matter most of all in leadership and life [Speech]. Democratic National Convention, Chicago, IL. In Micah L. Issitt (Ed.), *The reference shelf: Representative American speeches, 2023–2024* (pp. 44–46). Grey House Publishing. (Original work published 2024)

Democracy Must Be Preserved

By Joe Biden

"Typically Trump, once again, putting himself first and America last." President Joe Biden was a keynote speaker at the Democratic National Convention in Chicago, Illinois. Biden discussed his administration's efforts at border control, economic improvement, his record in office, and Trump's efforts to sideline those accomplishments to forward his agenda.

That was my daughter! Thank you. I love you. Thank you, thank you, thank you. I tell you what, to my dearest daughter Ashley. God, love you. You're incredible. Thank you for the introduction and for being my courageous heart, along with Hunter and our entire family, and especially our rock, Jill. It was those of you who know us, she still leaves me both breathless and speechless. Everybody knows her, I love her more than she loves me. She walks down the stairs, and I still get that going boom, boom, boom. You all who know me, know I'm not kidding. Let's give a special round of applause to our first lady Jill Biden.

My dad used to have an expression, for real, he'd say "Joey, family is the beginning, the middle and the end."

And I love you all, folks. And America, I love you! Folks, let me ask you. Let me ask you. Are you ready to vote for freedom?

Are you ready to vote for democracy and for America? Let me ask you. Are you ready to elect Kamala Harris and Tim Walz? As president and vice president of the United States.

My fellow Democrats, my fellow Americans, nearly four years ago, in winter, on the steps of the Capitol, on a cold January day I raised my right hand, and I swore on oath to you and to God to preserve, protect and defend the constitution and to faithfully execute the office of the president of the United States. In front of me, in front of me, was a city surrounded by the national guard, behind me a Capitol just two weeks before had been overrun by a violent mob.

But I knew then, from the bottom of my heart, that I knew now, there is no place in America for political violence. None. You cannot say you love your country only when you win. In that moment, I wasn't looking to the past, I was looking to the future.

I spoke to the work at hand. The moment we had to meet, it was, as I told you then, a winter of peril and possibility. Of peril and possibility.

We were in the grip of a once-in-a-century pandemic, historic joblessness, a call for racial justice long overdue, clear and present threats to our very democracy.

Delivered on August 19, 2024 at the Democratic National Convention, Chicago, IL.

The Democratic Campaign

And yet, and yet I believed then, and I believe now, that progress was and is possible just as it is achievable. And our best days are not behind us, they're before us. Now it's summer, the winter has passed. And with a grateful heart, I stand before you now on this August night to report that democracy has prevailed. Democracy, democracy has delivered. And now, democracy must be preserved.

You've heard me say it before, we're facing an inflection point, one of those rare moments in history when the decisions we make now will determine the fate of our nation and the world for decades to come.

That's not hyperbole; I mean it literally.

We're in the battle for the very soul of America.

I ran for president in 2020 because of what I saw at Charlottesville in August of 2017. Extremists coming out of the woods, carrying torches, their veins bulging from their necks, carrying Nazi swastikas and chanting the same exact antisemitic bile that was heard in Germany in the early thirties.

Neo-Nazis, white supremacists and the Ku Klux Klan, so emboldened by a president then in the White House that they saw as an ally. They didn't even bother to wear their hoods. Hate was on the march in America.

Old ghosts, and new garments, stirring up the oldest divisions, stoking the oldest fears, giving oxygen to the oldest forces that they long sought to tear apart America.

In the process, a young woman was killed. When I contacted her mother to ask about what happened, she told me. When the president was asked what he thought had happened. Donald Trump said, and I quote, "There were very fine people on both sides." My god. That's what he said. That is what he said and what he meant.

Thats's when I realized I had to listen to the admonition of my dead son. I could not stay on the sidelines, so I ran.

I had no intention of running again. I just lost part of my soul, but I ran with a deep conviction. An America I know and believe, and an America where honesty, dignity, decency still matter. An America where everyone has a fair shot, and hate has no safe harbor. An America where the fundamental creed of this nation that all of us are created equal is still very much alive.

And a broad coalition of Americans joined with me. 81 million voters voted for us. More than any time in all of history.

Because of all of you in this room and others, we came together in 2020 to save democracy. As your president, I been determined to keep America moving forward, not going back, to stand against hate and violence in all its forms, to be a nation where we not only live with but thrive on diversity, demonizing no one, leaving no one behind, and becoming the nation that we professed to be.

I also ran to rebuild the backbone of America—the middle class. I made a commitment to you that I'd be a president for all America, whether you voted for me or not.

We have done that. Studies show the major bills we have passed actually delivered more to red states than blue, because the job of the president is to deliver to all America.

Because of you, I'm not exaggerating, because of you, we've had one of the most extraordinary four years of progress ever. Period.

When I say we, I mean Kamala and me.

Just think about it. COVID no longer controls our lives. We've gone from economic crisis to the strongest economy in the entire world.

Record 60 million new jobs, record small business growth, record high stock market, record high 401Ks. Wages up, inflation down, way down, and continuing to go down. The smallest racial wealth gap in 20 years and yes, we both know we have more to do, but we're moving in the right direction.

More Americans have peace of mind that comes from having health insurance. More Americans have health insurance today than ever before in American history. And after, as a young senator beginning to fight, we got in a fight for 50 years to give Medicare the power to negotiate low-prescription drug prices, we finally beat Big Pharma.

And guess who cast the tie breaking vote? Vice President, soon to be President, Kamala Harris. And now it's the law of land. Instead of paying $400 a month for insulin seniors with diabetes, will pay $35 a month. The law we passed, already includes, starting in January, every seniors' total prescription cost can be capped at $2,000, no matter how expensive the drugs they have.

And what we don't focus on, and our Republican friends doesn't seem to understand, our reforms don't just save seniors money, they save the American taxpayers money.

You know what we just passed saved? It saved $160 billion dollars over the next decade.

That's not hyperbole. It's because Medicare no longer has to pay those exorbitant prices ... to the Big Pharma.

But look, folks. Thank you, Kamala, too. Look.

Folks, how can we have the strongest economy in the world without the best infrastructure in the world?

Donald Trump promised infrastructure week every week for four years, and he never built a damn thing.

But now because of Kamala and I've done, remember we're told we couldn't get it done, remember when we came into office, we couldn't get anything passed?

But right now, we're giving America an infrastructure decade, not week.

We're modernizing, our roads, our bridges, our ports, our airports, our trains, our buses.

Removing every lead pipe from schools and homes so every child can drink clean water. Providing affordable high-speed internet for every American no matter where they live. Unlike, not unlike, what Roosevelt did with electricity.

50   The Democratic Campaign

And so much more. We are uniting the country. We're growing our economy. We're improving our quality of life and we're building a better America. Because that's who we are.

How can we be the strongest nation in the world, without leading the world in science and technology?

After years of importing 90% of our semiconductor chips from abroad, which America invented those chips. Our CHIPS and Science Act meant the private companies from around the world are now investing literally 10's of billions of dollars to build new chip factories right here in America. And over that period, they'll create tens of thousands of jobs. And many of those jobs, so-called fabs, the buildings that make those chips, are being constructed now.

And guess what? The average salary in those fabs, the size of a football field, will be over $100,000 a year and you don't need a college degree.

Because of you and so many electeds out there, American manufacturing is back. Where those to say we wouldn't lead the world in manufacturing? 800,000 new manufacturing jobs. Our Republican friends, and others, made sure they'd go abroad to get the cheapest labor. We used to import products and export jobs, now we export American products and create American jobs. Right here in America, where jobs belong.

With every new job, with every new factory, pride and hope is being brought back to communities throughout the country that were left behind. You know, you're from them many of you, you know what it's like when that factory closed, where your mother, your father, your grandmother, grandfather worked, and now you're back, providing once again, proving that Wall Street didn't built America, the middle class built America and unions, unions built the middle class.

It's been my view since I came to the Senate. That's why I'm proud to have been the first president to walk the picket line and be labeled the most pro-union president in history. And I accept it. It's a fact. Because when unions do well, we all do well.

You got it man, you got it. I agree. I'm proud.

Look, remember we were told we couldn't get anything done. We couldn't get anything done in the Congress. Well with your support, we passed the most significant climate law in the history of mankind.

For $370 billion dollars, cutting carbon emissions in half by 2030, launching a climate corps, similar to AmeriCorps or Peace Corps creating tens of thousands of jobs for young people in the future who are going to make sure this continues.

Creating hundreds of thousands of jobs in clean energy for American workers including the IBW installing 500,000 charging stations all across America.

And in the process, reducing carbon emissions, and we're seeing it, we're seeing to it that the first beneficiaries environmental issues are those fence lines communities that have been smothered by the legacy of pollution. Louisiana and Delaware, Route nine, all the factories, all those chemical factories are right next to the poorest neighborhoods. They're the ones we're going to bring back.

And how, how can we be the greatest nation in the world without the best education system in the world?

Donald Trump and the Republican friends, that not only they can't think they can't read very well. Seriously, think about it.

Look at their Project 2025. Want to do away with the Department of Education.

Well during the pandemic, Kamala helped states and cities get back their get back their schools back open, and we gave public school teachers a raise, we created apprenticeships with businesses in the communities, putting students on path, to a good paying job, whether or not they go to college.

And by the way, we're making college a hell of a lot more affordable. Increasing Pell grants by $900. Over $15 billion dollars for HBCUs, minority service, including Hispanic institutions and tribal colleges.

We kept our commitment to provide more student relief than ever by lifting the burden of helping millions of families so they could get married, start a family, buy a home and begin to build family wealth and contribute to the community, and grow our economy.

It's not costing us, it's creating more wealth. We fundamentally transformed how our economy grows. From the middle out and the bottom up, instead of the top down.

You know, my dad used to say there wasn't a whole hell of a lot to drop down on my kitchen table at the end of the month. I come from basic middle-class family: Three-bedroom house, four kids, a grandpop living with us, decent neighborhood, but never a penny to spare. And look, that top-down notion, it never worked. Lota Democrats didn't think it worked, thought it worked, but it doesn't.

And when we did all that, what we've done, everybody could do well. Everybody. Donald Trump calls America a failing nation.

No, I'm serious. Think about this. Think about this. He publicly, he says to the whole world.

I'm going to say something outrageous, I know more foreign leaders by their first names than and know them well than anybody alive just because I'm so damn old.

And I'm not joking.

Think of the message he sends around the world, when he talks about America being a failing nation. He says we're losing. He's the loser. He's dead wrong. Many of you are very successful people who travel the world.

Name me a country in the world that doesn't think we're the leading nation in the world.

Without America, not a joke, think about it, I'm being literal, who could lead the world other than the United States of America? Well guess what? America's winning and the world's better off for it.

America is more prosperous, and Americans are safer today than under Donald Trump.

Trump continues to lie about crime in America, like everything else.

52 The Democratic Campaign

Guess what? On his watch, the murder rate went up 30%, the biggest increase in history. Meanwhile, we made the largest investment, Kamala and I, in public safety, ever. Now, the murder rate is falling faster than any time in history.

Violent crime has dropped to the lowest level in more than 50 years. And crime will keep coming down when we put a prosecutor in the oval office instead of a convicted felon.

Folks, distinguished senator from the Senate from California and I passed the first ban on assault weapons. And guess what? It worked. If we care about public safety, we need to prevent gun violence.

And what makes me ashamed when I travel the world, which I do, more children in America are killed by a gunshot than any other cause in the United States. More die from a bullet than cancer, accidents, than anything else in the United States of America. My god. That's why Kamala and I are proud, we beat the NRA and we passed the first major bipartisan gun-safety law in 30 years.

I'm serious. That comes from here. And now it's time to ban assault weapons again. And demand universal background checks. It's hard, I never thought I'd stand before a crowd of Democrats and refer to a president as a liar so many times. No, I'm not trying to be funny. It's sad.

Trump continues to lie about the border. Here's what he won't tell you. Trump killed the strongest bipartisan border deal in the history of the United States. That we negotiated with the Senate Republicans, took four weeks.

Once it passed, and everybody acknowledged most expansive border change in history, he called senators to say, "Don't support the bipartisan bill." He said, "It would help me politically and hurt him politically." My god. No, I'm serious. Think about it. Not a joke.

Not trying to be funny, but it's sad that Trump continues to lie about the border. Here's what he won't tell you: Trump killed the largest, strongest bipartisan border deal in the history of the United States that we negotiated with Senate Republicans in just four weeks. Once it passed and acknowledged the border change in American history, he called Senators and said, "Don't support the bipartisan Senate bill." He said it would help me politically and hurt him politically. My God. Seriously, think about it—it's not a joke. Even ask the press who don't like me, and they'll tell you that's true.

Typically Trump, once again putting himself first and America last. Then I had to take executive action. As a result of the executive action I took, border encounters have dropped over 50%. In fact, there are fewer border crossings today than when Donald Trump left office. And unlike Trump, we will not demonize immigrants, saying they are "poisoning the blood of America" or "poisoning the blood of our country." Kamala and I are committed to strengthening legal immigration, including protecting Dreamers and more.

And here's what else I believe in: protecting your freedom—your freedom to vote, your freedom to love who you love, and your freedom to choose. The decision to overturn *Roe v. Wade* that you heard earlier tonight—the U.S. Supreme Court majority wrote the following: "Women are not without electoral or political power." No kidding. MAGA Republicans found out the power of women in 2022, and Donald Trump is going to find out the power of women in 2024. Watch.

And Trump's MAGA Republican right-wingers seek to erase history. We Democrats continue to write history and make more history. I'm proud. I'm proud to have kept my commitment to appoint the first Black woman to the U.S. Supreme Court, Ketanji Brown Jackson, a symbol for every young woman in America that you can do anything. I'm proud I kept my commitment to have an administration that looks like America and that taps into the full talent of our nation. The most diverse Cabinet in history, including the first Black woman of South Asian descent to serve as Vice President—and who will soon serve as the 47th President of the United States. She is good.

Look... thank you. Folks, I've long said we have many obligations as a nation, but I got in trouble years ago for saying I make no apologies. We have only one truly sacred obligation: to prepare and equip those we send to war and care for them and their families when they come home—and when they don't. That's why I'm so proud to have written and signed the PACT Act, one of the most significant laws ever helping veterans and their families exposed to toxic materials like burn pits and Agent Orange.

I was around during the Vietnam War. It's hard—no one was able to prove that their illness was a consequence of Agent Orange, and no one was able to prove initially that because they lived near burn pits, like my son did in Iraq for a year, that it was the cause of their illness. But because of the PACT Act, a surviving spouse with two children is now eligible for a stipend of about $3,000 a month, and those children who lost a parent are eligible for tuition benefits to go to college and get job training. It's already helping over 1 million veterans and their families so far. Well, I love them, and I'm so proud of my son's service. We get it.

Guess who doesn't get it and doesn't respect our veterans? We know from his own chief of staff, four-star General John Kelly, that Trump, when in Europe, would not go to the gravesites in France of the brave service members who gave their lives for this country. He called them "suckers" and "losers." Who in the hell does he think he is? Who does he think he is? Those are not the words of a person worthy of being Commander-in-Chief—period. Not then, not now, not ever. I mean that. I mean that from the bottom of my heart. Just as no Commander-in-Chief should ever bow down to a dictator the way Trump bows down to Putin.

I never have, and I promise you, Kamala Harris never will. We will never bow down. When Trump left office, Europe and NATO were in tatters. Not a joke. The "America First" doctrine changed our whole image in the world. Well, I spent—they gave the hours, about 190 hours total—my counterparts, heads of state in Europe, to strengthen NATO. We did. We united Europe like it hadn't been united for years, adding Finland and Sweden to NATO. Ten days before he died, Henry Kissinger called and said, "Not since Napoleon has Europe not looked over their shoulder at Russia with dread."

54 The Democratic Campaign

Well, guess what? Putin thought he'd take Kyiv in three days. Three years later, Ukraine is still free! When I came to office, the conventional wisdom was that China would inevitably surpass the United States. They haven't. No one's saying that now!

We'll keep working to bring hostages home, end the war in Gaza, and bring peace and security to the Middle East. As you know, I wrote a peace treaty for Gaza. A few days ago, I put forward a proposal that brought us closer to that goal than we've been since October 7th.

We're working around the clock, my Secretary of State and I, to prevent a wider war, reunite hostages with their families, and surge humanitarian aid, health services, and food assistance into Gaza now. To end the civilian suffering of the Palestinian people, and finally, finally, finally deliver a ceasefire in this war.

Those protesters out in the street, they have a point. A lot of innocent people are being killed on both sides. Just as we worked around the clock to bring home wrongfully detained Americans and others from Russia, in one of the most complicated swaps in history, but they're home. Kamala and I are going to keep working to bring all Americans wrongfully detained around the world home. I mean it.

Folks, I've got five months left in my presidency. I've got a lot to do. I intend to get it done. It's been the honor of my lifetime to serve as your president. I love the job, but I love my country more.

All those people who said I should step down, that's not true. We love our country more, and we need to preserve our democracy. In 2024, we need you to vote. We need you to keep the Senate. We need you to win back the House of Representatives. We need you to beat Donald Trump.

Kamala and Tim, President and Vice President of the United States of America. Look, they'll continue to lead America forward, creating more jobs, standing up for workers, growing the economy, lowering the costs to American families so they just have a little more breathing room. We've made incredible progress with more work to do.

Kamala and Tim will continue to take on corporate greed and bring down the cost of insulin to $35 a month, not just for seniors, but for everyone in America. They'll cap prescription drug costs at a total of $2,000, not just for seniors, but for everyone. And folks, that's going to save Americans tens of billions of dollars.

Folks, they'll make housing more affordable, building 3 million new homes, providing $25,000 in down payment assistance for first-time home buyers, more than the $10,000 we approved. Donald Trump wants new taxes on imported goods, food, gas, clothing, and more. You know what that would cost the average family, according to the experts? $3,900 a year in taxes. No, that's just a fact. Kamala and Tim will make the child care tax credit permanent, lifting millions of children out of poverty and helping millions of families get ahead.

And you know what Trump did? He created the largest debt any president has in four years with his $2 trillion tax cut for the wealthy. Well, Trump has a new plan. He wants to provide a $5 billion tax cut for corporations that are very wealthy. Read it. It would put us further in debt. And folks, you know we have

1,000 billionaires in America. You know what their average tax rate is? 8.2%. If we just increase their taxes, as we proposed, to 25%, which isn't even the highest tax rate, it would raise $500 billion new dollars over 10 years. And they'd still be very wealthy. Look, Kamala and Tim are going to make them pay their fair share.

They'll protect Social Security and Medicare. Trump wants to cut Social Security and Medicare. Kamala and Tim will protect your freedom. They'll protect your right to vote. They'll protect your civil rights. And you know Trump will do everything he can to ban abortion nationwide. Oh, he will. You know Kamala and Tim will do everything they possibly can to stop him. And that's why you have to elect senators and representatives who will restore *Roe v. Wade*.

The ancient Greeks taught us that character is destiny. Character is destiny. For me and Jill, we know Kamala and Doug are people of character. It's been our honor to serve alongside them. And we know that Tim and Gwen Walz are also people of great character. Selecting Kamala was the very first decision I made when I became our nominee. And it was the best decision I made in my whole career.

Now that we've gotten to know each other, we've become close friends. She's tough. She's experienced. And she has enormous integrity. Her story represents the best American story. And like many of our best presidents, she was also vice president. But she'll be a president our children can look up to. She'll be a president respected by world leaders because she already is. She'll be a president we can all be proud of. And she will be a historic president who puts her stamp on America's future.

This will be the first presidential election since January 6th. On that day, we almost lost everything about who we are as a country. And that threat, this is not hyperbole, that threat is still very much alive. Donald Trump says he will refuse to accept the election result if he loses again. Think about that. He's promising a bloodbath if he loses, in his words. And that he'll be a dictator on day one, in his own words. By the way, this sucker means it. No, I'm not joking. Think about it. Anybody else said that in the past, you'd think he was crazy, you'd think it was an exaggeration, but he means it. We can't let that happen.

Folks, all of us carry a special obligation: Independents, Republicans, Democrats. We saved democracy in 2020, and now we must save it again in 2024. The vote each of us casts this year will determine whether democracy and freedom will prevail. It's that simple. It's that serious. The power is literally in your hands. History is in your hands. Not hyperbole. It's in your hands. America's future is in your hands.

Let me close with this. Nowhere else in the world could a kid with a stutter and modest beginnings in Scranton, Pennsylvania, and Claymont, Delaware, grow up to sit behind the Resolute desk in the Oval Office. That's because America is, and always has been, a nation of possibilities. Possibilities. We must never lose that. Never.

Kamala and Tim understand that this nation must continue to be a place of possibilities. Not just for a few of us, but for all of us. Join me in dedicating your whole heart to this effort. And with all my heart, I promise I'll be the best volunteer Harris and Walz camp have ever seen.

Each of us has our own American story. For me and my family, there's a song that means a lot to us. It captures the best of who we are as a nation. The song is called "American Anthem." There's one verse that stands out, and I can't sing worth a damn, so I'm not going to try. I'll just quote it: "The work and prayers of centuries have brought us to this day. What shall our legacy be? What will our children say? Let me know in my heart, when my days are through. America, America, I gave my best to you."

I've made a lot of mistakes in my career. But I gave my best to you. For 50 years, like many of you, I've given my heart and soul to our nation. And I've been blessed a million times in return for the support of the American people. I really have been too young to be in the Senate because I wasn't 30 yet, and now I'm too old to stay as president. But I hope you know how grateful I am to all of you.

I can honestly say, and I mean this from the bottom of my heart, giving my word as a Biden: I can honestly say I'm more optimistic about the future than I was when I was elected as a 29-year-old United States Senator. I mean it.

Folks, we just have to remember who we are. We're the United States of America! And there's nothing we cannot do when we do it together.

God bless you all, and may God protect our troops.

Thank you.

Print Citations

CMS: Biden, Joe. "Democracy Must Be Preserved." Keynote address at the Democratic National Convention, Chicago, IL, August 19, 2024. In *The Reference Shelf: Representative American Speeches, 2023–2024,* edited by Micah L. Issitt, 47–56. Amenia, NY: Grey House Publishing, 2024.

MLA: Biden, Joe. "Democracy Must Be Preserved." Democratic National Convention, 19 August 2024, Chicago, IL. Keynote address. *The Reference Shelf: Representative American Speeches, 2023–2024,* edited by Micah L. Issitt, Grey House Publishing, 2024, pp. 47–56.

APA: Biden, J. (2024). Democracy must be preserved [Keynote address]. Democratic National Convention, Chicago, IL. In Micah L. Issitt (Ed.), *The reference shelf: Representative American speeches, 2023–2024* (pp. 47–56). Grey House Publishing. (Original work published 2024)

2
The Republican Campaign

J. D. Vance at the 2024 People's Convention. Photo by Gage Skidmore, CC BY-SA 2.0, via Wikimedia.

Acceptance Speech for President

By Donald Trump

"Under our leadership. The United States will be respected again. No nation will question our power. No enemy will doubt our might. Our borders will be totally secure." Former president and businessman Donald Trump gave a speech accepting the Republican Party's nomination for the presidency at the Republican National Convention in Milwaukee, Wisconsin. Trump claims that a migrant crime wave and inflation have been caused by the Biden administration's mismanagement.

Thank you very much. Thank you very, very much. Wow. Thank you, Dana. Thank you, Kid Rock, sometimes referred to as Bob. Thank you, Lee, right from the beginning. Thank you very much. What a talent. What a beautiful, beautiful soul. Thank you.

Friends, delegates, and fellow citizens, I stand before you this evening with a message of confidence, strength, and hope. Four months from now, we will have an incredible victory, and we will begin the four greatest years in the history of our country. Together, we will launch a new era of safety, prosperity, and freedom for citizens of every race, religion, color, and creed. The discord and division in our society must be healed. We must heal it quickly.

As Americans, we are bound together by a single fate and a shared destiny. We rise together or we fall apart. I am running to be president for all of America, not half of America, because there is no victory in winning for half of America. Tonight, with faith and devotion, I proudly accept your nomination for President of the United States. Thank you. Thank you. Thank you very much.

Thank you very much, and we will do it right. We're going to do it right. Let me begin this evening by expressing my gratitude to the American people for your outpouring of love and support following the assassination attempt at my rally on Saturday. As you already know, the assassin's bullet came within a quarter of an inch of taking my life. So many people have asked me what happened, "Tell us what happened, please," and therefore, I will tell you exactly what happened, and you'll never hear it from me a second time because it's actually too painful to tell.

It was a warm, beautiful day in the early evening in Butler Township in the great commonwealth of Pennsylvania. Music was loudly playing and the campaign was doing really well. I went to the stage and the crowd was cheering wildly. Everybody was happy. I began speaking very strongly, powerfully, and happily because I was discussing the great job my administration did on immigration at the southern border. We were very proud of it.

Delivered on July 18, 2024 at the Republican National Convention, Milwaukee, WI.

60 The Republican Campaign

Behind me and to the right was a large screen that was displaying a chart of border crossings under my leadership. The numbers were absolutely amazing. In order to see the chart, I started to, like this, turn to my right and was ready to begin a little bit further turn, which I'm very lucky I didn't do, when I heard a loud, whizzing sound and felt something hit me really, really hard on my right ear. I said to myself, "Wow, what was that? It can only be a bullet," and moved my right hand to my ear, brought it down. My hand was covered with blood. Just absolutely blood all over the place. I immediately knew it was very serious, that we were under attack, and in one movement, proceeded to drop to the ground.

Bullets were continuing to fly as very brave Secret Service agents rushed to the stage. They really did, they rushed to the stage. These are great people at great risk, I will tell you, and pounced on top of me so that I would be protected. There was blood pouring everywhere, and yet, in a certain way, I felt very safe because I had God on my side. I felt that.

The amazing thing is that prior to the shot, if I had not moved my head at that very last instant, the assassin's bullet would have perfectly hit its mark, and I would not be here tonight. We would not be together. The most incredible aspect of what took place on that terrible evening in the fading sun was actually seen later. In almost all cases, as you probably know, and when even a single bullet is fired, just a single bullet, and we had many bullets that were being fired, crowds run for the exits or stampede, but not in this case. It's very unusual.

This massive crowd of tens of thousands of people stood by and didn't move an inch. In fact, many of them bravely, but automatically, stood up looking for where the sniper would be, they knew immediately it was a sniper, and then began pointing at him. You can see that if you look at the group behind me. That was just a small group compared to what was in front. Nobody ran, and by not stampeding, many lives were saved.

But that isn't the reason that they didn't move. The reason is that they knew I was in very serious trouble, they saw me go down, they saw the blood, and thought actually must dead, that I was dead. They knew it was a shot to the head. They saw the blood. There's interesting statistic. The ears are the bloodiest part. If something happens with the ears, they bleed more than any other part of the body. For whatever reason, the doctors told me that. I said, "Why is there so much blood?" He said, "It's the ears. They bleed more." We learned something.

But they just, this beautiful crowd, they didn't want to leave me. They knew I was in trouble. They didn't want to leave me. You can see that love written all over their faces. Incredible people. They're incredible people. Bullets were flying over us, yet I felt serene. But now the Secret Service agents were putting themselves in peril. They were in very dangerous territory. Bullets were flying right over them, missing them by a very small amount of inches. Then it all stopped. Our Secret Service sniper, from a much greater distance and with only one bullet used, took the assassin's life, took him out. I'm not supposed to be here tonight. Not supposed to be here.

Thank you. But I'm not. I'll tell you, I stand before you in this arena only by the grace of Almighty God. Watching the reports over the last few days, many people say it was a providential moment. Probably was. When I rose, surrounded by Secret Service, the crowd was confused because they thought I was dead and there was great, great sorrow. I could see that on their faces as I looked out. They didn't know I was looking out. They thought it was over. But I could see it and I wanted to do something to let them know I was okay. I raised my right arm, looked at the thousands and thousands of people that were breathlessly waiting and started shouting, "Fight, fight, fight."

Thank you. Once my clenched fist went up and it was high into the air, you've all seen that, the crowd realized I was okay and roared with pride for our country like no crowd I have ever heard before. Never heard anything like it. For the rest of my life, I will be grateful for the love shown by that giant audience of patriots that stood bravely on that fateful evening in Pennsylvania. Tragically, the shooter claimed the life of one of our fellow Americans, Corey Comperatore, unbelievable person, everybody tells me, unbelievable, and seriously wounded two other great warriors, I spoke to them today, David Dutch and James Copenhaver, two great people.

I also spoke to all three families of these tremendous people. Our love and prayers are with them and always will be. We're never going to forget them. They came for a great rally. They were serious Trumpsters, I want to tell you. They were serious Trumpsters and still are. But Corey, unfortunately, we have to use the past tense, he was incredible. He was a highly respected former fire chief, respected by everybody, was accompanied by his wife, Helen, incredible woman I spoke to today, devastated, and two precious daughters. He lost his life selflessly acting as a human shield to protect them from flying bullets. He went right over the top of them and was hit. What a fine man he was.

I want to thank the fire department and the family for sending his helmet, his outfit. It was just something, and they're going to do something very special when they get it. But we did something, which cannot match what happened. Not even close. But I am very proud to say that over the past few days, we've raised $6.3 million for the families of David, James, and Corey, including from a friend of mine, just called up. He sent me a check right here. I just got it. $1 million from Dan Newlin. Thank you, Dan. Again, when speaking to the family, I told them, I said, "Well, I'm going to be sending you a lot of money, but it can't compensate." They all said the same thing. "You're right, sir. We appreciate so much what you're doing, but nothing can take the place in the case of Corey." The other two, by the way, they were very, very seriously injured, but now they're doing very well. They're going to be okay. They're going to be doing very well. They're warriors. Now I ask that we observe a moment of silence in honor of our friend, Corey. There is no greater love than to lay down one's life for others. This is the spirit that forged America in her darkest hours. This is the love that will lead America back to the summit of human achievement and greatness. This is what we need.

62 The Republican Campaign

Despite such a heinous attack, we unite this evening more determined than ever. I am more determined than ever, and so are you, so is everybody in the USA.

Our resolve is unbroken and our purpose is unchanged to deliver a government that serves the American people better than ever before. Nothing will stop me in this mission because our vision is righteous and our cause is pure. No matter what obstacle comes our way, we will not break, we will not bend, we will not back down, and I will never stop fighting for you, your family, and our magnificent country. Never. Everything I have to give with all of the energy and fight in my heart and soul, I pledge to our nation tonight. Thank you very much. I pledge that to our nation. Going to turn our nation around and we're going to do it very quickly. Thank you.

This election should be about the issues facing our country and how to make America successful, safe, free, and great again. In an age when our politics too often divide us, now is the time to remember that we are all fellow citizens. We are one nation under God, indivisible, with liberty and justice for all. We must not criminalize, dissent, or demonize political disagreement, which is what's been happening in our country lately at a level that nobody has ever seen before. In that spirit, the Democrat Party should immediately stop weaponizing the justice system and labeling their political opponent as an enemy of democracy, especially since that is not true. In fact, I am the one saving democracy for the people of our country.

Very big news, as you probably just read. On Monday, a major ruling was handed down from a highly respected federal judge in Florida, Aileen Cannon, finding that the prosecutor and the fake documents case against me were totally unconstitutional, and the entire case was thrown out of court, with all of that publicity thrown out of court. If Democrats want to unify our country, they should drop these partisan witch hunts, which I have been going through for approximately eight years, and they should do that without delay and allow an election to proceed that is worthy of our people, we're going to win it anyway, but worthy of our people.

On this journey, I am deeply honored to be joined by my amazing wife, Melania. Melania, thank you very much. You also did something really beautiful, a letter to America calling for national unity. It really took the Republican Party by surprise. I will tell you, it was beautiful. In fact, some very serious people said that we should take that letter and put it as part of the Republican platform. That would be an honor, wouldn't it? Right, Mr. Congressman? But it captivated so many. I also want to thank my entire family for being here. Don, Kimberly, Ivanka and Jared, Eric and Lara, Tiffany and Michael, Barron, we love our Barron, and of course, my 10 wonderful grandchildren. You saw a few of them up there on my lap before. How good was Dana? Was Dana good? I mean, was he good? He was on probably the only vacation he's had in about maybe ever because he works, but about 10 years with his wife, very far away. I won't tell you where, but very, very far away. Beautiful place. My people called and he said, "Yeah, I won't be able to do it. This is many, many years. I promised my wife, I can't do it." They

Acceptance Speech for President **63**

came in, they said, "Dana won't be able to do it," because he was my first, second, and third choice. I said, "Well, you know, that's too bad, but I understand he's away and it's good. It's good for him." That was it. About 30 minutes later, she came back in. "Sir, Dana just called. He's going to do it." His wife, she said, "You can't turn him down. You just can't do it. You have to go." That's a good wife. He got on a plane. He got here a little while ago and now he's going to get on the plane in a little while and he's going to go back home to his wife. But they're great. I just want to thank her and him and their whole family because that's not easy. Kid Rock, same thing. Called, he said, "I want to be a part of it. I want to be a part..."

Kid does this great song, big, big monster song. I had no idea. He became a friend of mine over the last 10 years and he's amazing. Everyone loves him. I didn't even know how big he was. He has rallies, 35, 40,000 people he gets every time he goes out. I think he's making so much money he doesn't know what the hell to do with it. You want to know. And then we have my other friend and I've known him so long and we took that song and it was a big success, but we made that. I saw a chart of great songs to America. That was number one on the chart recently, number one. So that's Lee Greenwood, very special, beautiful person. He's a beautiful man.

But they all wanted to be here. They called. And how about the Hulkster? How good was he? You see that? Where is he? Boy, oh boy. They may call that entertainment. I know about entertainment, but when he used to lift a 350 pound man over his shoulders and then bench press him two rows into the audience, I said, "It may be entertainment, but he is one strong son of a gun." I will tell you, I watched it many times. There aren't a lot of entertainers that could do that, right? You were fantastic. Thank you very much. Followed by Eric. What was that all about? Boy, that was good. I didn't want to really come up here. But he was so great and he's such a good young man. He went through a lot of trouble. And Don last night was incredible. They went through so much trouble.

They got subpoenaed more than any people probably in the history of the United States. Every week they get another subpoena from the Democrats. Crazy Nancy Pelosi, the whole thing. Just boom, boom, boom. They've got to stop that because they're destroying our country. We have to work on making America great again, not on beating people. And we won. We beat them in all. We beat them on the impeachments. We beat them on indictments. We beat them. But the time that you have to spend, if they would devote that genius to helping our country, we'd have a much stronger and better country. And Jason, the biggest star in country music. Jason, thank you for being here. Jason, thank you very much. Jason Aldean, he's good. I like his wife even better by the way. She's here. Thank you, Jason. But I'm thrilled to have a new friend and partner fighting by my side, the next Vice President of the United States, the current Senator from Ohio, JD Vance and his incredible wife, Usha.

He's going to be a great vice president. He's going to be great. He'll be with this country and with this movement, greatest movement in the history of our

64 The Republican Campaign

country, make America great again. When they criticize it, they said, "We're going to try and stop MAGA." I said, "MAGA is Make America Great again. What are you going to stop? There's nothing to stop." Then they say, "Oh, that's right. It's very tough to fight it." And all of the people that did try and fight it have failed, but he's going to be with us for a long time and it was an honor to select him. Great, great student at Yale. His wife was a great student at Yale. They met at Yale. These are two smart people.

So JD, you're going to be doing this for a long time. Enjoy the ride. And a very special thank you to the extraordinary people of Milwaukee and the great state of... Oh, there they are. There they are. You are so easy to spot. And Green Bay's going to have a good team this year, right? They're going to have a good team. They're going to have a good team. Most of the audience doesn't like it, but it's true. You're going to have a very good team this year. And by the way, Wisconsin, we are spending over $250 million here creating jobs and other economic development all over the place. So I hope you'll remember this in November and give us your vote. I am trying to buy your vote. I'll be honest about that. And I promise we will make Wisconsin great again. We're going to make it.

Thank you, Mr. Governor. Thank you very much. Thank you. I'm here tonight to lay out a vision for the whole nation to every citizen, whether you're a young or old, man or woman, democrat, republican or independent, Black or white, Asian or Hispanic, I extend to you a hand of loyalty and of friendship. Together we will lead America to new heights of greatness like the world has never seen before. We were right there in the first term. We got hit with COVID. We did a great job. Nobody knew what it was, but nobody's ever seen an economy pre COVID. And then we handed over a stock market that was substantially higher than just prior to COVID coming in. Did a great job. Never got credit for that. We got credit for the war and defeating ISIS and so many things, the great economy, the biggest tax cuts ever, the biggest regulation cuts ever.

The creation of Space Force, the rebuilding of our military. We did so much. We did so much. Right to try, right to try is a big deal. We got right to try. They were trying to get that for 52 years. Somebody's terminally ill and hopefully there's nobody in this audience, but it does happen a lot. They're terminally ill and they can't use our new space age drugs and other things that we are way ahead. We are the greatest doctors in the world, the greatest laboratories in the world, and you can't do it. They've been trying to get that approved for 52 years. It wasn't that easy. The insurance companies didn't want to do it. They didn't want the risk.

The labs didn't want to do it because if it didn't work, people are pretty far down the line toward death. They didn't want to do it. The doctors didn't want to have it on their records. So I got everybody into an office. 52 years, they tried. Sounds simple, but it's not. And I got them to agree that somebody that needs it will. Instead of going to Asia, Europe or someplace, or if you have no money going home and dying, just die. We got them to sign an agreement, agree to it where they're not going to sue anybody. They're going to get all of this stuff. They're going to get it really fast. And what's happened is we're saving thousands and thousands of lives. It's incredible. Right to try. It's great feeling.

Under our leadership. The United States will be respected again. No nation will question our power. No enemy will doubt our might. Our borders will be totally secure. Our economy will soar. We will return law and order to our streets, patriotism to our schools, and importantly, we will restore peace, stability, and harmony all throughout the world. But to achieve this future, we must first rescue our nation from failed and even incompetent leadership. We have totally incompetent leadership. This will be the most important election in the history of our country. Under the current administration, we are indeed a nation in decline. We have an inflation crisis that is making life unaffordable, ravaging the incomes of working and low income families, and crushing, just simply crushing our people like never before. They've never seen anything like it. We also have an illegal immigration crisis and it's taking place right now as we sit here in this beautiful arena.

It's a massive invasion at our southern border that has spread misery, crime, poverty, disease, and destruction to communities all across our land. Nobody's ever seen anything like it. Then there's an international crisis, the likes of which the world has seldom been part of. Nobody can believe what's happening. War is now raging in Europe, in the Middle East. A growing specter of conflict hangs over Taiwan, Korea, the Philippines, and all of Asia. And our planet is teetering on the edge of World War III and this will be a war like no other war because of weaponry. The weapons are no longer army tanks going back and forth shooting at each other. These weapons are obliteration. It's time for a change. This administration can't come close to solving the problems. We're dealing with very tough, very fierce people. They're fierce people and we don't have fierce people. We have people that are a lot less than fierce except when it comes to cheating on elections and a couple of other things, then they're fierce. Then they're fierce. So tonight I make this pledge to the great people of America. I will end the devastating inflation crisis immediately bring down interest rates and lower the cost of energy. We will drill, baby, drill. Can you believe what they're doing? But by doing that, we will lead a large scale decline in prices. Prices will start to come down. Energy raised it. They took our energy policies and destroyed them. Then they immediately went back to them. But by that time, so much was lost. But we will do it at levels that nobody's ever seen before and we'll end lots of different things. We'll start paying off debt and start lowering taxes even further. We gave you the largest tax cut. We'll do it more. People don't realize I brought taxes way down, way, way down, and yet we took in more revenues the following year than we did when the tax rate was much higher. Most people said, "How did you do that?"

Because it was incentive. Everybody was coming to the country. They were bringing back billions and billions of dollars into our country. The companies made it impossible to bring it back. The tax rate was too high and the legal complications were far too great. I changed both of them and hundreds of billions of dollars by Apple and so many other companies were brought back into our nation. And we had an economy, the likes of which nobody, no nation had ever seen. China, we were beating them at levels that were incredible and they know it. They know it. We'll do it again, but we'll do it even better. I will end the illegal immigration crisis by closing our border and finishing the wall, most of which I've already built. On the wall, we were dealing with a very difficult Congress and I said, "Oh, that's okay. We won't go to Congress." I call it an invasion. We gave our military almost $800 billion.

I said, "I'm going to take a little of that money because this is an invasion." And most of the wall is already built and we built it through using the funds because what's better than that? We have to stop the invasion into our country that's killing hundreds of thousands of people a year. We're not going to let that happen. I will end every single international crisis that the current administration has created, including the horrible war with Russia and Ukraine, which would've never happened if I was president and the war caused by the attack on Israel, which would've never happened if I was president. Iran was broke. Iran had no money. Now Iran has $250 billion. They made it all over the last two and a half years. They were broke. I watched the other day on a show called Deface the Nation. Has anyone seen it? And they had a Congressman who was a Democrat, say, "Well, whether you like him or not, Iran was broke dealing with Trump."

I told China and other countries, "If you buy from Iran, we will not let you do any business in this country and we will put tariffs on every product you do send in of 100% or more." And they said to me, "Well, I think that's about it." They weren't going to buy any oil and they were ready to make a deal. Iran was going to make a deal with us. And then we had that horrible, horrible result that will never let happen again. The election result, we're never going to let that happen again. They use COVID to cheat. You're never going to let it happen again. And they took off all the sanctions and they did everything possible for Iran. And now Iran is very close to having a nuclear weapon, which would've never happened. This is a shame what this administration, the damage that this administration has done.

And I say it often, if you took the 10 worst presidents in the history of the United States, think of it, the 10 worst added them up, they will not have done the damage that Biden has done. Only going to use the term once. Biden. I'm not going to use the name anymore, just one time. The damage that he's done to this country is unthinkable. It's unthinkable. Together we will restore vision, strength, competence, and we're going to have a thing called common sense making most of our decisions. Actually, it's all common sense. Just a few short years ago, under my presidency, we had the most secure border and best economy in the history of our country, in the history of the world. We had the greatest economy in the history of the world. We had never done anything like it. We were beating every country, including China by leaps and bounds. Nobody had seen anything like it.

We had no inflation. Soaring incomes were going... Nobody can believe it. You can't believe what happened four years ago is happening now in reverse and the world was at peace. Inflation has been a killer for our country. No matter

Acceptance Speech for President **67**

what you make, it doesn't matter because inflation is eating you alive. People that were putting away money, they were making great wages, the highest they've ever made, but they were putting away a lot of money. Now they are just being destroyed. They're not putting away anything. They're barely living. They're going into savings accounts. They're taking out their money to live because of inflation. Inflation, remember it's called a country buster. You can go back to Germany from a hundred years ago. You can go back to any country that suffered great inflation. We've suffered the worst inflation we've ever had. But go back and see what's happened to those countries. We've had the worst inflation we've ever had under this person.

But in less than four years, our opponents have turned incredible success into unparalleled tragedy and failure. It's been a tremendous failure. Today, our cities are flooded with illegal aliens. Americans are being squeezed out of the labor force and their jobs are taken. And by the way, who's taking the jobs? The jobs that are created, 107% of those jobs are taken by illegal aliens. And you know who's being hurt the most by millions of people pouring into our country? The Black population and the Hispanic population because they're taking the jobs from our Black population, our Hispanic population, and they're also taking them from unions. The unions are suffering because of it. Thank you. Thank you. I like you too. Thank you very much. Inflation is wiped out the life savings of our citizens and forced the middle class into a state of depression and despair. That's what it is. It's despair and depression. We cannot and will not let this continue. Less than four years ago, we were a great nation and we will soon be a great nation again. We're going to be a great nation again, Thank you. With proper leadership, every disaster we are now enduring will be fixed and it will be fixed very, very quickly. So tonight, whether you've supported me in the past or not, I hope you will support me in the future because I will bring back the American dream. That's what we're going to do. You don't even hear about the American dream anymore. With great humility, I am asking you to be excited about the future of our country. Be excited, be excited. And by the way, the news reports... Oh, look at all of those big networks. Look at them. They're all here. But every one of them has said this could be the most organized, best run, and most enthusiastic convention of either party that ever seen. Every single one. And it's true. It's true. And there's love in the room. There's great love in the room. So I better finish strong. Otherwise, we'll blow it and we can't let that happen.

No, this was great. All of the great people that spoke and everybody hit a home run. I mean, there's not one that I can think of where I said, "Oh gee, that wasn't great." Every single person. I refuse to be the only one. Don't do that to me. They're already getting ready. See, I gave them an idea. No, this was a great convention. I think we're actually going to go home and miss it. Usually with a... First of all, look at these crowds. You'd never have this at a convention. Look at these crowds. Love. It's about love. This week, the entire Republican Party has formally adopted an agenda for America's renewal. And you saw that agenda and it's very short compared to the long, boring, meaningless agendas of the past,

68   The Republican Campaign

including the Democrats. They write these things that are hundreds of pages long and they never read them after they're done.

In their case fortunately, they don't read them because they're pretty bad. It's a series of bold promises that we will swiftly implement when you give us a Republican House. And Mr. Speaker, thank you very much. We have our great Speaker of the House with us tonight. Mr. Speaker, thank you very much. Thank you. A Republican Senate. We have many senators here. And send me back to our beautiful White House just a few short months from now. We're talking about just months. It can't come fast enough. We have to get it done. First, we must get economic relief to our citizens. Starting on day one, we will drive down prices and make America affordable again. We have to make it affordable. It's not affordable. People can't live like this.

Under this administration, our current administration, groceries are up 57%, gasoline is up 60 and 70%, mortgage rates have quadrupled. And the fact is it doesn't matter what they are because you can't get the money anyway. Can't buy houses. Young people can't get any financing to buy a house. The total household costs have increased an average of $28,000 per family under this administration. Republicans have a plan to bring down prices and bring them down very, very rapidly. By slashing energy costs, we will in turn reduce the cost of transportation, manufacturing, and all household goods. So much starts with energy. And remember, we have more liquid gold under our feet than any other country by far. We are a nation that has the opportunity to make an absolute fortune with its energy. We have it and China doesn't.

Under the Trump administration, just three and a half years ago, we were energy independent. But soon we will actually be better than that. We will be energy dominant and supply not only ourselves, but we will supply the rest of the world with numbers that nobody has ever seen, and we will reduce our debt $36 trillion. We will start reducing that and we will also reduce your taxes still further. Next, and by the way, they want to raise your taxes four times. Think of it. And all my life, I grew up watching politicians. I always loved politics. I guess I was on the other side. I'd watch and they were always talking about, "We will give you a tax cut. We will give you a tax cut." My whole life I was... watching, I will give you a tax cut, right, Mr. Congressman? That's all they talked about.

This is the only administration that said, "We're going to raise your taxes by four times what you're paying now." And people are supposed to vote for them? I've never heard it. You're paying too much. We're going to reduce your taxes still further. We gave you the biggest one, as I said, we're going to give you more and it's going to lead to tremendous growth. We want growth in our country. That's what's going to pay off our debt. And next, we will end the ridiculous and, actually, incredible waste of taxpayer dollars that is fueling the inflation crisis.

They spent trillions of dollars on things having to do with the Green New Scam. It's a scam. And that's caused tremendous inflationary pressures in addition to the cost of energy. And all of the trillions of dollars that are sitting there not yet spent, we will redirect that money for important projects like roads, bridges, and dams, and we will not allow it to be spent on meaningless Green New Scam ideas. And I will end the electric vehicle mandate on day one, thereby saving the US auto industry from complete obliteration, which is happening right now, and saving US customers thousands and thousands of dollars per car. And right now, as we speak, large factories that just started are being built across the border in Mexico. So with all the other things happening on our border.

And they're being built by China to make cars and to sell them into our country, no tax, no anything. The United Auto Workers ought to be ashamed for allowing this to happen. And the leader of the United Auto Workers should be fired immediately. And every single auto worker union and non-union should be voting for Donald Trump because we're going to bring back car manufacturing and we're going to bring it back fast. They're building some of the largest auto plants anywhere in the world. Think of it, in the world. And we're going to bring it back. We're going to make them. We don't mind that happening, but those plants are going to be built in the United States and our people are going to man those plants.

And if they don't agree with us, we'll put a tariff of approximately 100 to 200% on each car and they will be unsellable in the United States. We have long been taken advantage of by other countries. And think of it, oftentimes these other countries are considered so-called allies. They've taken advantage of us for years. We lose jobs, we lose revenue, and they gain everything and wipe out our businesses, wipe out our people. For four years, I stopped it. And we're really ready to make changes like nobody had seen before. And remember, at USMCA, I got rid of NAFTA, the worst trade deal ever made, and replaced it with USMCA, which is, they say, the best trade deal ever made.

Actually, probably the best trade deal was the deal I made with China where they buy $50 billion worth of our product. They were buying nothing. They buy $50 billion worth. They had to. But I don't even talk about it because of COVID. I don't even mention it, frankly, because of what happened with the China virus. We will not let countries come in, take our jobs, and plunder our nation. They plunder our nation. The way they will sell their product in America is to build it in America. Very simple. Build it in America and only in America.

And this very simple formula, and Congress has to go along with us and they will, this very simple formula will create massive numbers of jobs. We will take over the auto industry again and many, many hundreds of thousands of jobs. We lost so many jobs over the years. If you go back 20, 25 years, they've stolen, going to China and Mexico, about 68% of our auto industry manufacturing jobs. We're going to get them all back. We're going to get them all back, every one of them. At the center of our plan for economic relief, our massive tax cuts for workers that include something else that stood out to be very popular, actually. Here it's very popular, in this building and all those hotels that I saw that are so nice, I'm staying in a nice one, it's called no tax on tips. No tax on tips.

And I got that by having dinner recently in Nevada where we're leading by about 14 points. Hello. I'll see you there very soon, everybody. And we're having

70 The Republican Campaign

dinner at a beautiful restaurant in the Trump building on the Strip. And it's a great building. And the waitress comes over. "How's everything going?" A really nice person. "How's everything?" "Oh, sir, it's so tough. The government's after me all the time on tips, tips, tips." I said, "Well, they give you cash. Would they be able to find them?" She said, "Actually," and I didn't know this, she said, "very little cash is given. It's all put right on the check. And they come in and they take so much of our money, it's just ridiculous. And they don't believe anything we say. And they've just hired, as you know, 88,000 agents to go after them even more."

And this shows the level of most people who go out and they hire consultants they're paying millions of dollars. But I said to her, "Let me just ask you a question. Would you be happy if you had no tax on tips?" She said, "What a great idea." I got my information from a very smart waitress. That's better than spending millions of dollars. And everybody loves it, waitresses and caddies and drivers. There's a large group of people that are being really hurt badly. They make money, let them keep their money. I'm going to protect Social Security and Medicare. Democrats are going to destroy Social Security and Medicare because all of these people, by the millions, they're coming in, they're going to be on Social Security and Medicare and other things, and you're not able to afford it.

They are destroying your Social Security and your Medicare. Under my plan, incomes will skyrocket, inflation will vanish completely, jobs will come roaring back, and the middle class will prosper like never, ever before, and we're going to do it very rapidly. But no hope or dream we have for America can succeed unless we stop the illegal immigrant invasion, the worst that's ever been seen anywhere in the world. There's never been an invasion like this anywhere. Third-world countries would fight with sticks and stones not to let this happen. The invasion at our Southern Border, we will stop it and we will stop it quickly. You heard Tom Homan yesterday. Put him in charge and just sit back and watch. Brandon Judd for Border Patrol. He's incredible.

These guys, their job is a lot easier if they don't have to do anything, but they want to. Their patriots. Brandon Judd, Border Patrol. You have to see what ICE does with MS-13. These are probably the worst gang and ICE goes in there. And I know a lot of people on these rows here and they're very tough people, but they don't want to do this job. They'll go into a pack of MS-13 killers. They're probably the worst gangs in the world, and we have thousands of them. I moved thousands and thousands out in my four years. We moved them out and it was a pleasure. But ICE would go right into a pack of these killers and you see fists flying, you see everything flying, and then they take them, they put them in a paddy wagon, they take them back, and they get them out of our country.

And the other countries weren't accepting them back. And I called up and I said, "Tell them that we're not giving them economic aid anymore." And the next day I got calls from all of these countries that were terminated, billions of dollars we spent on economic aid to countries that does us, frankly, no good. And the next day I was called by everybody. I couldn't take all the calls, "Sir, what's the problem?" I said, "You won't take your killers back that you sent in caravans into America. You won't take them back." "Well, sir, if you'd like us to, we would give very serious consideration to doing that." And within 24 hours, they were being taken back. For years and years, when I first came in, they said, "President Obama tried to get them to go back and they wouldn't accept them."

They'd put planes on the runway so you couldn't lead the plane. They'd closed the road so you couldn't take the buses. They'd all have to turn back. As soon as I said, "No more economic aid of any kind to any country that does that," they called back and they said, "Sir, it would be our great honor to take MS-13. We love them very much. We love them very much, sir. We'll take them back." At the heart of the Republican platform is our pledge to end this border nightmare and fully restore the sacred and sovereign borders of the United States of America, and we're going to do that on day one. That means two things on day one, drill, baby drill, and close our borders. And by the way, and I think everybody as a Republican, as a patriot in this room, and most Democrats, we want people to come into our country, but they have to come into our country legally.

Less than four years ago, I handed this administration the strongest border in American history. But you can see on the chart that saved my life... That was the chart that saved my life. I said, "Look at it. I'm so proud of it." It was done by the Border Patrol. One of the greatest charts I've ever seen. It showed everything just like that. You know the chart. Oh, there it is. That's pretty good. Wow. The last time I put up that chart, I never really got to look at it. But without that chart, I would not be here today. I never got to look at it. I said, "You got to see this chart." I was so proud of it. And by the time I got there, I never got to see it that day, but I'm seeing it now and I was very proud. If you look at the arrow in the bottom, the heavy red arrow, that's the lowest level of illegal immigrants ever to come into our country in recorded history right there. And that was my last week in office.

And then you see what happened after I left. Look at the rest. And if you go out a little bit further, it's getting to be a little bit old, but I love it anyway. But you can go much higher with those numbers. Look what happened right after that. The invasion began. We had the opposite. We stopped the invasion. But the invasion that we stopped was peanuts by comparison to what happened after I left. Look at what happened after I left. They took over our country. We ended all catch-and-release. We shut down asylum fraud. We stopped human trafficking and forged historic agreements to keep illegal aliens on foreign soil. We want them to stay on their soil. Under the Trump administration, if you came in illegally, you were apprehended immediately and you were deported. You went right back. The current administration terminated every single one of those great Trump policies that I put in place to seal the border.

I wanted a sealed border. Again, come in, but come in legally. You know how unfair it is? Hundreds of thousands of people have been working for years to come into our country and now they see these people pour into our country at levels that are unprecedented. It's so unfair. And we're not going to do it. We're

72 The Republican Campaign

not going to stand for it. They suspended wall construction, ended Remain in Mexico. We had a policy, Remain in Mexico. You think that was easy to get from the Mexican government? But I said, "You must give it to us. If you don't give it to us, there will be repercussions." And they gave it to us, but not easy. Canceled our Safe Third agreements, demolished Title 42, implemented nationwide catch-and-release. That's catch-and-release where we catch them and release them into our country. We catch them and release them into Mexico. There's a slight difference.

And took 93, this is the previous administration, 93 executive actions to throw open our border to the world. The entire world is pouring into our country because of this very foolish administration. The greatest invasion in history is taking place right here in our country. They are coming in from every corner of the earth, not just from South America, but from Africa, Asia, and the Middle East. They're coming from everywhere. They're coming at levels that we've never seen before. It is an invasion indeed, and this administration does absolutely nothing to stop them. They're coming from prisons, they're coming from jails, they're coming from mental institutions, and insane asylums. The press is always on me because I say this, has anyone seen Silence of the Lambs? The late great Hannibal Lecter, he'd love to have you for dinner. That's insane asylums.

They're emptying out their insane asylums. And terrorists are coming in at numbers that we've never seen before. Bad things are going to happen. Meanwhile, our crime rate is going up while crime statistics all over the world are going down because they're taking their criminals and they're putting them into our country. A certain country, and I happen to like the president of that country very much, but he's been getting great publicity because he's a wonderful shepherd of the country. He says how well the country's doing because their crime rate is down. And he said he's training all of these rough people, they're rough, rough, rough, he's training them.

And I've been reading about this for two years and I think, "Oh, that's wonderful. Let's take a look at it." But then I realized he's not training them. He's sending all of his criminals, his drug dealers, his people that are in jails, he's sending them all to the United States, and he's different in that he doesn't say that. He's trying to convince everybody what a wonderful job he does in running the country. Well, he doesn't do a wonderful job. And by the way, if I ran one of the countries, many, many countries from all over, I would be worse than any of them. I would've had the place totally emptied out already. But we become a dumping ground for the rest of the world, which is laughing at us.

They think we're stupid and they can't believe that they're getting away with what they're getting away with, but they're not going to be getting away with it for long, that's what I can tell you. In Venezuela, Caracas, high crime. Caracas, Venezuela is really a dangerous place, but not anymore because in Venezuela, crime is down 72%. In fact, if they would ever win this election, I hate to even say that, we will have our next Republican convention in Venezuela because it will be safe. Our cities will be so unsafe, we will not be able to have it. There in El Salvador

Acceptance Speech for President **73**

murders are down by 70%. Why are they down? Now, he would have you convinced that because he's trained murderers to be wonderful people.

No, they're down because they're sending their murderers to the United States of America. This is going to be very bad. And bad things are going to happen, and you're seeing it happen all the time. That's why to keep our families safe, the Republican platform promises to launch the largest deportation operation in the history of our country. Even larger than that of President Dwight D. Eisenhower from many years ago. He was a moderate, but he believed very strongly in borders. He had the largest deportation operation we've ever had. Just recently, I spoke to the grieving mother of Jocelyn Nungaray, a wonderful woman. A precious 12-year-old girl from Houston who last month was tied up, assaulted, and strangled to death after walking to the convenience store just a block away from her house.

Her body was dumped near the side of the road in a shallow creek and found by some onlookers who couldn't believe what they had witnessed. Charged with Jocelyn's heinous murder are two illegal aliens from Venezuela who came across our border, were in custody, and were then released into the country by this horrible, horrible administration that we have right now. I also met recently with the heartbroken mother and sister of Rachel Morin. Rachel was a 37-year-old mom of five beautiful children who was brutally raped and murdered while out on a run. She wanted to keep herself in good shape. It was very important to her. She was murdered.

The monster responsible first killed another woman in El Salvador before he was led into America by the White House. This White House let them in. He then attacked a nine-year-old girl and her mother in a home invasion in Los Angeles before murdering Rachel in Maryland. He traveled all throughout the country doing tremendous damage. Rachel's mother will never be the same. I spent time with her. She will never be the same. I've also met with the wonderful family of Laken Riley, the brilliant 22-year-old nursing student. She was so proud of being first in her class, who was out for a jog on the campus of the University of Georgia when she was assaulted, beaten, and horrifically killed.

Yet another American life was stolen by a criminal alien set free by this administration. And these were incredible people we're talking about. These were incredible people who died. Tonight, America, this is my vow, I will not let these killers and criminals into our country. I will keep our sons and daughters safe. As we bring security to our streets, we will help bring stability to the world. I was the first president in modern times to start no new wars. We were the toughest, we were the most respected. And you saw this, Hungary, a strong country run by a very powerful, tough leader. He's a tough guy. The press doesn't like him because he's tough.

They were asking him at an interview, "The whole world is exploding. What's happening? What's going on?" Viktor Orbán, he's prime minister of Hungary, a very tough man. He said, "I don't want people coming into my country and blowing up our shopping centers and killing people." But they said to him, "Tell us what's going wrong. What's happening? What is it?" He said, "There's only one way you're going to solve it. You got to bring President Trump back to the United States because he kept everybody at bay." He used a word I wouldn't use because I can't use that word because you'd say it was braggadocious. The press would say, "He was a braggart."

I'm not a braggart, but Viktor Orbán said it. He said, "Russia was afraid of him, China was afraid of him, everybody was afraid of him. Nothing was going to happen. The whole world was at peace, and now the world is blowing up around us. All of these things that you read about were not going to happen." Under President Bush, Russia invaded Georgia. Under President Obama, Russia took Crimea. Under the current administration, Russia is after all of Ukraine. Under President Trump, Russia took nothing. We defeated 100% of ISIS in Syria and Iraq, something that was said to take five years. "It'll take five years, sir." We did it in a matter of a couple of months.

We have a great military. Our military is not woke. It's just some of the fools on top that are woke. I got along very well with North Korea. Kim Jong Un, I got along very well with him. The press hated when I said that. "How could you get along with him?"

Well, it's nice to get along with somebody that has a lot of nuclear weapons or otherwise, isn't it? See, in the old days you say, "That's a wonderful thing." Now they say, "How could you possibly do that?" But now I got along with them and we stopped the missile launches from North Korea. Now, North Korea is acting up again, but when we get back, I get along with him. He'd like to see me back too. I think he misses me, if you want to know the truth. Our opponents inherited a world at peace and turned it into a planet of war. We're in a planet of war. Look at that attack on Israel. Look at what's happening with Ukraine. The cities are just bombed out. How can people live like that where massive buildings are falling to the ground? It began to unravel with the disastrous withdrawal from Afghanistan, the worst humiliation in the history of our country. We have never had a humiliation like that. 13 heroic US service members were tragically and needlessly killed. 45 others were horrifically wounded. Nobody ever talks about them. No arms, no legs, face explosions, horrifically wounded. And by the way, we have a man in this room who's running for the US Senate from a great state, Nevada named Sam Brown, who paid the ultimate price. Thank you, Sam. Thank you, Sam. Thank you.

He paid the biggest price, probably ever paid by anybody that is running for office, and I think he's going to do great. He's running against a person that is not good, not respected, a total lightweight, but Sam, I think paid really. We were talking about it with some of the senators that are working so hard for Sam, but he paid the biggest price of any senator ever to run for the Senate. I don't think anybody's ever what he did. He was a real hero, a really great person, and he's running, and I hope that everybody gets out and votes for Sam Brown. And we also left behind $85 billion worth of military equipment along with many American citizens were left behind. Many, many American citizens emboldened by that

Acceptance Speech for President **75**

disaster. Russia invaded Ukraine. They saw this group of people that were incompetent. We took the soldiers out first. No, no, we're going to take the soldiers out second. If they would've followed my plan, we had a great plan, but the plan only kicked in if they did everything perfectly and they weren't doing things perfectly. So we said it doesn't kick in. 18 months in Afghanistan, we didn't have one… They were killing them left and right, snipers. And I spoke to the head of the Taliban. You've heard this story.

Abdul still there, still the head of the Taliban. The press called on me, "Why would you speak to him?" I said, "Because that's where the killing is. I don't have to speak to somebody that has nothing to do with it." And I told him, "Don't ever do that. Don't ever do that again. Don't ever, ever do that again. You've got to stop." Because during the Obama administration, many great people and soldiers, but a lot of soldiers were being killed from long distance. I said, "If you keep doing that, you're going to be hit harder than anybody's ever been hit by a country before." And he said, "I understand your excellency." He called me your excellency. I wonder if he calls the other guy your excellency. I doubt it. The other guy gave him everything. I mean, what kind of a deal was that? He walked out, gave him everything.

Do you know that right now, Afghanistan is one of the largest sellers of weapons in the world? They're selling the brand new beautiful weapons that we gave them. But think of it, he actually said to me, "But why do you show me a picture of my home?" I said, "You'll have to ask your people or one of your wives." But he could figure it out. And for 18 months, we had not one attack on an American soldier by the Taliban, 18 months. And then we had that horrible day where soldiers were killed. I was not there because of a ridiculous election, but we had that horrible attack. And they also gave up Bagram, one of the biggest bases anywhere in the world, air bases, anywhere in the world, the longest runways, most powerful hardened thickened runways. We gave it up, and I liked it, not because of Afghanistan, I liked it because of China. It's one hour away from where China makes their nuclear weapons.

And you know who has it now? China has it now. We were keeping that. And now China is likewise circling Taiwan and Russian warships and nuclear submarines are operating 60 miles off the coast in Cuba. Do you know that? The press refuses to write about it. If that were me running this country and we had nuclear submarines in Cuba, I will tell you that the headlines every day would be, "What's wrong with our president." You don't even hear this. You're not hearing about this. Russia has nuclear submarines and warships 60 miles away, Mr. Congressman, from Miami, by the way, it happens to be here, correct? In Cuba, that would not be stood for if it were somebody else. They don't want to mention it. But now maybe they will.

And the entire world, I tell you this, we want our hostages back and they better be back before I assume office, or you'll be paying a very big price. With our victory in November, the years of war, weakness and chaos will be over. I don't have wars. I had no wars other than ISIS, which I defeated but that was a

76 The Republican Campaign

war that was started. We had no wars. I could stop wars with a telephone call. If properly stated, it would never start. We will replenish our military and build an iron dome missile defense system to ensure that no enemy can strike our homeland. And this great iron dome will be built entirely in the USA. We're going to build it in USA. And Wisconsin, just like I gave you that massive ship contract, and you're doing a very nice job. Governor Wright. Thank you, governor. And they're doing a great job. In fact, I had a little design change and we gave them a tremendous for essentially what we used to call destroyers. These are now the most beautiful. They look like yachts. They said, "We have to take the bow and we have to make it a little nicer and a little point at the top instead of a flat nose." And the people at the shipyard said, "This guy knows what he's doing." We have the most beautiful ships, governor and everybody's sitting over there. And it was a big contract that everybody wanted. I gave it to Wisconsin. But we're going to have a lot of that built right here in the state of Wisconsin and all other states.

Israel has an iron dome. They have a missile defense system. 342 missiles were shot into Israel and only one got through a little bit. It was badly wounded. It fell to the ground but most of them are. And Ronald Reagan wanted this many years ago, but we really didn't have the technology many years ago. Remember they called it starship, spaceship, anything to mock him. But he was a very good president, very, very good. But now we have unbelievable technology. And why should other countries have this and we don't? No, no. We're going to build an iron dome over our country and we're going to be sure that nothing can come and harm our people.

And again, from an economic development standpoint, we're going to make it all right here. No more sending it out to other countries in order to help. It's America first. We will unleash the power of American innovation. And as we do, we will soon be on the verge of finding the cures to cancer, Alzheimer's disease and many other diseases. We're going to get to the bottom of it. You remember this gentleman that I don't want to mention other than one time I had to because when you say you're the 10 worst, I had to do it. I didn't want anybody to be confused. But this man said, "We're going to find a cure to cancer." Nothing happened. We're going to get to the cure for cancer and Alzheimer's and so many other things. We're so close to doing something great, but we need a leader that will let it be done. We will not have men playing in women's sports. That will end immediately.

And we will restore and renovate our nation's once great cities, making them safe, clean, and beautiful again. And that includes our nation's Capitol, which is a horrible killing field. So many things. They leave from Wisconsin. They go to look at the Washington Monument. They end up getting stabbed, killed or shot. We will be very soon very proud of our Capitol, again, Washington, DC.

America's on the cusp of a new golden age. But we will have the courage to seize it. We're going to take it. We're going to make it a current... I mean, we're going to bring this into a golden age like never seen before. Remember this. China wants to do it. Japan wants to do it. All of these countries want to do it.

We have to produce massive amounts of energy if we're going to produce the new... If you look at some of the things that have been done and some of the things that we're going to do, but AI needs literally twice the electricity that's available now in our country. Can you imagine?

But instead, we're spending places where they recharge electric cars. They built eight chargers at a certain location toward the Midwest. Eight charges for $9 billion. Think of them as a tank for filling up your guess. Think of it. They spent $9 billion on eight charges, three of which didn't work. And if you are going to do this all over our country, this crazy electric mandate, if you're going to do this all... And by the way, I'm all for electric. They have their application. But if somebody wants to buy a gas powered car, gasoline powered car or a hybrid, they're going to be able to do it. And we're going to make that change on day one.

So to conclude, just a few short days ago, my journey with you nearly ended. We know that. And yet here we are tonight, all gathered together talking about the future promise and a total renewal of a thing we love very much. It's called America. We live in a world of miracles. None of us knows God's plan or where life's adventure will take us. I want to thank Franklin Graham for being here tonight. He's an outstanding man. He wrote me a note recently. I have a lot of respect for him. "Sir, I love your storytelling. I think it's great in front of these big rallies. But sir, please do me one favor. It won't make any difference. Please, don't use any foul language."

I was a little embarrassed. He said, "It won't make any difference." Actually, it does. The story's not quite as good, but I've been very good. The story is not quite as good to be honest. I've got to have a little talk with Franklin. But he was great. He's a great gentleman. His father was so incredible, Billy Graham. My father used to love taking me to see Billy Graham. My father would take me to see Billy Graham at Yankee Stadium. He had the biggest rallies you've ever seen. He was a good rally guy too, but he'd get up and he was a fantastic guy. My father loved Billy Graham. But I love Franklin Graham. I think Franklin's been fantastic and I'm working so hard to adhere to his note to me. I'm working hard on it, Franklin. But if the events of last Saturday make anything clear, it is that every single moment we have on earth is a gift from God. We have to make the most of every day for the people and for the country that we love.

The attacker in Pennsylvania wanted to stop our movement, but the truth is the movement has never been about me. It has always been about you. It's your movement. It's the biggest movement in the history of our country by far. Can't be stopped. It can't be stopped. It has always been about the hardworking, patriotic citizens of America. For too long, our nation has settled for too little. We settle for too little. We've given everything to other nations, to other people. You have been told to lower your expectations and to accept less for your families. I am here tonight with the opposite message. Your expectations are not big enough. They're not big enough.

It is time to start expecting and demanding the best leadership in the world. Leadership that is bold, dynamic, relentless and fearless. We can do that. We are

Americans. Ambition is our heritage. Greatness is our birthright. But as long as our energies are spent fighting each other, our destiny will remain out of reach. And that's not acceptable. We must instead take that energy and use it to realize our country's true potential and write our own thrilling chapter of the American story. We can do it together. We will unite. We are going to come together and success will bring us together. It is a story of love, sacrifice and so many other things. And remember the word devotion. It's unmatched devotion. Our American ancestors crossed the Delaware, survived the icy winter at Valley Forge and defeated a mighty empire to establish our cherished republic. They fought so hard, they lost so many. They pushed thousands and thousands of miles across a dangerous frontier, taming the wilderness to build a life and a magnificent home for their family. They packed their families into covered wagons, trekked across hazardous trails, scaled towering mountains and brave rivers and rapids to stake their claim on the wide open, new and very beautiful frontier. When our way of life was threatened, American patriots marched onto the battlefield, raced into enemy strongholds, and stared down death and stared down those enemies to keep alive the flame of freedom. At Yorktown, Gettysburg and Midway, they joined the roll call of immortal heroes. Just so many heroes, so many great, great people. And we have to cherish those people. We can't forget those people. We have to cherish those people. And building monuments to those great people is a good thing, not a bad thing. They saved our country.

No challenge was too much. No hardship was too great. No enemy was too fierce. Together these patriots soldiered on and endured and they prevailed because they had faith in each other, faith in their country. And above all, they had faith in their God. Just like our ancestors, we must now come together, rise above past differences, any disagreements have to be put aside and go forward united as one people, one nation, pledging allegiance to one great, beautiful, I think it's so beautiful, American flag. Tonight I ask for your partnership, for your support. And I am humbly asking for your vote. I want your vote. I'm going to make our country great again. Every day I will strive to honor the trust you have placed in me. And I will never ever let you down. I promise that, I will never let you down. To all of the forgotten men and women who have been neglected, abandoned, and left behind, you'll be forgotten no longer. We will press forward and together we will win, win, win. Win, win, win, win, win, win, win. Nothing will sway us, nothing will slow us, and no one will ever stop us. No matter what dangers come our way, no matter what obstacles lie in our path, we will keep striving toward our shared and glorious destiny. And we will not fail. We will not fail Together, we will save this country. We will restore the republic and we will usher in the rich and wonderful tomorrows that our people so truly deserve. America's future will be bigger, better, bolder, brighter, happier, stronger, freer, greater and more united than ever before. And quite simply put, we will very quickly make America great again. Thank you very much. Thank you very much, Wisconsin. God bless you. God bless you, Wisconsin. And God bless the United States of America, our great country. Thank you very much everybody. Thank you.

Print Citations

CMS: Trump, Donald. "Acceptance Speech for President." Speech at the Republican National Convention, Milwaukee, WI, July 18, 2024. In *The Reference Shelf: Representative American Speeches, 2023–2024,* edited by Micah L. Issitt, 59–79. Amenia, NY: Grey House Publishing, 2024.

MLA: Trump, Donald. "Acceptance Speech for President." Republican National Convention, 18 July 2024, Milwaukee, WI. Speech. *The Reference Shelf: Representative American Speeches, 2023–2024,* edited by Micah L. Issitt, Grey House Publishing, 2024, pp. 59–79.

APA: Trump, D. (2024). Acceptance speech for president [Speech]. Republican National Convention, Milwaukee, WI. In Micah L. Issitt (Ed.), *The reference shelf: Representative American speeches, 2023–2024* (pp. 59–79). Grey House Publishing. (Original work published 2024)

Address at the National Rifle Association's Annual Meeting

By Donald Trump

"We're under siege with the guns, the rifles, and everything else. We're under siege. But they didn't move us an inch, and we have to stand strong." Republican Presidential Nominee Donald Trump spoke at the National Rifle Association (NRA) annual meeting in May of 2024. Trump claimed that gun rights are being threatened and urged gun owners to vote for him to protect their freedoms to own weapons.

Well, thank you very much, and thank you, Randy. It's a true honor to be here today to receive the endorsement of the proud American patriots at the NRA. These are great patriots. These are great people, and we're going to do things like nobody can believe. We're going to win this election at levels that nobody's ever seen before. Thank you very much for that endorsement. It means a lot to me.

When I started off, as you know, in 2016, I got that endorsement early, and I got it. Some people thought they had it made, but we got it. We got it again, and we've lived up to everything, as you know, everything I said. We're under siege with the guns, the rifles, and everything else. We're under siege. But they didn't move us an inch, and we have to stand strong. You know that we have to stand very strong. So thank you very much, everybody. I appreciate it.

The NRA has stood with me from the very beginning, and with your vote, I will stand strong for your rights and liberties. Four or more years in the White House, we're going to do things like nobody can believe. We're going to turn our country around. We're going to, quite simply, make America great again. But one thing I'll say, and I say it as friends, we've got to get gun owners to vote because you know what? I don't know what it is.

Perhaps it's a form of rebellion because you're rebellious people, aren't you? But gun owners don't vote. What is that all about? I've heard that. I heard it a few weeks ago. If the gun owners voted, we would swamp them at levels that nobody's ever seen before. So I think you're a rebellious bunch, but let's be rebellious and vote this time. Okay? If you go out and vote ... I understand exactly why you don't, but we have to win this election. It's the most important election in the history of our country.

You've got to get all your friends, all the gun owners. They have to go, and they have to vote. If they vote, there's nobody that can beat us, nobody. So it's very important, and I want to thank the NRA president, Charles Cotton, your first

---

Delivered on May 20, 2024 at the National Rifle Association's Annual Meeting, Kay Bailey Hutchinson Center, Dallas, TX.

vice president, Bob Barr, and interim executive vice president, Andrew Arulanandam. That's a terrific group of people.

We're also grateful to be joined by a very special man. He's a hot politician, very hot, Governor Greg Abbott. Where is he? He's are around here someplace. He's around here. Thank you, Greg. You're a hot politician, Greg. You know why he's hot? Because he's doing a good job. That's a good reason, right? Right, [inaudible]? Thank you very much, Greg. Appreciate it. Great job.

Also, a friend of mine is the chairman of our campaign in Texas. We're 2 and 0, and we have lots of people running. So far, I think we're 51 and 0 in Texas. I don't know. I like Texas, and they like me. Somehow it works together. But this man is very, very strong, very popular. Lieutenant Governor Dan Patrick. Thank you, Dan. Very strong guy, very popular guy.

Thank you very much. Great job. How are we doing, Dan? Are we doing okay? We're way up in Texas. We're way up. Thank you very much. Members of Congress here, we have a lot of them, but a few of them I'm going to introduce. We also have senators, and we're going to just introduce a small group because we have to get on about our business, don't we? Members of Congress.

The only man to hit a ball in Washington out of the stadium, he hit a home run, slow pitch. They play the Democrats and ... Slow pitch meaning about 55 or 60 miles an hour, not that slow. But nobody's ever hit a home run over the fences except this one man, and he was wearing a MAGA hat. I didn't know him at the time, but I said, "Who's the guy that hit the home run?" This was a couple of years ago. He hit it right over the fences in the deepest part of the park.

That's not an easy thing to do for a civilian. If you're a baseball player, you could do it. If you're a civilian, you're not supposed to be able to do it. But he was wearing that beautiful red MAGA hat, and I said, "Who is that guy?" His name's Greg Steube, and he's here today. He's my friend with his incredible wife. Thank you, Greg Steube. Where are you, Greg? Where's Greg? What a shot that was. When they wear a hat that says MAGA that means they're with us all the way. Thank you, Greg.

Also a terrific congressman and a friend of yours, very good friend of you in the state and the country, Pat Fallon. Pat. Pat. Thank you, Pat. Great, Pat. Great job. Another man, he was the doctor for ... I don't think any of you have ever heard of this gentleman, Barack Hussein Obama. Has anyone ever heard of Barack? No, he was a doctor. Very talented doctor, too. He's got a lot of things on his resume. He was a great doctor. He was a great admiral, and now he's a great congressman.

Before I introduce him, I just want to say, when he was the doctor at the White House, they asked him, "Who's healthier? Who's a better physical specimen? Is it Trump or is it Obama?" And he said, "It's not even close. It's Donald Trump. Not even close." I said, "I love this guy." Dr. Ronny Jackson, your congressman, great congressman from Texas. Then he had to louse it up. You know what he did? He said, "And he'd live for 200 years, except he likes junk food, so

The Republican Campaign

he might only live to 110." Can you believe? Huh? I do like junk food. Who doesn't?

A real good friend of mine, an incredible Republican, conservative, really a person that loves our country more than anything else, happens to solidly reside in the state of Texas, the president of the America First Policy Institute, what she's done is incredible. She has taken the Policy Institute and brought it to a level that nobody thought possible, and fairly quickly, too, I would say. Brooke Rollins. Brooke? Thank you. Thank you, Brooke. She could run any company in America, but I don't want to say that because I don't want her stolen away from me.

Texas legislature candidates who have my complete and total endorsement, David Covey, Alan Schoolcraft. Where is Alan? Alan Schoolcraft, Helen Kerwin, and Brent Hagenbuch. Where are you? Stand up. Oh, there they are. David is leading very substantially an absolutely terrible speaker of the house who didn't want to go into voter fraud. He didn't want to do it. Raise your hand, David. Because David's leading very, very substantially against your speaker of the house.

I see the recent polls. But still, it's about a week away. They all have my complete and total endorsement. They're phenomenal people, and they're going to do really, really well. We appreciate you being with us. Thank you, and good luck in a week from now. Good luck. You're going to win big. You're all going to win big. We have to get your speaker out of there so that we can go into voter fraud.

Because even though we win Texas, Dallas and Houston, those areas, a lot of bad things happening. Right, Dan? They have a lot of bad things happening, and we got to stop it before it gets out of control. They will do that. Also, a man, he was operating a piece of equipment, a big haul or a big truck. He was a truck guy. A real truck guy, not like Biden. Biden says, "I drive trucks. I drive trucks. I used to drive an 18-wheeler." He doesn't know what he's ... He didn't. No. He always says that.

He said, "I used to drive an 18-wheeler." When the truckers come in, that's what he says. When the pilots come in, "I used to fly a plane." No, it's true. Misinformation. I was going to say he's full of bullshit, but I don't want to use bad language because there are a lot of young ... No, I don't want to. I don't want to do that.

Well, I played golf today with a really good golfer, Tony Romo. Do you know Tony Romo? He may be a better golfer than a football player. I don't know. But we played really today. We were talking about the state. We were talking about a lot of things, and we were at a wonderful course, very nearby. We had a tremendous amount of support from the people at that club. I'll tell you, it's amazing. They love this state. They love your governor, your lieutenant governor.

They love this country. It's a beautiful thing to see. Really beautiful. But Biden, he said his biggest lie of all because I'm a nice golfer is the expression. We have another nice golfer here, by the way, Mr. Steve Witkoff and his son, Alex. He's a nice golfer, and he's one of the most successful businessmen in the country. He flew in just to spend some time because he's a big believer in the NRA.

But Biden, his biggest lie of all, he said he's a 6.2 handicap golfer. This guy couldn't break 200. I really mean it. He actually challenged me last week. We're going to have debates with him, and it was good. That's good. I think we're going to. He's still looking for that white stuff that was found in the White House. He's saying, "It never arrived. It never arrived." They can't find it. Everyone thought it was for Hunter. Maybe it wasn't for Hunter. I think it was for somebody else.

But he said 6.2. Usually, a guy's a six or a seven or an eighter. I've played golf for a long time. I won a lot of golf. 31 club championships, can you believe it? He challenged me to a golf match. He said, "I'll give him three aside." The guy can't break 200. Here's his swing. I'm very good at imitating swings. Well, you ask Tony Romo about that. He'll tell you about Trump. No, but that's his biggest lie, 6.2. He's got to be 6.2. You know why? 6.2 is totally accurate. Down 0.2. I never even heard of that before. Who's a 6.2?

But this gentleman that is from North Carolina got up and made a speech and the place said, "Why aren't you running for office?" And he gave it a shot. He ran for lieutenant governor, so he went from a truck tractor ... He was a very good operator right here. It was a forklift and a good one, a big one. He had a great job, but he made his speech. I think he was protesting taxes or something in North Carolina, and he took the place by storm, one of the most beautiful, resonant voices you've ever heard.

He stood up. I said, "I think I'm going to really insult him by saying this. It's possible that I will." I didn't want to do that. You know we're doing well with the Black voter. They can't even believe it. They love Trump, and I love them. But I said to this man, and when he endorsed me, he gave a speech. I said, "You are Dr. Martin Luther King on steroids. That's how good you are. You are unbelievable as a speaker."

He got up, and he's doing fantastically well in North Carolina. I think he's going to be the next governor of North Carolina, Mark Robinson, and a very popular guy. How's it going? Good? The polls are looking good, I hear. Yes? You got to hear this guy speak. Anyway, he's going to be speaking at the convention very loudly and beautifully, and we look forward to that. We're going to have a great convention in Milwaukee, and we're not doing one.

They're going to do a Zoom convention, I hear, because they're blaming the pickets, the riots, whatever they might want to blame. The real problem is he doesn't want to get up and speak. He doesn't want to walk. He can't walk from that stair to this podium. He can't put two sentences together. Even his challenge on the debate, it took him seven shots. They have seven different clips.

For more than 150 years, the NRA has been defined by men and women, like all of you, loyal, hardworking citizens who believe in defending your families and your communities and our country. RFK Jr., I call him Junior ... By the way, he's radical left. Don't think about it. Don't waste your vote. We need a conservative person with common sense. This guy is radical left who destroyed New York. They're taking down all of the energy components. We have the highest, and all of New England actually. He's a disaster.

He's radical left. RFK Jr. is radical left. He reminds me of this fly that's driving me crazy up here. This fly is brutal. I don't like flies. But RFK Jr. calls you a terrorist group. He calls you a terrorist group. Can't vote for him. You can't. Somebody said, "Well, they like his policy on vaccine." The other day, he said, no, no, he'll go for the vaccine. He's got no policy on anything. He's radical left. He always has been.

His family is angry at him because he's doing this. They won't talk to him because they said, "Where the hell did this come from?" For some reason, he's getting probably a little bit more Biden, hurting Biden a little bit more, but we can't waste any votes. We have to make sure we win. I don't know if you read, but I'm meeting next week, very soon, with the Libertarians because, largely, they have so much of what we have.

They're also people of common sense, speaking. They have a couple of things that are a little different, but we have to join with them because they get their 3% every year, no matter who's running. We have to get that 3% because we can't take a chance on Joe Biden winning. He's the worst president in the history of our country by far. We can't have it.

But RFK Jr. says bad, bad things. He calls you a terrorist group, and I call you the backbone of America. That's a big difference, wouldn't you say? But under crooked Joe Biden, everything you stand for is under threat like never before. Our Second Amendment, which is largely why you're here, I mean that's the biggest statement for you. When I go and make speeches at different places, it's always important. But today, this is the big statement. It's under siege.

Second Amendment is under siege. Our constitution is being run through the shredder. Our borders have been obliterated. Inflation continued to rage, and it's raging right now again. They shouldn't lower the interest rates because they're going to have to stop it, but he's going to lower it just for purposes of trying to win an election, just like he went into the strategic reserves to try and win an election and let this stuff that's supposed to be used for war and national emergencies, to try and keep the gas prices down.

Now we have the lowest strategic reserves we've ever had. Our country is going to hell. Rapacious gangs and ruthless criminals are terrorizing our streets and crooked Joe Biden's weakness has us teetering on the edge of World War III. I've gotten to know the leaders of the world very well, the ones in South America that are sending all of their criminals and their prisoners and their gangs into our country, intelligently. I'd do the same thing if I was there. I'd do it faster than them.

But they're sending everybody into our country. I mean think of it. We have these people coming into our country. We don't want them in our country. They're from prison. They're gang members. They're drug dealers. They're rapists. We have people coming into our country. No country could sustain what's happening to us. They don't check them. They have no idea who they are. It's not just South America. It's all over the world.

It's time for a president who will replace weakness with strength, turn poverty to prosperity, and vanquish Joe Biden's corrupt tyranny with a great restoration of American freedom. We have to do that. From the very first day that we take back the White House, I believe we are going to have the four greatest years in the history of our country. It's hard to believe when you look at what's happening right now with the inflation and the bad economy.

I'll just say Scott. I call him Scott. He's one of the great prognosticators on Wall Street, one of the smartest people on Wall Street. He said, "The only reason the stock market's doing well is because Trump is leading in all of the polls. If Trump wasn't leading in all of the polls, and if Trump doesn't win, you're going to have a collapse like in 1929." So just remember. He said it, but I said it, too. I really believe it. I believe it.

That's the only thing that's doing well is the stock market. It's doing well because we're doing well. We had a great stock market. But if it didn't happen, it's going to be a very bad time, I think, for our country. But to achieve the future, you have to march into the voting booth, and you have to tell crooked Joe Biden, "Joe, you're doing a horrible job. You're a horrible president." Like the Apprentice, "Joe, you're fired. Get out of here, Joe. You're fired."

Let there be no doubt the survival of our Second Amendment is very much on the ballot. You know what they want to do. If they get in, our country's going to be destroyed in so many ways. But the second Amendment will be ... It's under siege. But with me, they never get anywhere. We need that Second Amendment for safety, forgetting about even going hunting and all of the things that you do. We need it for safety because the bad guys are not giving up their guns. You know that.

The bad ones are not giving up their guns. Oh, they will be so happy. If the Biden regime gets four more years, they are coming for your guns, 100% certain. Crooked Joe has a 40-year record of trying to rip firearms out of the hands of law-abiding citizens. He's always wanted to do that. You can't do it. We're the party of common sense now. I call it the party of common sense. We're conservative and all of that, but we want borders. We want good elections.

We have to have a Second Amendment that's meaningful. If we don't, we're going to have levels of death and destruction like this country has never seen before. We're the party of common sense. As we speak, the Biden administration is trying to crush independent firearms dealers by revoking their licenses if they make a single error, even in very unimportant paperwork. You know that. Are there any people in here that have that happen? Five hands go up. It's sad.

No, they want to take away your rights. Well, I know that better than anybody. They want to take away my rights better than anybody, worse than Alphonse Capone. Al Capone was indicted twice. I got indicted four times. I never heard the word. What's an indictment? What's an indictment, please? Think of it. I go years and years. I go through all sorts of stuff in New York. I built buildings with the unions, with all the people that are involved. It's a rough business.

86   The Republican Campaign

I never had a question about me. All of a sudden, within a period of this little tiny period, I got indicted four times, and on a civil basis, four or five times with it all being run from the White House and the DOJ. I say Alphonse Capone, the meanest, roughest, most horrendous. I'm looking at some of the people here like this gentleman, rough guy, rough guy. Stand up.

But you know what? You don't want to have dinner with Al Capone. I can tell you that, right? He wouldn't like you look too good. He wouldn't like you. He'd say, "Let's get rid of that guy." Al Capone. Remember Scarface, right? Scarface. He has a scar that went from here to here, and he was rough. He got indicted less than I did. Think of this. My father is up in heaven, and my mother. My father was tough, but he was a good man. He was a good person, so I know he's in heaven. My mother, I guarantee it. My father, I think. I'm pretty sure. But he was great. He was a great guy.

They're looking down on me right now. They say, "Can you believe it, darling? My son." I got indicted so much. I heard they were going to try and do it a couple of more times, the White House said, "Don't do it. Don't do it. You're indicting this guy into the White House." There's a little truth of that. There's a little truth. But we have the highest poll numbers we've ever had. We have the highest poll numbers we've ever had.

I don't want to ever say this. Bing, bing. I don't know if this is wood or plastic. You can't tell nowadays. I think it's plastic. Is there any wood around? Oh, there's a piece. But we have the best poll numbers we've ever had, and I think a lot of it is the weaponization of justice, or as I call it, the weaponization of injustice because that's what it is. They'll use that on these great congressmen that I just introduced because I have a platform that's a very big platform, and I can tell and talk to the voters, whether it's on television or I can do whatever I want.

I can get it out, and I have done it and probably a pretty good job. You see this case that's in New York, this fake case with a highly conflicted judge, so conflicted. There's probably no judge maybe in history that's been as conflicted as this guy, and he refuses to recuse himself. But I'm able to talk about things, although I do have a gag order. I can't talk about the things I want to talk about because what I talk about is just on the surface because if I go in, they want to put me in jail.

Can you believe they want to put me in jail if I say the truth? So I can't talk about certain things. It says, "You can't talk about this. You can't talk about that." But those are the best things. But we talk about the things I can talk about. It has to be unconstitutional. Can you imagine? You've won the Republican nomination for president of the United States, and you have a local judge appointed by Democrat politicians. He was appointed. He didn't win the election. He's appointed ... And he says, "I'm going to put a gag order on the Republican Party's presidential candidate." Think of that, "I'm going to put a gag order." So when people ask me questions, I'll have to say, "I'm sorry. I can't answer that question." And they're easy questions, they're like softballs, they're so easy to answer. But I'm able to speak to the people and the people understand. And we're well into the 80s, and even more than that, and they see how fake it is. And so many of the politicians... like the ones I just mentioned, and others, many of them that aren't here from all over the country... they go to the trial and they watch what's going on.

But we had a big day on Friday, didn't we? Didn't we have a big day? But they want to rig that just like they rigged the presidential election of 2020. They want to rig it. This is their form of rigging and it only happens in third-world countries. Never happened here. It's a disgrace what's going on. But with me and the White House, the radical gun-grabbers will run straight into a very, very powerful brick wall. Their dreams have taken away your God-given rights will die. When the polls close on November 5th, 2024, those dreams that they have will be dead. They will be dead dreams.

Every promise I made, every single promise I made to you as a candidate, I kept as your President. Look at all the things we did. Taxes. Think of it. Biggest tax cut in history. Biggest regulation cuts in history. Greatest economy in the history of our country.

Larry Kudlow was on last night. He was on I think Sean Hannity, another great guy. A lot of good people out there. We have a lot of great people that get the word out. But Larry Kudlow was out, and he was comparing our economy to Biden's economy, and he says, "Not even close." I mean we had the greatest economy ever, and he's got an economy that is so bad with inflation. No matter what happened, you can never override. Inflation is a country-buster; it has been for hundreds of years. You go back to Germany of old. It's a country-buster, and it's busting our country, and it's destroying our people.

Just as I pledged back in 2016, I appointed nearly 300 pro-Constitution judges to interpret the law as written. It's a record, by the way. And I faced down vile attacks from the radical left to confirm three great Supreme Court justices: Neil Gorsuch, Brett Kavanaugh, and Amy Coney Barrett. They're great. Oh, they were thrilled when I got three. A lot of presidents get none because they stay in office; they're usually appointed at a young age.

It's interesting. I have a friend in New York, he wanted to be a judge so bad, and when I... Great lawyer, actually. When I won, he called me. He said, "Wow." Do you believe it? A big real estate lawyer, phenomenal talent, and 69 years old. He said, "Unbelievable how you did this. Can I be honest? I'd love to give up my practice." He makes a lot of money, "I'd like to give up my practice and I'd like to run. I'd like to be a judge. I'd be a great judge," and he would be a great judge, and I called my people. I told him, "Don't worry about it. You're going to be a judge. Congratulations."

Then I called up my people and I said, "I have a guy from New York who's an incredible lawyer. He's got the right temperament. He'd be a really great judge," "Oh, good, sir. How old is he?" I said, "He's 69." "Sir, so he's going to be there for two, three, four years. We like people in their 30s so they're there for 50 years or 40 years. We don't want..." And as soon as they said that, I realized, "Yeah, they're exactly right." So I called up my friend. I said, "You're phenomenal. We love you, love you, love you. But will you guarantee that you're going to be there for 25

88   The Republican Campaign

years?" "Well, I can't do that." "Good, then I can't appoint you." It's sort of a shame, actually. He would have been great. But after three, four years, they'll say, "I think I want to go to... I want to move to Texas and I want to retire in Texas."

A lot of people have Moving to Texas. Standing before you at the NRA Leadership Forum in 2019, I revoked America's signature from the globalist United Nations Armed Trade Treaty, which was one of the worst things to happen, but we revoked it. I stood up for our hunters, fishers, and sportsmen like never before. No President has ever stood up for you, the people in this room, like I did, opening up millions of acres of federal land, and rolling back Barack Hussein Obama's assault on hunting, fishing and trapping. It was an assault. He didn't want you to hunt. Why? I don't know. They usually blame the environment, "It's the environment."

And I stopped cold their efforts to take away your ammunition. You know those efforts are big, the ammunition. Has anyone noticed it's been... They're going after the ammunition. When the radical-left Democrats tried to use COVID to shut down gun sales during the China virus, I proudly designated gun and ammunition retailers as critical infrastructure so they couldn't touch it. They tried. Many of the gun dealers are in this room. They came up to me backstage, a couple of my men. I said, "I was so honored to be called critical." I was critical. It was critical. I've never been called critical in my life. You gave me this powerful designation, but we did that and it really worked. The word critical was very important because that's what it is. We have to save our country.

My administration also petitioned the Supreme Court to overturn New York City's unconstitutional ban on transporting handguns outside the home. They say, "You can't do it," and we overturned it. And in a landmark case two years ago, the court affirmed that the right to self-defense does not end when you step outside the front door of your house. We won it. In my second term, we will roll back every Biden attack on the Second Amendment, the attacks are fast and furious, starting the minute that Crooked Joe shuffles his way out of the White House. At noon on Inauguration Day, we will sack the anti-gun fanatic, Steve Dettelbach. Have you ever heard of him? He's a disaster. And replace him with an ATF director who respects the sacred rights to keep and bear arms. And remember every single thing I told you, I did. That's one of the big things is that when I first ran... We ran, and when I first ran nobody... You know, I did great in business, and did a lot of success even in show business with The Apprentice and all, but I never did this before. And I said I was going to do certain things: every single thing, virtually every single thing that I said... I said, "We're going to give you the biggest tax cuts." I said, "We're going to give you the biggest regulation cuts." I said, "We're going to give you Space Force. We're going to rebuild our military," which we did. I said, "We're going to build hundreds of miles of wall," which we did. We had 200 miles of wall ready to go, and they decided... Then we had the rigged election and they decided not to put them up and they sold that very expensive wall. It's exactly what the border patrol wanted. Exactly.

I wanted nice, beautiful 40-, 50-foot concrete plank; they didn't like that. And I did everything they wanted, even the repellent panel on the top. It stops you. It's called an anti-climb panel. You can't climb over it. We had people that climbed Mount Everest. We had all different walls built so that we got the best one. They couldn't climb this one, and the anti... I didn't like the panel on top. I don't know if you know what I'm talking about, but there's an anti-climb panel on top, but it makes it very hard for people to get over the wall. They could scoot up those walls; it was incredible. And we built everything.

And now you know what they did? We had 200 miles that would have been put up. We built 571 miles of wall, and we had the safest border in history. I got Mexico to give us soldiers. All of the things I did. But these people, they took the 200 miles of wall that could have been flipped up and thrown up, and they were sitting there ready to be installed, and they sold it for 5 cents on the dollar. I don't even know what the hell does anybody want that wall for, right? Maybe other countries are buying it use for their wall. Probably that's it, for 5 cents on the dollar.

On day one, we will seal the border, we will stop the invasion, and we will send Joe Biden's illegal aliens back home right where they belong. Right where they belong. They're going back home where they belong. And we start with the criminals; and there are many, many criminals. Less than four years ago, we had the most secure border in US history, we ended catch-and-release, built tremendous numbers of miles of border wall like nobody thought possible. I took it out of the military because I considered it an invasion of our country, and I got Mexico to send 28,000 soldiers to our border free of charge. Do you think that was easy to do? I told the President of Mexico, "I need 28,000 soldiers free of charge to guard our border." "Oh, Donald. Oh, President." He was laughing. He thought I was kidding. I said, "No, they have to be free of charge. You'll do it. I know you'll do it. There's no question that you're going to do it."

They come through Mexico along with the drugs which, by the way, are now 10 times greater coming through, fentanyl and all, coming through our border than it was just four years ago: 10 times greater. It's even more than that, I believe, but they're estimating at least 10 times. But I said, "I need your soldiers and you'll give them to us free of charge." He said, "No, no, no. I will not do that, Donald. Ha, ha, ha, ha." He thought it was so funny. I said, "Do me a favor..." And he's a friend of mine. He's a good guy. He's a radical socialist and that's fine. I don't care. I don't care. But he was a good guy. I said, "Do me a favor. Look, I don't like negotiating with you. It's sort of unpleasant. I want to negotiate with your people." And I said, "So do you have somebody that can negotiate a little bit on this subject, and others?" and he said, "Yes, I will send Jose..." whoever, "to see you."

And a few days later a man comes into Washington. He had the most beautiful clothing I've ever seen, I'm telling you. He was wearing suits. In fact, other than it probably would sound bad for the negotiation, I wanted to ask him, "Who's your tailor?" but I didn't think that was a good way to start off the

90 The Republican Campaign

negotiation. And I said to him, "I want to do this." I went to the border patrol and ICE, who are phenomenal people, and I went to everybody who has anything to do with the border, and our country and safety and immigration, I said, "Give me a top 10 list. I want everything. I want everything. I'll get it all." "Sir. You won't get any of this stuff. We've been trying to get it for 30 years from Mexico." I said, "That's okay. 100% I'll get it."

Anyway, they gave us the stay-in-Mexico policy. In other words, people have to stay in Mexico. They don't come into our country; they stay in Mexico. And they gave us catch-and-release into Mexico, not catch-and-release into our country. They gave us many things, various illness situation, where people that are ill with contagious diseases... Right, Doc Ronny? They pour into our country. It's like, "Let's just accept everybody and let's spread illness all over our country," so we had that taken care of. We had everything. We had 10.

So the guy comes in from Mexico, and I say, "Here's what I want. I want 28,000 soldiers free of charge. I want Remain in Mexico. I want catch-and-release into Mexico." They never heard of this. And he's like, "Ha, ha, ha." He's going, "President, we won't do that. Why would we do this? Are we stupid? Why would we do this?" I said, "You're going to do it 100%. What, you don't think you're going to do it? Of course you're going to do it." "No, I'm not going to do it." I said, "Yes, you are going to do it 100%." He goes, "No way." I said, "Way." I said, "Way. You're going to do it." And now he's not laughing anymore because he's trying to figure, "What the hell is going on with this guy?" He's saying no and I'm saying yes. I said, "No, 100% you're going to do it." He said, "No, I'm not." And I said, "Here's what's happening. It's Friday evening. On Monday morning at seven o'clock, every single car that you send into our country..." You know they've stolen 32% of our car industry over the years. Not during my administration, by the way. But over the years they've taken a huge chunk out of Michigan. And by the way, that's why I'm leading in Michigan, because people see what they've done to the jobs and the cars. And the building, the manufacturing of cars, is just horrible. And Mexico has taken a tremendous amount of that business away. They're building massive car plants again in Mexico. I had it stopped. Some of the biggest plants in the world. You know who's building a lot of them? China is building car plants in Mexico to sell cars into the United States. And I told them the other day, "Don't do it because you're going to be charged 100% tariff, which makes it impossible to sell the cars into our... And you're building these big monster plants, and you're wasting a lot of money doing it because we're not going to accept any of those cars."

We're not going to lose our jobs to monster plants that are being built along the border to sell into the United States because they have a guy like Crooked Joe Biden as President who's accepted money. He's a Manchurian candidate. He's accepted money from China, from Russia, from Ukraine, from everywhere. If that were a Republican, he would have been given the electric chair. They would have brought back the death penalty. What he's gotten away... He's the most crooked. He's also the most crooked President we've ever had. And to spin it a little bit, he's a threat to democracy. You know they like to say I'm a threat to democracy. What the hell have I done? All I've done is we had no wars, except we defeated ISIS, and we defeated them brutally and quickly. Quickly. . . .

But remember what they're going to do if this horrible low-IQ individual who's representing us... If this horrible person, who's done such a bad job, worst President of history by far: if this horrible individual finishes the debate, which I think he will... if he's standing, if he's standing... they'll say, "It was a brilliant performance." It was a brilliant performance. They've never seen anything like it. Very much reminiscent of the days of FDR. You know, FDR was a beautiful... had a beautiful patrician voice, magnificent voice, great debater, a very smart man. FDR, 16 years, almost 16 years, he was four-term. I don't know, are we going to be considered three-term or two-term? You tell me. Ronny, what do you think? Are we three-term or two-term if we win?... but think of it, they're going to say wonderful. Now he did the State of the Union the other day, he was high as a kite. So, I think we should call for drug tests on the debate. We're going to call for drug tests. We're going to call for drug tests. So anyway, so Macron calls, you know what I mean. Even I say to myself, you're a freaking genius. Hey, look, I had an uncle, my father's brother, who's the longest serving professor, he's the longest serving professor in the history of MIT. He graduated, he was a phenomenal student. A real genius. Really brilliant guy. And I believe in the racehorse theory, fast horses produced fast horses. He went to MIT, graduated, they said, we'd love to have you be a professor. He was there for, I think, 41 years. He's the longest serving professor in the history of MIT.

It's nice to know. Do you think Biden has that in his family? I don't think so. I don't think so. I may be wrong. Let's check. Let's check. So, Macron calls me back, see, this is the final of the stories. Macron calls me back, calls me back, and he said, "Donald, Donald, we have agreed to do what you want. We will not charge the tax." How sad is that? There are so many different things like buying Air Force One saying, I'm not going to pay for it and not signing the contract. I said, who negotiated the contract? Barack Hussein Obama. Then I'm not signing it. Well, why would you do that? Because I know it's too expensive. I didn't know anything about the plane. It's too expensive, and I was able to cut $1.6 billion off the price over a period of two months with Boeing.

We have a lot of stories we could tell out, but the saddest thing of all is that crooked Joe Biden has turned your state, and the entire country, into a dumping ground for the world. In Venezuela, violent crime is down at levels that they've never seen before. It was 67%, three weeks ago, it's now down to 72%. It's down. Violent crime is down. Would you ever hear that? If it goes down 1%, we say, oh, it's so great. Down 72% because all of their inmates, their mental patients, and the DREC, from deep in the basements of their most vile prisons, and they're depositing them all into our country. All their gang members in Caracas, Venezuela, Caracas wonderful city if you'd like to... actually, it's going to turn out to be a lot safer than our cities because all the criminals are being sent to us.

The Republican Campaign

In fact, I'll invite you. In fact, I have an idea for the NRA. Let's have the next year's meeting in Venezuela, where it's going to be a lot safer than our country. Venezuela will have no crime because all of their criminals will be deposited, so Ronnie, we'll go together. Okay. Congressman Fallon, we're going to go together. We'll all take a trip together and we're going to go and we're going to get Dan and the whole group, and we're going to go to Venezuela because we want a crime- free environment. Okay? That's what's happening. That's what's happening. Think of it, they're down 72% now from last year in violent crime. Biden wants to disarm American citizens while he floods our country with Biden-migrant crime....

We will fight for America like no one has ever fought before. 2024 is our final battle. With you at my side, we will demolish the deep state. We will expel the warmongers from our government. We will drive out the globalists, we will cast out the communists, Marxists, and fascists. We will throw off the sick political class that hates our country. We will route the fake news media. We will drain the swamp and we will liberate our country from these tyrants and villains once and for all. Like those patriots before us, we will not bend, we will not break, we will not yield. We will never give in. We will never give up. We will never, ever, ever, ever back down. With your support, we will go on to victory in the likes of which no one has ever seen, and we will evict crooked Joe Biden from the White House on November 5th, 2024. The great silent majority is rising like never before. And under our leadership, the forgotten man and woman will be forgotten no longer. We are one movement, one people, one family, and one glorious nation under God. And together, we will make America powerful again. We will make America wealthy again. We will make America strong again. We will make America proud again. We will make America safe again. We will make America free again. And we will make America great again. Thank you very much to the NRA, and thank you, Texas. Thank you very much. God bless you all. God bless you all. Thank you. Thank you.

Print Citations

CMS: Trump, Donald. "Address at the National Rifle Association's Annual Meeting." Speech at the Kay Bailey Hutchinson Center, Dallas, TX, May 20, 2024. In *The Reference Shelf: Representative American Speeches, 2023–2024,* edited by Micah L. Issitt, 80–92. Amenia, NY: Grey House Publishing, 2024.

MLA: Trump, Donald. "Address at the National Rifle Association's Annual Meeting." Kay Bailey Hutchinson Center, 20 May 2024, Dallas, TX. Speech. *The Reference Shelf: Representative American Speeches, 2023–2024,* edited by Micah L. Issitt, Grey House Publishing, 2024, pp. 80–92.

APA: Trump, D. (2024). Address at the National Rifle Association's annual meeting [Speech]. Kay Bailey Hutchinson Center, Dallas, TX. In Micah L. Issitt (Ed.), *The reference shelf: Representative American speeches, 2023–2024* (pp. 80–92). Grey House Publishing. (Original work published 2024)

Hulk Hogan Says Donald Trump Is the Toughest of Them All

By Terry Bollea

Terry Bollea, a seventy-one-year-old professional wrestler better known as "Hulk Hogan" for his television wrestling persona, spoke at the Republican National Convention in Milwaukee, Wisconsin. He made comparisons between his scripted victory matches as a professional wrestler, and Trump's political career and claimed that a Trump victory would allow "Trumpites" to run wild.

Well, let me tell you something, brother. You know something? When I came here tonight, there was so much energy in this room. I felt maybe I was in Madison Square Garden getting ready to win another world title or maybe I thought... The vibe was so intense, the energy was so crazy, it felt like maybe I was going to press that no good, sticky giant over my head and slam him through the mat, brother.

But what I found out was I was in a room full of real Americans, brother, and at the end of the day, with our leader up there, my hero, that gladiator, we're going to bring America back together one real American at a time, brother.

You know something? I've seen some great tag teams in my time. Hulk Hogan and oh yeah, the macho man, Randy Savage. But you know something? I see the greatest tag team of my life standing upon us getting ready to straighten this country out for all the real Americans. Even though you guys are real Americans, you better get ready because when Donald J. Trump becomes the President of the United States, all the real Americans are going to be nicknamed Trumpites because all the Trumpites are going to be running wild for four years. With the power of Donald J. Trump and all the Trumpites running wild, America is going to get back on track and like Donald J. Trump said, America is going to be great again.

When I look out and I see all the real Americans, I think about how Donald Trump, his family was compromised. When I look out there and I see Donald Trump, I think about how his business was compromised. But what happened last week when they took a shot at my hero and they tried to kill the next President of the United States, enough was enough. I said, "Let Trump-a-mania run wild, brother! Let Trump-a-mania rule again. Let Trump-a-mania, make America great again."

You know something, Trumpites? I didn't come here as Hulk Hogan, but I just had to give you a little taste. My name is Terry Bollea, and as an entertainer... I love you too. As an entertainer, I try to stay out of politics, but after everything

---

Delivered on July 18, 2024 at the Republican National Convention, Milwaukee, WI.

that's happened to our country over the past four years and everything that happened last weekend, I can no longer stay silent. I'm here tonight because I want the world to know that Donald Trump is a real American hero, and I'm proud to support my hero as the next president of this United States.

Guys, I've known Donald Trump for over 35 years. Hold on a second. Hold on. I just had a flashback. I just had a flashback, man. This is really tripping. The last time I was up on stage, Donald Trump was sitting at ringside at the Trump Plaza. I was bleeding like a pig, and I won the world title right in front of Donald J. Trump. You know something? He's going to win in November and we're all going to be champions again when he wins.

Like I said, I've known that man for over 35 years, and he's always been the biggest patriot, and he still is. He's always told you exactly what he thought, and he still does, brother. No matter the odds, he always finds a way to win. When he's back in our White House, America is going to start winning again.

You know, guys, over my career, I've been in the ring with some of the biggest, some of the baddest dudes on the planet, and I've squared off against warriors, ooh, yeah, savages, and I've even, like I said, body slammed giants in the middle of the ring. I know tough guys but let me tell you something, brother, Donald Trump is the toughest of them all.

They've thrown everything at Donald Trump. All the investigations, the impeachments, the court cases, and he's still standing and kicking their butts. We never had it better than the Trump years. Back then, we had a thriving economy, we had strong borders, we had safe streets, we had peace and respect around the world, but then we lost it all in a blink of an eye. Crime is out of control, the border is out of control, the price of food and gas, and housing is out of control, and the only person who can clean this up is Donald Trump.

Guys, I really, really love this country, and I've lived the American dream. I want my kids, your kids, and all those little teeny Hulk-a-maniacs out there to live the American dream, too. This November, guys, we can save the American dream for everyone, and Donald Trump is the president who will get the job done. All you criminals, all you lowlifes, all you scumbags, all you drug dealers, and all you crooked politicians need to answer one question, brother. Whatchya gonna do when Donald Trump and all the Trump-a-maniacs run wild on you, brother? God bless you, and thank you.

Print Citations

CMS: Bollea, Terry. "Hulk Hogan Says Trump Is the Toughest of Them All." Speech at the Republican National Convention, Milwaukee, WI, July 18, 2024. In *The Reference Shelf: Representative American Speeches, 2023–2024,* edited by Micah L. Issitt, 93–95. Amenia, NY: Grey House Publishing, 2024.

MLA: Bollea, Terry. "Hulk Hogan Says Trump Is the Toughest of Them All." Republican National Convention, 18 July 2024, Milwaukee, WI. Speech. *The Reference Shelf: Representative American Speeches, 2023–2024,* edited by Micah L. Issitt, Grey House Publishing, 2024, pp. 93–95.

APA: Bollea, T. (2024). Hulk Hogan says Trump is the toughest of them all [Speech]. Republican National Convention, Milwaukee, WI. In Micah L. Issitt (Ed.), *The reference shelf: Representative American speeches, 2023–2024* (pp. 93–95). Grey House Publishing. (Original work published 2024)

We Must Elect Leaders Who Will Preserve the Bill of Rights

By Robert F. Kennedy Jr.

"Tens of millions of Americans are waking up to the fact that they were lied to, the fact that they were manipulated, that they were gaslit, except for a narrow elite that's still promoting it, mainly in the media." Robert F. Kennedy Jr., son of former US attorney general and senator Robert F. Kennedy, and a popular conspiracy theorist, spoke at the Libertarian National Convention in May of 2024. He claims that both the Trump and Biden governments violated constitutional rights in pushing a false narrative about the COVID-19 pandemic.

Can you hear me? I am very, very happy to be here today. I'm going to speak about the United States Constitution and particularly the Bill of Rights. A lot of people don't realize that the Articles of the Constitution don't grant citizens any rights or freedoms whatsoever. That was a real problem to some of the Founding Fathers, particularly to George Mason. Mason wrote a pamphlet during the Constitutional Convention that opposed the new government. And that pamphlet was so convincing that the other Framers of the Constitution felt that it was too much of a hazard and that the Constitution was in danger at that point of not being ratified. And that's when James Madison came to the rescue by drafting the Bill of Rights, the first 10 Amendments to the United States Constitution.

Originally, Madison felt that the Bill of Rights were unnecessary because it was obvious to him that the government couldn't exert powers that the Constitution had not assigned to it. But everybody in this hall knows governments don't like to limit themselves. Instead, they're constantly moving to exert and appropriate new powers. But the Patriots in 1791 vividly remembered the British tyranny and they knew that every power that a government takes, it will never voluntarily relinquish. And every power a government takes, it will ultimately abuse to the ultimate extent possible. And that's why the delegates to the Constitutional Convention balked at a Constitution that only enumerated government powers but nowhere limit them. And so thanks to George Mason, the Bill of Rights was enshrined in our nation's founding documents. The main Articles of the Constitution enumerate what the government can do. The Bill of Rights is the opposite; it enumerates what the government cannot do.

It's the Bill of Rights that earned America the reputation as the Land of Liberty. The problem is the Bill of Rights is only a document. It doesn't have any

---

Delivered on May 26, 2024 at the Libertarian National Convention, Washington, DC.

magical powers to force government officials to respect it. And I'm sorry to say that again and again throughout our history, our leaders have failed to respect it. Again and again they have cited some pretext to suspend and violate our constitutional rights. There's always a reason why right now the rights are an inconvenience that we can't afford. It was the Red Scare in the 1920s. It was Joe McCarthy in the 1950s. It was civil rights protests and the Vietnam War protesters in the 1960s. It was the War on Drug in the 1970s. It was the War on Terror after 2001, and most recently it was the COVID pandemic. Maybe a brain worm ate that part of my memory, but I don't recall any part of the United States Constitution where there's an exemption for pandemics. And in fact, there's not one of the Amendments of the Bill of Rights as a preamble that says, except when officials choose to declare a public health emergency. They all say very simply, the government shall not infringe on these rights no matter what. If the government can take them away at will, then they're not rights at all. They're really just privileges that are granted and revoked by an authority. Is that the kind of country that you want to live in?

And every time they suspend rights and then pretend to give them back again, they establish a dangerous precedent. The rights they give back are never quite as strong as the ones that they took away.

Obviously, it's not the piece of paper called the Bill of Rights that protects our freedoms. We have to actually believe in it. Our leaders have to believe it with sufficient loyalty to counterbalance the temptations of power. And even more importantly, our citizens have to believe that their rights so loyally that they stand up for them even when it means taking a personal risk. After all, the Constitution isn't just a legal document; it's also an inspirational document. And that's why if you treasure your freedom, you better elect leaders who are inspired by it and who will wield it to inspire others. Leaders who believe in freedoms and hold the Bill of Rights in reverence.

I'm sorry to say that neither President Trump nor President Biden pass this critical examination. Neither of them upheld the Constitution when it really counted. Let's start with President Trump. I think he had the right instinct when he came into office. He was initially very reluctant to impose lockdowns, but then he got rolled by his bureaucrats. He caved in and many of our most fundamental rights disappeared practically overnight. It all started with the social media and the mainstream media, apparently without any government prompting, began censoring any speech that departed from the government's official orthodoxies. It's critical to the survival of any democracy that the free press maintains a posture of fear skepticism toward government pronouncements and towards large agglomerations of government and political and economic and corporate power.

But suddenly, America's free press was no longer speaking truth to power. Instead, it made itself a vessel for government propaganda. It began suppressing the voices of dissents and silencing and gaslighting the powerless. Oh, Hamilton, Madison, and Adams said that they had put the right of free expression into the

First Amendment because all of the other rights depended on it. A government that has the capacity to silence its critics has license for any kind of atrocity.

I grew up reading Aldous Huxley and Robert Heinlein and Arthur Koestler and Franz Kafka and Alexander Solzhenitsyn and George Orwell. And the consistent theme in all of those works was the presumption that censorship of speech was always wrong, that it was always the first step down on the slippery slope toward tyranny and totalitarianism. There is no time when we look back at history and we say that the people who were censoring speech were the good guys. They're always the bad guys.

The Framers didn't write the First Amendment to protect convenient or desirable speech. They wrote it to protect the kind of speech that nobody wants to hear. They wrote it to protect incendiary speech. They wrote it to protect insults. They wrote it to protect misinformation and disinformation and malinformation and even lies. All of those are protected by the First Amendment. There were no exceptions. The Constitution doesn't have exemptions for wars or resurrections or financial crises or pandemics. The Framers wrote the Constitution for hard times.

During the American Civil War the Confederate states were sending up agents provocateurs to the northern cities like Boston and New York and inciting draft riots and they were destroying northern morale at a critical time during the war. This was a war that almost destroyed our nation. For three years, that war, nobody had any idea whether the United States of America would exist after the war was over. There was even money on it. There were 659,000 Americans who died during that war. It's the equivalent of 7.2 million today.

So Lincoln and the northern military knew who these agent provocateurs were as soon as they entered the cities, and they began arresting them before they could give these speeches. And the Chief Justice of the Supreme Court, Roger Taney, said, you can't do that. That is an assault against free speech and habeas corpus. And he said, "Even if the life of the nation is at stake, even if hundreds of thousands of lives are at stake, you cannot suppress our Constitution. It is above everything." So they wrote it for hard times. They didn't write it for easy times. The United States Bill of Rights was written for the most difficult times, and no matter how difficult they are, they are indomitable. We're not allowed to suppress them.

But the moment the White House officials satisfied themselves that the American people would accept censorship by the end of February of 2020, they took hammer and tongs to the rest of the Constitution. President Trump allowed his health regulators to mandate a science-free social distancing, which undermined our First Amendment rights to freedom of assembly. We could no longer peacefully gather. So that was the first two legs of the First Amendment, freedom of assembly, freedom of speech. And they went after the third leg of the First Amendment, which is freedom of worship. They closed every church in this country for a year with no due process, with no scientific citation, with no public hearings, no notice and comment rulemaking, no environmental impact statements. All of the process of democracy that I've been suing companies and governments for 40 years because they forgot to do one of those things, and all of our constitutional rights were plowed under.

They closed all the churches, but they kept open the Walmarts and the liquor stores. And the Fifth Amendment says that no one shall be deprived of life, liberty, or property unless convicted of a crime. Yet President Trump shut down 3.3 million business. President Trump said that he was going to run America like a business, and he came in and he gave the keys to all of our businesses, to a 50-year bureaucrat who'd never been elected to anything and had no accountability. He closed down 3.3 million businesses with no due process, no just compensation in violation of the Fifth Amendment. With the lockdowns, the mass mandates, the travel restrictions, President Trump presided over the greatest restriction on individual liberties this country has ever known. He didn't stand up for the Constitution when it really mattered.

Next, President Trump's beloved Operation Warp Speed shut down jury trials for any corporation that was involved in COVID countermeasures. Here's what the Seventh Amendment says: No American shall be denied the right of a trial before a jury of his peers in cases or controversies exceeding $25. There is no pandemic exception.

And by the way, the framers knew all about pandemics. There were two pandemics during the Revolutionary War, one that decimated the armies of Virginia, the other that destroyed for a long time the army of New England at the very time when Benedict Arnold's army had conquered Montreal. So they had gone into the inner city, taken away from the British, and they owned it, but they had to withdraw because they did not have the troop strength to defend it because of the smallpox epidemic. Otherwise, Canada today would be part of the United States. And all of the framers knew that. And between the end of the war, the Revolutionary War in 1780, ratification of the Bill of Rights in 1791, there were pandemics in every city in our country, Boston Philadelphia, New York, North Carolina, South Carolina, all the major cities had cholera epidemics, yellow fever epidemics, malaria epidemics that killed tens of thousands of people, almost all of the framers and had family members or friends who died in those pandemics. Yet they did not put a pandemic exemption in the United States Constitution.

And the waiver of the Seventh Amendment for corporations that were involved in countermeasures meant that no matter how reckless the corporation behaved, no matter how negligent it was, no matter how toxic or unnecessary the ingredients, no matter how shoddy the testing, no matter how grievous your injury, you could not sue that company. They had a ticket to make anything they want without any kind of accountability.

The Trump White House also went after the Fourth Amendment prohibitions against warrantless searches and seizures with this intrusive track and trace surveillance systems that obliterated our rights to privacy in this country. The only amendment that did not come under attack during the COVID pandemic was the Second Amendment, and many Americans believe that the reason for that is because we have a Second Amendment.

Incidentally, President Trump also assaulted the First Amendment, failed to defend press freedom when he continued President Obama's persecution and prosecution of Julian Assange. Assange should be celebrated as a hero for doing exactly what journalists are supposed to do, which is to expose government corruption. We shouldn't be putting them in prison; we should have a monument to him here in Washington, DC.

The same is true for Edward Snowden who exposed illegal spying by the NSA. Congress went ahead and passed legislation because of the findings of Edward Snowden. If he hadn't told us, we wouldn't know about it. He's a hero, not a criminal. So I'm going to tell you what I'm going to do. I'm going to do what President Trump should have done. On my first day in office, I'm going to pardon Edward Snowden and I'm going to drop charges, all charges against Julian Assange.

I'm curious to know how President Trump is going to defend his attacks on the Constitution when I meet him on the debating stage. I invited him to debate in front of you, in front of the members of this party, but he declined. At some point, I hope that he has the courage to stand up there so that we can all talk about these issues and to make sure that these assaults on our Constitution never, ever happen again. We need to have a civics lesson for the American people to make sure this is never repeated. When President Trump left office, the assault on the Constitution intensified. President Biden violated a freedom so fundamental that James Madison didn't even think to put it in the Bill of Rights. He never imagined that the government could mandate medical procedures to unwilling Americans in violation of bodily autonomy. But that's what happened during the pandemic, a program of coercion and information chaos and information control that prevented the public from making fully informed choices.

But that wasn't the worst of it. He put the power of his office behind the assault of the one freedom upon which all their freedoms rely: the freedom of the press. We now know from the Twitter Files, from the discovery in the Murthy V. Biden case, and from my own case, which is now in front of the Supreme Court, Kennedy V. Biden that 37 hours after he took the oath of office, President Biden was colluding with the FBI to coerce the social media sites, Google, Twitter, Facebook, YouTube, Instagram to open portals to allow the federal agencies to censor political speech of Americans. The FBI opened this portal to the CIA, to CISA, to NIH, to the IRS, to the CDC, to the DHS, and about a half dozen other agencies in an obscene orgy of federal censorship that was unprecedented in the American experience.

It started with what they called medical misinformation, and it wasn't even misinformation. There's a dialogue between Facebook and the White House at that time in which Facebook is saying a lot of this information, including from me, the stuff that they were suppressing is actually factually accurate. And the White House, they coined a new name, a new word called "malinformation," which is information that is factually accurate, but is nevertheless inconvenient to government authorities. And pretty soon an entire censorship industrial complex had grown up, which was billion dollars spent that involved the government agencies, the universities, NGOs and tech companies, and the stuff that they censored, they started with medical, so-called medical misinformation. They then widened that to all kinds of political issues, including censorship about criticism of the war in Ukraine and other government programs.

Going back to at least the FISA Act under President George W. Bush, Democratic and Republican administrations have taken turns assaulting our Constitutional rights and freedoms. You know that, that's why you joined the Libertarian Party. Well, I stand with you in valuing personal liberty, and I promise you that when I'm President, I'm going to protect your right to speak freely. I'm going to protect your right to assemble peacefully. I will protect your freedom to worship. I will protect your right to keep and bear arms. I will protect your right to a trial before jury. I will protect your privacy against unreasonable searches and seizures. I will protect your private property and your right to operate a business. And that's not all.

Two of the most overlooked amendments in the Bill of Rights are the ninth and 10th. And those amendments essentially say that just because we've listed all of those rights by name, it doesn't mean that those are all the rights that you have. That any power, they say everything else, right, any power that is not explicitly given to the federal government remains with the individual or the states, and I will always protect those rights.

As I mentioned before, the Constitution is more than a legal document. It's meant to inspire us. It's a recitation of the most fundamental moral truths that govern human conduct. It reminds us of the central proposition and only under a system which maximizes the personal freedoms that God intended for us when He gave us free will and we achieve our potential for creativity, for prosperity, for the ultimate elevation of the human spirit. The Constitution embodies the very soul of our nation as first invoked in the Declaration of Independence. Let me read you now its most famous passage, which comes in the second paragraph. "We hold these truths to be self-evident, that all men are created equal, that they are endowed by their Creator with certain unalienable rights, and that among these are life, liberty, and the pursuit of happiness." I get goose bumps when I read those words. Those words change the world forever.

The Bill of Rights endowed them with a legal existence and a legal reality, but we need to take them further. Some people argue that it's fine for social media platforms to censor speech. After all, they're private companies, and they can do as they please. Well, that argument falls apart when the government is bribing, threatening and cajoling them to censor speech and to deplatform dissidents. It also falls apart if they have monopolistic control over the public space. But aside from that, yeah, they do have a legal right to censor. It is legally acceptable, but is it morally acceptable? Is it socially acceptable?

It shouldn't be in an authoritarian country like China or Japan, or sorry, Iran, censorship is socially acceptable. People take it for granted. It's in the air they breathe. In this country, to the extent that we still cherish the spirit of our

102   The Republican Campaign

founders, the Bill of Rights, the Declaration of Independence, we do not take it for granted. Instead, we greet censorship with outrage. We greet it with indignation. We greet it with contempt. We fiercely reject it. If the day comes when we do not, our descent into tyranny is inevitable.

What disturbed me most during the pandemic was not what the government was trying to do and what it succeeded in doing, it was really how the public complied.

But now, except for the people in this room. I'm going tell you something that when I was researching my book on Dr. Fauci, I did a chapter on these old CIA programs at MKUltra, MKUltra, MKNaomi, MKDietrich. These were the MK stands for, "Mind control," and they were a series of experiments that the CIA, they had other programs too, Operation Bluebird, Operation Artichoke, that were all designed to manipulate human behavior, individual behavior through the use of hypnosis, through psychiatric drugs, through sensory deprivation, through noise torture, through information, confusion, and the experiments in how to manipulate entire societies in order to impose control from above. They were doing all these weird experiments and creating Manchurian candidates, and it all came out in 1973, between '73 and '77 with the Church Committee and the House Select Committee on Assassinations.

One of the famous experiments that I during in my book was able to connect to MKUltra was the Milgram experiment. The Milgram experiment was, as many of you know, it was an experiment that was part of this program. It was conducted by a young associate professor at Yale University who recruited about 70 people from every walk of life, Blacks, whites, teachers, students, business people, laborers, and he would put the subjects on a chair in one room and they had a dial on the table in front of him, and they were told that that dial was applying a shock, an electric shock to a subject who sat in the other room who was actually a confederate of Dr. Milgram. He was an actor, but he pretended to be tied to a chair. And when the electricity went up, he would scream. He would see what level it was and scream appropriately, and struggle, and plead and beg and cry.

And many of the subjects, when they were told to do it, Dr. Milgram would stand behind him with his white lab uniform on and all that, or the iconography of authority, of medical authority. He'd stand behind them and he'd say, "Turn it up, turn it down, turn it higher, turn it down, or turn it higher." Many of the subjects were weeping. They were pleading with him, "Don't make me turn it up more." And when he told him to turn it up, they did so anyway, and 67% of the people, the subjects who he recruited, turned it up to 250 volts where it was marked potentially fatal. And what Milgram concluded is that most people, 67% of the people will allow people in authority to overwhelm and subvert their most closely held values. They all knew it was wrong, but they did it because they were told to do it. The good news is that 33% of those people stood up and walked out of the room, and I think that those were the Libertarians.

Those are the people in this room. Most Americans accepted the orthodoxy and we watched this happening with dismay. We watch families separated and fighting with each other. I know you all knew people whose relationships changed because of your skepticism and their feeling of safety when they were subsumed in that orthodoxy, and now things are changing. Tens of millions of Americans are waking up to the fact that they were lied to, the fact that they were manipulated, that they were gaslit, except for a narrow elite that's still promoting it, mainly in the media. Americans have lost all trust in our public institutions.

About two months ago, the CDC made an official recommendation for the ninth COVID booster. 90% of Americans are saying, "We're not going to do it." Do you want a government that is telling you you can't go to work unless you submit to that? But that's what they did to us two years ago. And now most Americans are realizing, are losing their faith in those institutions and with good reason, and I'm going to restore faith in those institutions. I'm not going to do it by telling people, "You ought to be censored. You ought to believe in it." I'm going to do it by making them tell the truth, and giving us good science and changing the corrupt cultures that have put them under the control of corporations. The President of the United States is more than just a legal authority occupying the bully pulpit. He sets an example for the nation, for good or for ill. So I want to tell you the kind of example that I'm going to set for America. Yes, I'm going to uphold the Constitution, and protect every freedom and the Bill of Rights. I'll also strive to represent the principle that animates those freedoms. And I believe this is the same principle that lies at the heart of the libertarian philosophy, it is the principle of respect. It is the respect for each individual as a full and sovereign being. Think about it; censorship for example, is just another form of disrespect. It says, "I'm going to decide which kind of information you should and shouldn't hear. I'm going to protect you from dangerous thoughts."

I'm going to protect you from subversive information. It's patronizing, right? All of our cherished rights embody respect for the individual. That's why we uphold equality under the law. No one is to be locked up arbitrarily. No one is to be deprived... Happy to talk afterwards. No one is to be deprived of their property. No one is to be subjected to humiliating searches without reasonable suspicion of having committed a crime. No one is to be prevented from worshiping God in the manner that they believe. Why is that? Because I respect your right to explore and define your own relationship with God. And no one is coerced into submitting to unwanted medical procedures. No one is required to participate against their will in scientific experiments. And each person is trusted with a responsibility to bear arms by default unless he violates that trust.

This is the spiritual principle. Prior, even to the Constitution, all men are created equal. It originally applied just to property owners, then to just white men, then to all men, and then to women. Today we understand that right to include every human being. My promise to you is that as president, I will uphold the principle of respect for each human being as an equal before God and an equal before the law. That's why my campaign never paints our opponents as monsters. That's why I never weaponize. I will never weaponize the justice system, the

104 The Republican Campaign

federal agencies like the IRS, the FBI, or the CIA, or the Secret Service against my political adversaries.

Everyone is equal under the law, period. No special favors for the big banks or the corporations. No more regulations tilted to destroy small businesses. No more extravagant subsidies to mature industries. No more corporate welfare. No more surveillance of private citizens. No more propaganda. No more secrecy and no more lies. My first day of office after pardoning Snowden and Assange, I'm going to issue.

I'm going to issue an executive order forbidding the National Security Agency or any of the intelligence agencies from propagandizing of the American people. I'm going to issue an executive order against any federal employee from collaborating with media or social media to censor Americans. And I'm going to issue an executive order that any federal official who lies to the American people in conjunction with his official duties will immediately be fired.

Let me add that respect for the sanctity of the sovereign individual knows no national boundaries. Murder is not okay anywhere in any form. That is why I will end the forever wars. I will end the regime change wars, the wars that have bankrupted our nation and ruined our reputation abroad. Finally, I want to say one thing about authority. I don't know what libertarian philosophy says about it, but I believe in a healthy respect for authority. However, authority must be earned, not forced. We must not confuse respect for fear.

This has been the mistake of American foreign policy. I grew up in an era when people around the world were hungry for American leadership that they understood the difference between leadership and bullying. And that's a lesson that our leadership, both Republicans and Democrats have now forgotten. Other nations may fear us today, but they no longer respect us. And why is that? Because we've waged a series of unjust wars, because we violated our own principles of freedom and democracy. We have forfeited our moral authority because we have supported dictators and corrupt regimes and subverted democracy around the globe.

And just as we have lost respect globally, we've also lost it at home. We have lost respect for ourselves. American children overwhelmingly say that they are not proud to be Americans. There was a poll that came out in 2013 in which Americans under the age of 35 were asked, "Are you proud of the United States of America?" 85% said yes. The same poll taken five months ago. 18% said yes. So somehow in the administration of the last two presidents, this young generation has completely lost faith in our country and they've lost hope for their own futures. Now is the time to restore that hope, that admiration, that pride and respect. The only way to do that is to return to the founding spirit of our country, to return to the spirit that animated the Declaration of Independence and the Bill of Rights. If we're faithful to those, we will regain our pride as a nation. We'll regain our prosperity. We'll regain the respect of the world and we'll regain our self-respect. We gain self-esteem by doing estimable things and that means complying with our own constitution above all.

In the summer of 2020, I traveled, this was at the height of the pandemic. I traveled to Berlin to speak to a group about 1.3 million people from all over Europe in a peaceful demonstration. And an NBC film crew came up to me during that convocation and they asked me why I wasn't wearing a mask, which nobody was except for the NBC film crew. And they said it wasn't I scared of dying of COVID. And I said to them, "There's a lot worse things than dying." And they said to me, "Like what?" And I said, "Like living like a slave. Like having my children grow up in an America where the Bill of Rights is just an empty piece of paper."

In 1776, it was a generation of Americans that were willing to sacrifice their lives, their jobs, their property, their fortunes to give us this bill of rights. And upwards of 20,000 of them died to give us this gift, and we managed to keep it for two centuries. And then in eight short years during the administrations of two presidents, we gave it all away without putting up a fight. Thomas Jefferson said that the Tree of Liberty has to be watered with the blood of every generation, but we don't have to die to preserve our Bill of Rights, but we have to be willing to make sacrifices. And the sacrifices we're being asked to make are very, very trivial compared to what they made in 1776.

We're being asked to endure the scolding or the disapprobation of the public, the defamation of the press, the antipathy of our government. That's not a big deal. We all need to be able to put our self-interest aside if we're going to maintain these rights for future generations. And all of you who come here for the Libertarian party, you all disagree about many things. Many of you don't disagree who don't agree with me on a lot of stuff. We all agree on one thing, which is we have to fight with a Bill of Rights... Without the Bill of Rights, we have nothing in this country and we all need to be united because there are a lot of people out there that don't understand what America is supposed to look like. And the people in this convocation do. Our public officials have forgotten that vision for America and it's time that we remind them. We can only do that by electing leaders who understand the necessity for personal sacrifices to preserve the Bill of Rights. That's the path to restoring our national greatness. That will be my promise to you as President of the United States. Thank you all very much and God bless you.

Print Citations

CMS: Kennedy, Jr., Robert F. "We Must Elect Leaders Who Will Preserve the Bill of Rights." Speech at the Libertarian National Convention, Washington, DC, May 26, 2024. In *The Reference Shelf: Representative American Speeches, 2023–2024,* edited by Micah L. Issitt, 96–105. Amenia, NY: Grey House Publishing, 2024.

MLA: Kennedy, Jr., Robert F. "We Must Elect Leaders Who Will Preserve the Bill of Rights." Libertarian National Convention, 26 May 2024, Washington, DC. Speech. *The Reference Shelf: Representative American Speeches, 2023–2024,* edited by Micah L. Issitt, Grey House Publishing, 2024, pp. 96–105.

APA: Kennedy, Jr., R. F. (2024). We must elect leaders who will preserve the Bill of Rights [Speech]. Speech at the Libertarian National Convention, Washington, DC. In Micah L. Issitt (Ed.), *The reference shelf: Representative American speeches, 2023–2024* (pp. 96–105). Grey House Publishing. (Original work published 2024)

Elect Trump President Again and America Will Be Unstoppable

By Matt Gaetz

"Under Trump we prospered, we were richer. Inflation was low, and there were two genders." Matt Gaetz, Representative from Florida, endorsed Donald Trump at the Republican National Convention in Milwaukee, Wisconsin. In a short speech, Gaetz hit popular Republican talking points, claimed that Trump will end alleged corruption under the Biden administration, and suggested that Trump will oppose gender identity politics.

Donald Trump is unstoppable. Elect him president again, and America will be unstoppable too. Meanwhile, Joe Biden's been out of it. Democrats have been hiding the real Biden for years. We saw people in the Witness Protection Program more often than we saw unscripted Biden. Under Biden-Harris, America has fallen sicker, lonelier, and poorer. Under Trump we prospered, we were richer. Inflation was low, and there were two genders. Under Biden-Harris, inflation has gotten so bad, you can no longer bribe Democrat senators with cash alone. You have to use gold bars just so the bribes hold value. Oh, the swamp draining will recommence soon, and I will be President Trump's strongest ally in Congress to pass term limits, to stop taxpayer funding for political campaigns, to ban members of Congress for life from becoming lobbyists. And for the same reason you don't let the referee bet on the game, ban members of Congress from trading individual stocks.

I am proud to stand before you. The only Republican in Congress who takes no lobbyist money, no PAC money. It's not good for me, I work for you, not them. President Trump, he'll never defund our police but he will defund foreign aid to countries that hate us. And President Trump understands that if it isn't racist to check ID for a hunting license or welfare benefits or a fishing license, then it is okay to demand an ID to vote everywhere in this country and every election itself.

A Democrat congressman recently said that any criticism of Joe Biden is ableist. I don't think it's too much to ask that the American president be able to do the job. Kamala Harris isn't able to do any job. She was appointed Border Czar. Appointing Kamala Harris to oversee the border is like appointing Bernie Madoff to oversee your retirement plan. President Trump has shown the world what he is made of, and now we will show the world what America is made of by having his back. And how about the choice President Trump made for a running

---

Delivered on July 17, 2024 at the Republican National Convention, Milwaukee, WI.

mate? J.D. Looks like a young Abraham Lincoln, but he's from Ohio, like General Grant. And like General Grant, J.D. Vance knows how to fight. So they can run Biden from the nursing home. Harris, George Clooney, Robert De Niro, whoever they want to run, we are on a mission to rescue and save this country, and we ride or die with Donald John Trump to the end. Thank you all so much. Thank you for having my back. Let's go get them.

Print Citations

CMS: Gaetz, Matt. "Elect Trump President Again and America Will Be Unstoppable." Speech at the Republican National Convention, Milwaukee, WI, July 17, 2024. In *The Reference Shelf: Representative American Speeches, 2023–2024*, edited by Micah L. Issitt, 106–107. Amenia, NY: Grey House Publishing, 2024.

MLA: Gaetz, Matt. "Elect Trump President Again and America Will Be Unstoppable." Republican National Convention, 17 July 2024, Milwaukee, WI. Speech. *The Reference Shelf: Representative American Speeches, 2023–2024*, edited by Micah L. Issitt, Grey House Publishing, 2024, pp. 106–107.

APA: Gaetz, M. (2024). Elect Trump president again and America will be unstoppable. [Speech]. Republican National Convention, Milwaukee, WI. In Micah L. Issitt (Ed.), *The reference shelf: Representative American speeches, 2023–2024* (pp. 106–107). Grey House Publishing. (Original work published 2024)

Presidential Candidate Suspends His Campaign and Endorses Donald Trump

By Robert F. Kennedy Jr.

"Ultimately, the future, however it happens is in God's hands and in the hands of the American voters and those of President Trump." Robert F. Kennedy Jr. delivered a speech to officially suspend his presidential campaign and endorsed Donald Trump, after Trump reached out to Kennedy to offer him a cabinet position. Kennedy also made misleading claims about the nature of neurological illness in the United States and claimed that the Trump administration would cure chronic illness among children.

The party, which I pledged my own allegiance to long before I was old enough to vote. I attended my first Democratic convention at the age of six, in 1960. And back then, the Democrats were the champions of the Constitution, of civil rights. The Democrats stood against authoritarianism, against censorship, against colonialism, imperialism, and unjust wars. We were the party of labor, of the working class. The Democrats were the party of government transparency and the champion of the environment. Our party was the bulwark against big money interests and corporate power. True to its name, it was the party of democracy.

As you know, I left that party in October because it had departed so dramatically from the core values that I grew up with. It had become the party of war, censorship, corruption, Big Pharma, Big Tech, Big Ag, and big money. When it abandoned democracy by canceling the primary to conceal the cognitive decline of the sitting president, I left the party to run as an independent. The mainstream of American politics and journalism derided my decision. Conventional wisdom said that it would be impossible even to get on the ballot as an independent, because each state poses an insurmountable tangle of arbitrary rules for collecting signatures. I would need over a million signatures: something no presidential candidate in history had ever achieved. And then I'd need a team of attorneys and millions of dollars to handle all the legal challenges from the DNC. The naysayers told us that we were climbing a glass version of Mount Impossible.

So, the first thing I want to tell you is that we proved them wrong. We did it because beneath the radar of mainstream media organs, we inspired a massive independent political movement. More than 100,000 volunteers sprang into action, hopeful that they could reverse our nation's decline. Many worked 10-hour days, sometimes in blizzards and blazing heat. They sacrificed family

---

Delivered on August 23, 2024 at a Trump rally, Phoenix, AZ.

time, personal commitments, and sleep, month after month, energized by a shared vision of a nation healed of its divisions. They set up tables at churches and farmers' markets. They canvassed door to door. In Utah and in New Hampshire, volunteers collected signatures in snowstorms, convincing each supporter to stop in the frigid cold, to take off their gloves, and to sign legibly. During a heat wave in Nevada, I met a tall athletic volunteer who cheerfully told me that he had lost 25 pounds collecting signatures in 117 degree heat.

To finance this effort, young Americans donated their lunch money, and senior citizens gave up part of their Social Security checks. Our 50-state organization collected those millions of signatures and more, and no presidential campaign in American political history has ever done that. And so I want to thank all of those dedicated volunteers, and congratulate the campaign staff who coordinated this enormous logistical feat. Your accomplishments were regarded as impossible. You carried me up that glass mountain. You pulled off a miracle. You achieved what all the pundits said could never be done. You have my deepest gratitude, and I'm never going to forget that; not just for what you did for my campaign, but for the sacrifices you made because you love our country. You showed everyone that democracy is still possible here. It continues to survive in the press and in the idealistic human energies that still thrive beneath a canvas of neglect and of official and institutional corruption.

Today, I'm here to tell you that I will not allow your efforts to go to waste. I'm here to tell you that I will leverage your tremendous accomplishments to serve the ideals that we share: the ideals of peace, of prosperity, of freedom, of health, all the ideals that motivated my campaign. I'm here today to describe the path forward that you've opened with your commitment and with your hard labors.

Now, in an honest system, I believe that I would've won the election. In a system that my father and my uncles thrived in, a system with open debates, with fair primaries, with regularly scheduled debates, with fair primaries, and with a truly independent media, untainted by government propaganda and censorship, in a system of nonpartisan courts and election boards, everything would be different. After all, the polls consistently showed me beating each of the other candidates, both in favorability and also in head-to-head match-ups. But I'm sorry to say that while democracy may still be alive at the grassroots, it has become a little more than a slogan for our political institutions, for our media, and for our government, and most sadly of all, for me, the Democratic Party.

In the name of saving democracy, the Democratic Party set itself to dismantling it. Lacking confidence that its candidate could win in a fair election at the voting booth, the DNC waged continual legal warfare against both President Trump and myself. Each time that our volunteers turned in those towering boxes of signatures needed to get on the ballot, the DNC dragged us into court, state after state, attempting to erase their work, and to subvert the will of the voters who had signed those petitions. It deployed DNC-aligned judges to throw me and other candidates off the ballot, and to throw President Trump in jail. It ran a sham primary that was rigged to prevent any serious challenge to President

110   The Republican Campaign

Biden. Then, when a predictably bungled debate performance precipitated the palace coup against President Biden, the same shadowy DNC operatives appointed his successor, also without an election. They installed a candidate who was so unpopular with voters that she dropped out in 2020 without winning a single delegate.

My uncle and my father both relished debate. They prided themselves on their capacity to go toe-to-toe with any opponent in a battle over ideas. They would be astonished to learn of a Democratic Party presidential nominee who, like Vice President Harris, has not appeared in a single interview or an unscripted encounter with voters for 35 days. This is profoundly undemocratic. How are people to choose when they don't know whom they are choosing? And how can this look to the rest of the world? My father and my uncle were always conscious of America's image abroad because of our nation's role as the template for democracy, a role model for democratic processes, and the leader of the free world. Instead of showing us her substance and character, the DNC and its media organs engineered a surge of popularity for Vice President Harris based upon nothing. No policies, no interviews, no debates, only smoke and mirrors and balloons in a highly-produced Chicago circus. There in Chicago, a string of Democratic speakers mentioned Donald Trump 147 times just on the first day. Who needs a policy, when you have Trump to hate? In contrast, at the RNC Convention, President Biden was mentioned only twice in four days.

I do interviews every day. Many of you have interviewed me. Anybody who asks gets to interview me. Some days I do as many as 10. President Trump, who actually was nominated and won an election, also does interviews daily. How did the Democratic Party choose a candidate that has never done an interview or debate during the entire election cycle? We know the answers. They did it by weaponizing the government agencies. They did it by abandoning democracy. They did it by suing the opposition, and by disenfranchising American voters. What most alarms me isn't how the Democratic Party conducts its internal affairs or runs its candidates. What alarms me is the resort to censorship, and media control, and the weaponization of the federal agencies. When a US president colludes with, or outright coerces, media companies to censor political speech, it's an attack on our most sacred right of free expression, and that's the very right upon which all of our other constitutional rights rest.

President Biden mocked Vladimir Putin's 88% landslide in the Russian elections, observing that Putin and his party controlled the Russian press, and that Putin prevented serious opponents from appearing on the ballot. But here in America, the DNC also prevented opponents from appearing on the ballot, and our television networks exposed themselves as Democratic Party organs. Over the course of more than a year, in a campaign where my poll numbers reached, at times, in the high twenties, the DNC-aligned mainstream media networks maintain a near-perfect embargo on interviews with me. During his ten-month presidential campaign in 1992, Ross Perot gave 34 interviews on mainstream networks. In contrast, during the 16 months since I declared, ABC, NBC, CBS,

MSNBC, and CNN, combined, gave only two live interviews from me. Those networks instead ran a continuous deluge of hit pieces with inaccurate, often vile, pejoratives and defamatory smears.

Some of those same networks then colluded with the DNC to keep me off the debate stage. Representatives of those networks are in this room right now, and I'll just take a moment to ask you to consider the many ways that your institutions have abdicated this really sacred responsibility: the duty of a free press to safeguard democracy and to challenge, always, the party in power. Instead of maintaining that posture of fierce skepticism toward authority, your institutions have made themselves government mouthpieces and stenographers for the organs of power. You didn't alone cause the devolution of American democracy, but you could have prevented it.

The Democratic Party's censorship of social media was even more of a naked exercise of executive power. This week, a federal judge, Judge Terry Doughty, upheld my injunction against President Biden calling the White House's Censorship Project, "The most egregious violation of the First Amendment in the history of the United States of America." Doughty's previous 155-page decision details how just 37 hours after he took the oath of office, swearing to uphold the Constitution, President Biden and his White House opened up a portal and then invited the CIA, the FBI, CISA, which is a censorship agency, it's the center of the censorship industrial complex, DHS, the IRS and other agencies, to censor me and other political dissidents on social media. Even today, users who try to post my campaign videos to Facebook or YouTube get messages that this content violates community standards. Two days after Judge Doughty rendered his decision this week, Facebook was still attaching warning labels to an online petition calling on ABC to include me in the upcoming debate. They said that violates community standards, their community standards. The mainstream media was once the guardian of the First Amendment and Democratic principles and has joined this systemic attack on democracy.

It also, the media justifies their censorship on the grounds of combating misinformation. But governments and oppressors don't censor lies. They don't fear lies. They fear the truth, and that's what they censor. And I don't want any of this to sound like a personal complaint because it's not. For me, it is all part of a journey, and it's a journey that I signed up with. But I need to make these observations because I think they're critical for us doing the thing that we need to do as citizens and a democracy to assess where we are in this country and what our democracy still looks like, and the assumptions about US leadership around the globe. And are we really still a role model for democracy in this country or have we made it a kind of a joke?

Now here's the good news. While mainstream outlets denied me a critical platform, they didn't shut down my ideas, which have especially flourished among young voters and independent voters. Thanks to the alternative media, many months ago, I promised the American people that I would from the race if I became a spoiler. A spoiler is someone will alter the outcome of the election, but

112 The Republican Campaign

has no chance of winning. In my heart, I no longer believe that I have a realistic path to electoral victory in the face of this relentless systematic censorship and media control. So I cannot in in good conscience, ask my staff and volunteers to keep working their long hours or ask my donors to keep giving when I cannot honestly tell them that I have a real path to the White House. Furthermore, our polling consistently showed that by staying on the ballot in the battleground states, I would likely hand the election over to the Democrats with whom I disagree on the most existential issues: censorship, war and chronic disease. I want everyone to know that I am not terminating my campaign. I am simply suspending it and not ending it.

My name will remain on the ballot in most states. If you live in a blue state, you can vote for me without harming or helping President Trump or Vice President Harris. In red states, the same will apply. I encourage you to vote for me and if enough of you do vote for me and neither of the major party candidates win 270 votes, which is quite possible. In fact, today our polling shows them tying it 269 to 269 and I could conceivably still end up in the White House in a contingent election. But in about 10 battleground states where my presence would be a spoiler, I'm going to remove my name and I've already started that process and urge voters not to vote for me. It's with a sense of victory and not defeat that I'm suspending my campaign activities. Not only did we do the impossible by collecting a million signatures. We changed the national political conversation forever.

Chronic disease, free speech, government corruption, breaking our addiction to war have moved to the center of politics. I can say to all who have worked so hard in the last year and a half, thank you for a job well done. Three great causes drove me to enter this race in the first place primarily. And these are the principle causes that persuaded me to leave the Democratic Party and run as an independent, and now to throw my support to President Trump. The clauses were free speech, the war in Ukraine and the war on our children. I've already described some of my personal experiences and struggles with the government's censorship industrial complex.

I want to say a word about the Ukraine war. The military industrial complex has provided us with a familiar comic book justification like they do on every war, that this one is a noble effort to stop a super villain, Vladimir Putin, invading the Ukraine and then to thwart his Hitler-like march across Europe. In fact, tiny Ukraine is a proxy in a geopolitical struggle initiated by the ambitions of the US neocons or American global hegemony. I'm not excusing Putin for invading Ukraine. He had other options, but the war is Russia's predictable response to the reckless neocon project of extending NATO to encircle Russia, a hostile act. The credulous media rarely explained to Americans that we unilaterally walked away from two intermediate nuclear weapons treaties with Russia and then put nuclear-ready Aegis missile systems in Romania and Poland. This is a hostile, hostile act, and that the Biden White House repeatedly spurned Russia's offer to settle this war peacefully.

The Ukraine war began in 2014 when US agencies overthrew the democratically elected government of Ukraine and installed a hand-picked, pro-Western government that launched a deadly civil war against ethnic Russians in Ukraine. In 2019, America walked away from a peace treaty, the Minsk agreement that had been negotiated between Russia and Ukraine by European nations. And then in April of 2022, we wanted the war. In April of 2022, President Biden sent Boris Johnson to Ukraine to force President Zelenskyy to tear up a peace agreement that he and the Russians had already signed, and the Russians were withdrawing troops, Kyiv, Donbas and Luhansk, and that peace agreement would've bought peace to the region and would've allowed Donbas and Luhansk to remain part of Ukraine.

President Biden stated that month that his objective in the war was regime change in Russia. His defense secretary Lloyd Austin simultaneously explained that America's purpose in the war was to exhaust the Russian army, to degrade its capacity to fight anywhere else in the world. These objectives, of course, have nothing to do with what they were telling Americans about protecting Ukraine's sovereignty. Ukraine is a victim in this war and it's a victim of the West. Since then ... And both Russia and the West. Since then, we have since tearing up that agreement, forcing Zelenskyy to tear up the agreement. We've squandered the flower of Ukrainian youth, as many as 600,000 Ukrainian kids and over a 100,000 Russian kids, all of whom we should be mourning have died and the Ukraine's infrastructure is destroyed.

The war has been a disaster for our country as well. We squandered nearly $200 billion already, and these are badly needed dollars in our communities, suffering communities all over our country. The Nord Stream pipeline sabotage and the sanctions have destroyed Europe's industrial base, which formed the bulwark of US national security. A strong Germany with a strong industry is a much, much stronger deterrent to Russia and a Germany that is de-industrialized and turned into just an extension of US military base. We've pushed Russia into a disastrous alliance with China and Iran. We're closer to the brink of nuclear exchange than at any time since 1962. And the neocons and the White House don't seem to care at all.

Our moral authority and our economy are in shambles, and the war gave rise to the emergence of BRICS, which now threatens to replace the dollar as the global reserve currency. This is a first-class calamity for our country. Judging by her bellicose, belligerent speech last night in Chicago, we can assume that President Harris will be an enthusiastic advocate for this and other neocon military adventures. And President Trump says that he will reopen negotiations with President Putin and end the war overnight as soon as he becomes president. This alone would justify my support for his campaign.

Last summer, it looked like no candidate was willing to negotiate a quick end of the Ukraine war, to tackle chronic disease epidemic, to protect free speech, our constitutional freedoms, to clean corporate influence out of our government, or to defy the neocons in their agenda of endless military adventurism. But now,

114   The Republican Campaign

one of the two candidates has adopted these issues as his own to the point where he has asked to enlist me in his administration. I'm speaking of course of Donald Trump.

Less than two hours after President Trump narrowly escaped assassination, Calley Means called me on my cell phone. I was in Las Vegas. Calley is arguably the leading advocate for food safety, for soil regeneration, and for ending the chronic disease epidemic that is destroying America's health and ruining our economy. Calley has exposed the insidious corruption at the FDA, the NIH, the HHS, and the USDA that has caused the epidemic. Calley had been working on and off for my campaign advising me on those subjects since the beginning, and those subjects have been my primary focus for the last 20 years. I was delighted when Calley told me that day that he had also been advising President Trump. He told me President Trump was anxious to talk to me about chronic disease and other subjects and to explore avenues of cooperation. . . he asked if I would take a call from the President. President Trump telephoned me a few minutes later and I met with him the following day. A few weeks later, I met again with President Trump and his family members and close his advisors in Florida. In a series of long, intense discussions, I was surprised to discover that we are aligned on many key issues In those meetings. He suggested that we join forces as a unity party. We talked about Abraham Lincoln's team of rivals.

That arrangement would allow us to disagree publicly and privately and fiercely if need be on issues over which we differ, while working together on the existential issues upon which we are in concordance. I was a ferocious critic of many of the policies during his first administration, and there are still issues and approaches upon which we continue to have very serious differences. But we are aligned with each other on other key issues, like ending the forever wars, ending the childhood disease epidemic, securing the border, protecting freedom of speech, unraveling the corporate capture of our regulatory agencies, getting the US intelligence agencies out of the business of propagandizing and censoring and surveilling Americans and interfering with our elections.

Following my first discussion with President Trump, I tried unsuccessfully to open similar discussions with Vice President Harris. Vice President Harris declined to meet or even to speak with me. Suspending my candidacy is a hard-rending decision for me, but I'm convinced that it's the best hope for ending the Ukraine war and ending the chronic disease epidemic that is eroding our nation's vitality from the inside, and for finally protecting free speech. I feel a moral obligation to use this opportunity to save millions of American children above all things. In case some of you don't realize how dire the condition is of our children's health and chronic disease in general, I would urge you to view Dr. Carlson's recent interview with Kelly Means and his sister Dr. Casey Means who is the top graduate of her class at Stanford Medical School. This is an issue that affects all of us far more directly and urgently than any culture war issue and all the other issues that we obsess on and that are tearing apart our country.

This is the most important issue, therefore, it has the potential to bring us together. So let me share a little bit about why I believe it's so urgent. Today, two-thirds... We spend more on healthcare than any country on Earth, twice what they pay in Europe, and yet we have the worst health outcomes of any nation in the world. We're about 79th in health outcomes behind Costa Rica and Nicaragua and Mongolia and other countries. Nobody has a chronic disease burden like we have. And during the COVID epidemic, we had the highest body count of any country in the world. We had 16% of the COVID deaths and we only have 4.2% of the world's population. And CDC says that's because we are the sickest people on earth. We have the highest chronic disease rate on Earth, and the average American who died of COVID had 3.8 chronic diseases.

So these were people who had immune system collapse, who had mitochondrial dysfunction, and no other country has anything like this. Two-thirds of American adults and children suffer from chronic health issues. 50 years ago, that number was less than 1%. So we've gone from 1% to 66%. In America, 74% of Americans are now overweight or obese, and 50% of our children. 120 years ago, when somebody was obese, they were sent to the circus. Literally there were case reports done about them. Obesity was almost unknown. In Japan, the childhood obesity rate is 3% compared to 50% here. Half of Americans have pre-diabetes or type two diabetes. When my uncle was President and I was a boy, juvenile diabetes was effectively non-existent. A typical pediatrician would see one case of diabetes during his entire career, a 40 or 50 year career. Today, one out of every three kids who walks through his office door is diabetic or pre-diabetic, and the mitochondrial disorder that caused diabetes also causing Alzheimer's, which is now classified as diabetes and it's causing this country more than our military budget.

Every year there's been an explosion of neurological illnesses that I never saw as a kid. ADD, ADHD, speech delay, language delay, Tourette's syndrome, narcolepsy, ASD, Asperger's, autism. In the year 2000, the autism rate was one in 1500. Now autism rates and kids are one in 36 according to CDC nationally, nobody's talking about this. One in every 22 kids in California has autism. And this is a crisis that 77% of our kids are too disabled to serve in the United States military. What is happening to our country and why isn't this in the headlines every single day? There's nobody else in the world that is experiencing this. This is only happening in America. About 18%... And by the way, there has been no change in diagnosis, which the industry sometimes like to say. There has been no change in screening. This is a change in incidence. In my generation seventy-year-old men, the autism rates are about one in 10,000. In my kids' generation, one in 34. I'll repeat. In California, one in 22.

Why are we letting this happen? Why are we allowing this to happen to our children? These are the most precious assets that we have in this country. How can we let this happen to them? About 18% of American teens now have fatty liver disease. That's like one out of every five. That disease when I was a kid only affected late-stage alcoholics who were elderly. Cancer rates are skyrocketing in the young and the old. Young adult cancers are up 79%. One in four American women is on antidepressant medication. 40% of teens have a mental health diagnosis and 15% of high schoolers are on Adderall and half a million children on SSRIs. So what's causing this suffering? I'll name two culprits. First and the worst is ultra-processed food. About 70% of American children's diet is ultra-processed. That means industrial manufactured in a factory. These foods consist primarily of processed sugar, ultra-processed grains and seed oils.

Laboratory scientists, many of them formerly worked for the cigarette industry, which purchased all the big food companies in the 1970s and eighties, deployed thousands of scientists to figure out chemicals, new chemicals to make the food more addictive. And these ingredients didn't exist a hundred years ago. Humans aren't biologically adapted to eat them. Hundreds of these chemicals are now banned in Europe, but ubiquitous in American processed foods. The second culprit is toxic chemicals in our food and our medicine, in our environment. Pesticides, food additives, pharmaceutical drugs and toxic waste permeate every cell of our bodies. The assault on our children's cells and hormones is unrelenting. The name just one problem. Many of these chemicals increase estrogen. Because young children are ingesting so many of these hormone disruptors, America's puberty rate is now occurring at age 10 to 13, which is six years earlier than girls were reaching puberty in 1900.

Our country has the earliest puberty rates of any continent on the earth, and no, this isn't because of better nutrition. This is not normal. Breast cancer is also estrogen driven and now strikes one in eight women. We are mass poisoning all of our children and our adults. Considering the grievous human cause of this tragic epidemic of chronic disease, it seems almost crass to mention the damage it does to our economy. But I'll say it is crippling the nation's finances. When my uncle was President of our country, we spent $0 on chronic disease. Today, government healthcare spending is almost all for chronic disease and it's double the military budget, and it is the fastest growing budget item in the federal budget. Chronic disease costs more to the economy as a whole, costs at least $4 trillion, five times our military budget. And that's a 20% drag on everything we do and everything we aspire to.

More in minority communities suffer disproportionately. People who worry about DEI or about bigotry of any kind. This dwarfs anything. We are poisoning the poor. We are systematically poisoning minorities across this country. Industry lobbyists have made sure that most of the food stamp lunch program, 70 or 77% of school lunches are processed foods. There's no vegetables, there's nothing that you would want to eat. We are just poisoning the poor citizens, and that's why they have the highest chronic disease burden of anybody, any demographic in our country and the highest in the world. The same food industry lobbied to make sure that nearly all agricultural subsidies go to commodity crops that are the feedstock of processed food industry. These policies are destroying small farms and they're destroying our soils.

We give about, I think eight times as much in subsidies to tobacco than we do to fruits and vegetables. It makes no sense, if we want a healthy country. The good news is that we can change all this and we can change it very, very quickly. America can get healthy again. To do that, we need to do three things. First, we need to root out the corruption in our health agencies. Second, we need to change incentives in our healthcare system. And third, we need to inspire Americans to get healthy again. 80% of NIH grants go to people who have conflicts of interest. These are the people... Virtually everybody who sits... And Joe Biden just appointed a new panel to NIH to decide the food recommendations. And they're all people who are from the industry. They're all people who are from the processed food companies. They're deciding what Americans hear is healthy and the recommendations on the food pyramid and what goes to our school lunch programs, what go to the Swiss program, the food stamp programs. They are all corrupted and conflicted individuals, these agencies. The FDA, USDA, and CDC, all of them are controlled by giant, for-profit corporations. 75% of the FDA's funding doesn't come from taxpayer, it comes from pharma. And pharma executives and consultants and lobbyists cycle in and out of these agencies.

With President Trump's backing, I'm going to change that. We're going to staff these agencies with honest scientists and doctors who are free from industry funding. We're going to make sure the decisions of consumers, doctors, and patients are informed by unbiased science. A sick child is the best thing for the pharmaceutical industry. When American children or adults get sick with a chronic condition, they're put on medication for their entire life. Imagine what will happen when Medicare starts paying for Ozempic, which costs $1,500 a month and it's being recommended for children as young as six, all for a condition, obesity, that is completely preventable and barely even existed 100 years ago.

Since 74% of Americans are obese, the cost if all of them took their Ozempic prescription is $3 trillion a year. This is a drug that is made by Novo Nordisk, the biggest company in Europe. It's a Danish company and the Danish government does not recommend it. It recommends change in diet to treat obesity, and exercise. And in our country the recommendation now is for Ozempic to children at age six. Novo Nordisk, the biggest company in Europe, and virtually its entire value is based upon its projections of what it's going to sell, the Ozempic it's going to sell to America.

And the food lobbyists have a bill in front of Congress today that is backed by the White House, backed by Vice President Harris and President Biden to allow this to happen. This is a $3 trillion clause that is going to bankrupt our country. For a fraction of that amount we could buy organic food for every American family, three meals a day, and eliminate diabetes altogether. We're going to bring healthy food back to school lunches. We're going to stop subsidizing the worst foods with our agricultural subsidies. We're going to get toxic chemicals out of our food. We're going to reform the entire food system, and for that we need new leadership in Washington because, unfortunately, both the Democrats and the

Republican parties are in cahoots with the big food producers, big pharma, and big ag, which are among the DNC's major donors.

Vice President Harris has expressed no interest in addressing this issue. Four more years of Democratic rule will complete the consolidation of corporate and neocon power, and our children will be the ones who suffer most. I got involved with chronic disease 20 years ago, not because I chose to or wanted to. It was essentially thrust upon me. It was an issue that should've been central to the environmental movement. I was a central leader at that time, but it was widely ignored by all the institutions, including the NGOs, who should have been protecting our kids against toxins. It was an orphaned issue, and I had a weakness for orphans. I watched generations of children get sicker and sicker.

I had 11 siblings, and I had seven kids myself, and I was conscious of what was happening in their classrooms and to their friends. And I watched these sick kids, these damaged kids in that generation. Almost all of them are damaged, and nobody in power seemed to care or to even notice. For 19 years I prayed every morning that God would put me in a position to end this calamity. The chronic disease crisis was one of the primary reasons for my running for president, along with ending censorship and the Ukraine war.

It's the reason I've made the heart-wrenching decision to suspend my campaign and to support President Trump. This decision is agonizing for me because of the difficulties it causes my wife and my children and my friends, but I have the certainty that this is what I'm meant to do, and that certainty gives me internal peace, even in storms. If I'm given the chance to fix the chronic disease crisis and reform our food production, I promise that within two years we will watch chronic disease burden lift dramatically. We will make Americans healthy again.

Within four years America will be a healthy country. We will be stronger, more resilient, more optimistic, and happier. I won't fail in doing this. Ultimately, the future, however it happens is in God's hands and in the hands of the American voters and those of President Trump. If President Trump is elected and honors his word, the vast burden of chronic disease that now demoralizes and bankrupts the country will disappear. This is a spiritual journey for me. I reached my decision through deep prayer, through hard-nosed logic, and I asked myself, what choices must I make to maximize my chances to save America's children and restore national health?

I felt that if I refused this opportunity I would not be able to look myself in the mirror, knowing that I could've saved lives of countless children and reversed this country's chronic disease epidemic. I'm 70 years old. I may have a decade to be effective. I can't imagine that President Harris, President Harris, would allow me or anyone to solve these dire problems. After eight years of President Harris any opportunity for me to fix the problem will be out of my reach forever.

President Trump has told me that he wants this to be his legacy. I'm choosing to believe that this time he will follow through. His son, his biggest donors, his closest friends all support this objective. My joining the Trump campaign will be a difficult sacrifice for my wife and children, but worthwhile if there's even a small chance of saving these kids. Ultimately, the only thing that will save our country and our children is if we choose to love our kids more than we hate each other.

That's why I launched my campaign, to unify America. My dad and uncle made such an enduring mark on the character of our nation, not so much because of any particular policies that they promoted but because they were able to inspire profound love for our country and to fortify our sense of ourselves as a national community held together by ideals. They were able to put their love into the intentions and hearts of ordinary Americans and to unify a national populist movement of Americans, blacks and whites, Hispanics, urban and rural Americans, inspired affection and love and high hopes and a culture of kindness that continue to radiate among Americans from their memory.

That's the spirit on which I ran my campaign and that I intend to bring into the campaign of President Trump. Instead of vitriol and polarization, I will appeal to the values that unite us, the goals that we could achieve if only we weren't at each other's throats. Most unifying theme for all Americans is that we all love our children. If we all unite around that issue now we can finally give them the protection, the health, and the future that they deserve. Thank you all very much. Thank you everybody for attending. This concludes our program for the day. Thank you, sir.

Print Citations

CMS: Kennedy, Jr., Robert F. "Presidential Candidate Suspends His Campaign and Endorses Donald Trump." Speech presented at a Trump rally, Phoenix, AZ, August 23, 2024. In *The Reference Shelf: Representative American Speeches, 2023–2024*, edited by Micah L. Issitt, 108–119. Amenia, NY: Grey House Publishing, 2024.

MLA: Kennedy, Jr., Robert F. "Presidential Candidate Suspends His Campaign and Endorses Donald Trump." Trump rally, 23 August 2024, Phoenix, AZ. Speech. *The Reference Shelf: Representative American Speeches, 2023–2024*, edited by Micah L. Issitt, Grey House Publishing, 2024, pp. 108–119.

APA: Kennedy, Jr., R. F. (2024). Presidential candidate suspends his campaign and endorses Donald Trump [Speech]. Trump rally, Phoenix, AZ. In Micah L. Issitt (Ed.), *The reference shelf: Representative American speeches, 2023–2024* (pp. 108–119). Grey House Publishing. (Original work published 2024)

Vice Presidential Nominee's Remarks on the Economy, Inflation, and Manufacturing

By J.D. Vance

"So while Americans were getting richer, a lot of bureaucrats and globalists were getting poor." James David "J.D." Vance, author and politician who has served as a US senator representing the state of Ohio since 2023 and became Donald Trump's vice presidential candidate in 2024, spoke at a rally in Michigan. Vance claimed that the Biden-Harris campaign has undone the accomplishments of Donald Trump and their administration's corruption has fueled wealth inequality.

Wow. Hello. It is great to be in the great state of Michigan. In 69 days, my friends, we're going to take this country back. We're going to elect Donald J. Trump President of the United States, and it is going to start right here with the great people of Michigan.

Now, last week, the biggest heist in American history happened right under Kamala Harris's nose. Somebody stole 818,000 jobs that she and Tim Walz had been bragging about. Did you all see that? Where'd they go? Now, you may not have heard this because our friends in the back, the media, doesn't like to talk about it, but what really happened is this. The Harris Administration had to admit that more than a quarter of all the jobs that had supposedly been created last year were actually fake. They never existed. It was the biggest revision to the job numbers since the financial crisis back in 2008–2009. In other words, what it means is they are cooking the books to hide how bad the economy really is under Kamala Harris. I promise you this: on November 5th, there is one job that is definitely going to vanish, and that is when we tell Kamala Harris, "You are fired," and send her back to San Francisco.

Now, you all are fired up and it's hot out here. Kamala Harris, she needs a rock star to get a crowd like this. We just come out here because we're patriots and we want to save this country.

Now, Kamala, I don't know if you noticed, if you paid attention to the news lately. Kamala has decided that the American people don't like her policies, and she's exactly right about that. Just take one, immigration. Kamala Harris, remember, she suspended deportations on day one. She stopped Donald Trump's Remain in Mexico policy. That was on day one, and that's why we have a

---

Delivered on August 27, 2024 at a Vance rally, Big Rapids, MI.

wide-open southern border. But I read a story this morning that her advisors are considering just copying all of Donald Trump's policies. They're more popular.

In fact, I've heard that for her debate in just a couple of weeks, she's going to put on a Navy suit, a long red tie, and adopt the slogan "Make America Great Again." But we're not going to let the American people forget that Kamala Harris is the candidate of American decline. She cast the tie-breaking vote for the Inflation Explosion Act. She cast the tie-breaking vote to send interest rates and mortgages through the roof. She opened that border on day one, and as much as fake Kamala wants to pretend that she now agrees with Donald Trump, we've got to remind her, she's the Vice President right now. Stop talking about what you're going to do. Start talking about what you are going to do right now because you're the Vice President. And what she has done has been a disaster. Now, I will confess that in some ways, I have a soft heart, ladies and gentlemen. In some ways, I feel bad for Kamala Harris.

They don't. You don't. But I'm not sure that this is a woman who knows what she actually believes. If you think about it, she's just a cog in the wheel of a very corrupt system. Now, let's go back in time a few years and just remember the formula of Kamala Harris and her handlers and what it wrecked. Now, remember, step one was to ship all of our good manufacturing jobs to Mexico, to China, to far-flung corners all over the world. Remember, Kamala Harris supported the reauthorization of NAFTA, which has been terrible for the state of Michigan, the state of Ohio, and the state of Pennsylvania. Proud towns became ghost towns. Dignified American workers became dependent on the government and families, including a lot of families like mine, fell apart under financial stress. Now, that was step one. Did we ask for any of that?

Now, here's step two. Step two is open our border to millions of illegal immigrants, and into that void of joblessness, pour drugs and a lot of cheap labor. Our leadership, including Kamala Harris, they said it was compassionate, but it was a lie. What they really wanted, my friends, was millions of voters for Democrat policies, and they wanted millions of cheap laborers. American wages went down and our leaders learned they could ignore their own citizens and their quest for power. Now, that was step two, and I ask, did we ask for that?

Now, the next step was a lot of stupid foreign policy. Our leaders couldn't deliver prosperity, but they could deliver war and conflict. So we invaded countries all over the world and then we invited other countries to invade us through illegal immigration. Our people got poorer, our leaders got richer, and they got more powerful. Now, that was step three, and I ask, did we ask for that?

Now, I have lived, and I know a lot of us in this crowd have lived, the consequences of these failures, and I saw it very personally, my friends. My parents divorced. My family began to struggle. My mom, God love her, she found solace in the prescription pain pills that a lot of kids and a lot of adults were getting hooked on, and then eventually she moved on to some harder stuff. Now, I will tell you that I thought I would lose my mom when I was a kid, and I prayed every single day that she would somehow find her way to a second chance. And I'm

122　The Republican Campaign

very proud, my friends, to tell you, not only did my mom find a second chance, but she's here with us today, campaigning with me in the state of Michigan.

Now she is, I will say, the best grandmother that my kids could ask for. They are seven, four, and two. Spoils them a little bit too much. Mom, no more Pokemon cards. In front of a thousand people, no more Pokemon cards. The kids have got enough. But I know that a lot of Americans prayed for that second chance, and thank God, we got it. But a lot of Americans prayed for other things. They prayed for good jobs. They prayed for their towns to have prosperity. They prayed for their parents to overcome the scourge of addiction. And in 2016, a lot of those prayers were answered, my friends, weren't they?

After a generation of Americans being ignored by their leaders, Americans spoke with a unified voice, and you know what they said? They said, "No more bullshit," and they sent Donald J. Trump to the White House.

Now, the same people who screwed this country up for 30 years said President Donald Trump would fail. Remember that? And I remember, I was myself... I didn't fully believe in the promises of Donald Trump. He persuaded me because he did such a good job. What happened next? Let's all remember. Gas was $2 a gallon. Housing was affordable for young and old alike. Wages were rising. And this word inflation that's all people talk about now, it wasn't even an issue. We had broad prosperity for every American, rich and poor. Donald Trump stopped the stupid wars and stood up to the bad guys all over the world. He recognized what our failed leadership didn't: that weakness invites American boys and girls to wars that they shouldn't have to fight. American strength promotes peace, and we had a hell of a lot of peace when Donald J. Trump was the President of the United States.

I got to get whatever we fed these guys behind me. They're having a good time. My friends, our border was secure. Overdose deaths were coming down where they had gone up for 15 years and a lot of people who struggled in my hometown had good jobs and good prosperity, and it happened all across the state of Michigan and Ohio. My mom, she got clean and she stayed clean. That was my personal victory that happened. And remember, for every lie they told about Donald J. Trump, he just kept on plugging away at doing the American people's business. He did it so well we had take-home pay rising faster than it had in 30 years. Remember this. Our corrupt leadership said, "If you put tariffs on China, prices will go up." Instead. Donald Trump did exactly that, manufacturing came back and prices went down for American citizens. They went up for the Chinese, but they went down for our people.

Because when you make your own stuff with the hands of American workers, the whole country prospers. We know that in Michigan better than anywhere. Now, our corrupt leadership said, "If you enforce the border, people south of the border are going to suffer." But Donald Trump recognized that his first responsibility as President was to the American citizen and not to anybody else. So he shut down that border. He shut off the drug trade, he drove the cartels out of business, and he had overdose deaths falling in this country. What an amazing thing it was.

Remember, our corrupt leadership said that you can't defeat ISIS. Remember that? Just a few years ago, they said, "We're going to have to re-invade Iraq to defeat ISIS." Donald Trump defeated ISIS in a matter of weeks, and then he brought America's sons and daughters home. What an amazing, amazing track record of leadership.

But let's be honest. The country wasn't broken in four years, and four years was not enough time to root out all of the corruption. So while Americans were getting richer, a lot of bureaucrats and globalists were getting poor. That was the story of Trump's term. So Kamala Harris, she and her corrupt handlers, they came up with a plan. Now, they couldn't beat Donald Trump in an honest debate, so they decided to engage in censorship. They were going to censor Donald Trump and they were going to censor his supporters.

Now remember, back in 2020, they lied about Biden's corruption and covered up the fact that his family got rich by selling access to the United States government, and Kamala Harris was there for all of it. They lied about the Hunter Biden laptop and encouraged big tech to silence the story. And they did. They lied about Covid coming from a Chinese lab, and they censored anybody who disagreed. Kamala Harris even went on national TV and said Joe Biden was as sharp as a tack, even he was clearly mentally incompetent to do the job. And so it's obvious what's been going on, right? Kamala Harris has been calling the shots. And by lying about his mental fitness for the job, she got what she always wanted, which was more power.

And what was the result? On her watch, gas prices are up 50%. Housing costs have doubled. You talk to a young person today; young people cannot afford to buy a home in their own country. We're turning a generation of 20- and 30-year-olds into permanent debtors. Donald Trump and I believe young people ought to own a stake in their own country, be able to build a life and start a family. That's what we're fighting for.

Grocery prices under Kamala Harris are up 21%, and I think that undercounts it. A record number of Americans are working multiple jobs, the housing market is as unaffordable as it has ever been, and the average new car costs nearly $50,000. Americans, this is heartbreaking. We now owe more than $1 trillion in credit-card debt, a record high at a time when interest rates are going up and up.

That's not all she did, my friends. She isn't just causing high prices. She's undoing the incredible work that Donald Trump did to rebuild American manufacturing. Now we stand very close, of course, to the new Goshen factory, right? That's right. And remember the tie-breaking vote that she cast to send inflation through the roof? Remember that vote? That vote also made Chinese companies like Goshen eligible for millions of your taxpayer dollars.

Now, the great Mike Rogers, who's running for Senate, has been a champion on this issue. Thank you, Mike, for doing what you do. There we go. Stand up. But it's not just the really good ones like Mike Rogers. Even some of the folks in

124 The Republican Campaign

Obama's administration said that the Goshen factory plant is a threat to America's national security. Even Obama's leadership. But Kamala Harris not only wants to allow the Chinese Communist Party to build factories on American soil; she wants to pay them to do it with our tax money.

Now, China has also, of course, stolen from Michigan car companies and unfairly subsidized its auto industry for years. That is the wreckage of what the Chinese have been doing. And now Democrats in this state, and including Kamala Harris, want to give them hundreds of millions of dollars to those same companies that have been undercutting Michigan auto workers. What a disaster, isn't it?

Now, I know, like I said, we've got some great leadership like Mike Rogers who are helping us in this fight. We've also got Chairman Pete Hoekstra, who will help turn Michigan red. Where's Pete at? Thank you, Pete. We've got the great Tudor Dixon. Where is Tudor at? I saw Tudor earlier. There's Tudor Dixon.

Now, they all know firsthand the Democrats are helping China destroy and replace our auto industry from the inside out, and we're going to stop it. The Democrats are helping China, and it's not just in Goshen, okay? They're doing a lot more beyond that. In fact, just a few weeks ago you probably saw this: Stellantis announced that it would lay off nearly 2,500 proud Michigan auto workers making the iconic Ram 1500 Classic.

Now, that is the record of Kamala Harris shipping American jobs to China and paying them to do it with your tax dollars. And what did she talk about at her convention speech? I just saw that. Did you see Kamala's convention speech?

Well, that was smart of you for not seeing it, but I'm in this business. I have to. Now, Kamala Harris said, "When we fight, we win." This is one of her favorite tag lines.

And I don't know if you saw it, but then Tim Walz stood up and shouted, "And even when we don't fight." That's what Tim Walz said. Now, he lies about everything, of course. He calls me weird, but then he lies about how his kids were conceived. Who does that? That's just the weirdest thing I've ever seen. He said he served in combat, but the closest Tim Walz ever came to combat is when he let rioters burn Minneapolis to the ground and did absolutely nothing to stop it.

And I know we have got a lot of veterans out there. I served in the United States Marine Corps, and I did go to Iraq when my country asked me, and I'm proud of it. And I know a lot of veterans who take offense.

But there are a lot of veterans from across our military who don't like it when other people lie about their service for military gain, and that's exactly what Tim Walz said. It is a slap in the face to all veterans, and it's not just from Tim Walz. Kamala Harris not only chooses to stand by this man, because in spite of his dishonesty, she actually chose him to become her Vice President to begin with.

Now, while we're on the subject of their convention, she said something else at her convention. And I don't know if you paid attention here. She said, "There are going to be extremely serious consequences for voting for Donald Trump." Now Kamala, I've got two responses to that. First of all, that is not a very presidential thing to say. Is she the Vice President or the Vice Principal, warning about very serious consequences, whining at people for telling a joke instead of trying to persuade them that she deserves to be their president? I'm sick of people like that.

But second, it's the substance, because the extremely serious consequences, Kamala, have come from your leadership as Vice President of the United States. Americans can't afford groceries because of your leadership, Kamala. Young people can't afford homes because of the policies that you have enacted as Vice President. Now, the only serious consequence in November that I'm worried about is giving Kamala Harris a disastrous promotion. Let's say to Kamala Harris, "You are fired. We are not sending you to the Oval Office."

Now, my favorite line from Kamala is she says if you elect her president, she is going to fix it all on day one. Well, Kamala, I hate to break it to you, but day one was 1,300 days ago. You've been Vice President for three and a half years. What the hell have you been doing during all that time? The message from this crowd and this state of Michigan is you had your chance, your failed, and we're not giving you a promotion.

And Donald J. Trump is coming back to clean up your mess, Kamala Harris, and it's going to start right here in the state of Michigan.

Now, Kamala Harris has run her entire campaign on the idea that she's joyful. But ask yourself, are you better off than you were four years ago?

The only person in America who could possibly answer yes to that question is probably Kamala Harris herself. She went from getting no votes for president and having to drop out to getting no votes for president and becoming the Democrat nominee, all without lifting a finger. No wonder Kamala is joyful. Now, never mind the fact that Americans can't afford groceries. Kamala got her promotion. Never mind that our fellow citizens can't afford their rent, because Kamala, she's having fun. And never mind that Kamala Harris is on the cusp of running us into World War III. Kamala will laugh all the way to the bank while her donors get rich, and we know it's not going to be her family sacrificing to pick up the mess.

But I got to tell you, as much as I am frustrated with Kamala Harris, I am so hopeful about the future of our country. We have the most beautiful country in the entire world, don't we?

I've been flying around the country, I've been driving around the country, and you get a new perspective running to be the next vice president that I'm so grateful for. We've got natural resources all across this country that are the envy of the world, my friends. We just need better leadership. It is that simple. Better leadership. That's all we need to fix this country. So here's what we're going to do, and we'll offer a little contrast. Kamala Harris wants to open the border on day one. Donald Trump is going to close the southern border, and his message to every illegal immigrant is pack your bags because you're going home.

Kamala Harris wants to bankrupt Medicare by giving it to illegal aliens. Donald Trump is going to fight to safeguard Medicare and all of our great programs so that it only goes to the American citizens who paid into it, not to illegal aliens who are going to bankrupt it. Now, Kamala Harris wants to shut down American energy and drive manufacturing out of this country. Donald Trump has a different idea. He is going to drill, baby, drill. We're going to unleash American workers and bring back those great factories. Kamala Harris wants to reward companies that ship American jobs overseas, and she wants to raise taxes on American workers. Donald Trump is going to cut taxes for American workers, cut taxes for the businesses that hire them, and raise the tariffs on the companies that are shipping jobs overseas. That's our promise, and that's exactly what Donald Trump's going to do.

And so while Donald Trump is the people's President and Kamala Harris is running on a fake joy, Donald Trump is going to offer something very, very different. He's going to offer a very real hope for the future of this country. Hope that we can reignite our economy and bring back prosperity. Hope that we can raise our kids in secure neighborhoods with safe borders. Hope that we can renew the patriotism that binds us together as one nation under God.

My friends, the American Dream right now, it probably seems a little out of reach to a lot of us, but in 69 days, we're going to save every single American Dream. We're going to save this country for the citizens of this land, and we are going to lead, together with President Donald J. Trump, a great American comeback. So I want us to send a message. I want us to send a message. They can hear it all the way in San Francisco. They can hear it in Tim Walz's Minneapolis. They can hear it all across this country that Michigan is going red, Michigan is leading the Great American comeback, and Michigan is going to elect Donald J. Trump the next President of the United States. God bless you all, thank you all, and thank you for having me in this beautiful country. God bless you all.

Print Citations

CMS: Vance, J.D. "Vice Presidential Nominee's Remarks on the Economy, Inflation, and Manufacturing." Speech at a Vance rally, Big Rapids, MI, August 27, 2024. In *The Reference Shelf: Representative American Speeches, 2023–2024,* edited by Micah L. Issitt, 120–126. Amenia, NY: Grey House Publishing, 2024.

MLA: Vance, J.D. "Vice Presidential Nominee's Remarks on the Economy, Inflation, and Manufacturing." Vance rally, 27 August 2024, Big Rapids, MI. Speech. *The Reference Shelf: Representative American Speeches, 2023–2024,* edited by Micah L. Issitt, Grey House Publishing, 2024, pp. 120–126.

APA: Vance, J.D. (2024). Vice presidential nominee's remarks on the economy, inflation, and manufacturing [Speech]. Vance rally, Big Rapids, MI. In Micah L. Issitt (Ed.), *The reference shelf: Representative American speeches, 2023–2024* (pp. 120–126). Grey House Publishing. (Original work published 2024)

3
U.S. Issues

Greg Abbott at the World Travel and Tourism Council conference (2016). Photo by World Travel & Tourism Council, CC BY 2.0, via Wikimedia.

Texas Governor Speaks to Republican Governors at the US-Mexico Border

By Greg Abbott

"There is extraordinary danger, imminent danger, crossing our border all the time." Texas Governor Greg Abbott addressed Republican governors at the US border with Mexico in February of 2024. He discussed illegal border crossing, suggested that terrorists and violent criminals are coming into the country in higher numbers, and accused the Biden-Harris administration of failing to address the alleged problem.

Governor Greg Abbott: Let me start by thanking everybody for being here, but more important than that, I want to thank the governors of the United States of America who are standing with Texas. Half of the governors of the United States have joined with Texas in our cause to make sure states can do everything possible to secure our border. Half of the governors that have joined the cause to support Texas are joining us at this event today, and we are here to send a loud and clear message that we are banning together to fight to ensure that we will be able to maintain our constitutional guarantee that states will be able to defend against any type of imminent danger or an invasion that has been threatened by Joe Biden and his abject refusal to enforce the immigration laws of the United States of America.

The laws of the United States passed by Congress, they require the President to deny illegal entry. To the contrary of denying illegal entry, he has aided and abetted that illegal entry. If somebody makes it across the border illegally, the president has the responsibility imposed by Congress to detain any illegal immigrant who has come here. As opposed to detaining any illegal immigrant, Biden instead has let them all loose across the entire country with no ability to accurately determine their whereabouts or what they may be doing. Because of this, we've seen the catastrophic consequences of Joe Biden's open border policies over the tenure of Joe Biden. We've had three Houstons cross the border illegally, all-time records, and we see the dangers every single day.

Just to recount a few that happened just this past year. The Texas Department of Public Safety, they arrested an MS 13 gang member who was on the terrorist watch list. Know this, there are people on the terrorist watch list that are apprehended all the time and coming across the border. These are people who pay extra money not to be caught. The United States of America and the President do not know how many people have crossed the border illegally who are on the

---

Delivered on February 4, 2024 at the US-Mexico border, Eagle Pass, TX.

terrorist watch list and have never been seen. They do not know the imminent dangers that we may be facing.

Another example is, once again, the Texas Department of Public Safety. They arrested somebody who came across the border illegally who had served in the army, in the military for Iran. Why is this person here? Why were they trying to sneak in illegally? What were they going to try to do? We were fortunate to be able to apprehend him, but who knows what would've happened had we not apprehended him?

And then you see the deadly loss of life. We saw it just outside of the Houston area last year when we saw an illegal immigrant who had come across the border illegally four times, murder five people outside of Houston, Texas. These are crimes that don't happen now and then, these are crimes that happen all the time. Part it is because it is set forth by the Texas Department of Public Safety. We have people who are coming across our border who were released from prison in other countries. There was a person who was apprehended who was wanted for rape charges, another who was wanted for murder charges. There is extraordinary danger, imminent danger, crossing our border all the time.

And of course, Americans are not going to soon forget what they saw happen in New York City, where we saw illegal immigrants brutalize and beat up police officers in New York City, only to be immediately released on bail back out on the streets, causing no one knows what level of mayhem because of the extraordinary dangers that the state of Texas is sustaining as well as states across the country. And because Joe Biden has completely abdicated and abandoned his responsibility to enforce the laws of the United States, I have used a clause in the Constitution that empowers states to defend themselves. It is Article one, section 10, clause three of the United States Constitution, where a state can defend itself and its citizens to protect their safety from the imminent danger that we are facing and from an invasion of millions of people coming from across the globe into our country who are unaccounted for whatsoever.

I applaud and thank the members of the governors who are with us here today for stepping up and standing beside behind and with Texas in this effort. We're all fighting for a safer, more secure border and country and I thank them for all they do.

Now, I'm going to turn it over to Bill Lee, the governor of the great state of Tennessee. A state, by the way, that from the very beginning of Texas history has always been here for the great state of Texas.

Governor Bill Lee: Thank you, Governor, and Tennessee will continue. We are the Volunteer state, we have had hundreds of troops on the border, we are prepared even today to send additional troops working with the Texas Department of Military to do just that.

I'm here today as the chairman of the Republican Governor Association, number one to say thank you to Governor Abbott who has done everything within his power to provide an improvement to the situation at the border, to provide safety and security for Texans, for Americans. The federal government has failed Texans and Americans in providing that security and that safety. That's why these governors are here together today, to do our job, which is the job that the federal government has failed to do, and that is to protect this country. Each one of us understand the devastating effects that the border policy has had on every one of our states individually, and we're here together to collaboratively work to support Texas and to provide for the safety and security of people all across the country.

This experiment in an open border policy has catastrophically failed America, and this country is in desperate need of leadership as it relates to this issue. Governor Abbott has had unwavering and shown unwavering leadership, and we stand in support of that leadership, each of us today. Governor Kemp from Georgia has also been leader in this issue, providing not only troops but resources. Governor Kemp, would you like to say a few things?

Governor Brian Kemp: Thank you Governor Lee. Governor Abbott, we are here with our fellow governors today standing with you, and many governors that are not. Because every state in our country now is a border state because of what is happening. When you think about the amount of fentanyl, the human trafficking that is coming, they're coming to every state in the country and every governor is having to deal with it. We're standing with Governor Abbott today because if our border is not secure, our country is not secure, and Joe Biden's policies are making our country less safe. That's what we're here documenting today and standing with Governor Abbott who's trying to do something about that.

We just had a great briefing. There's been 169 people in 2023 that were on the GBI terrorist watch list apprehended. How many of those are in our country that we didn't, or Governor Abbott's people didn't apprehend? 458 million lethal doses of fentanyl that have been detained at this border. Think about the doses that were not. Every governor is dealing with that.

$51 million in cash. 56,000 pounds of methamphetamine that every state in the country is having to deal with. This is ruining lives in our states, it's ruining our communities, and it's taking a toll on our families. It is time that something was done about this. That is why we are standing here as governors, making sure that that gets done. Every state in the country is depending on Joe Biden acting, and if he does not, then we will continue to do so, and we stand with Governor Abbott and what he is doing. It is now my honor to introduce you to Arkansas's Governor, Sarah Huckabee Sanders.

Governor Sarah Huckabee Sanders: Thank you. Glad the wind picked up just as I stepped up here. I would have gladly borrowed a hat, but they all have the wrong states on them, so.

Thank you all for coming out today. Obviously, I think by the strong showing and the sheer number of governors that are stepping up across the country, it's very clear that this is not just a fight that Texas is having. This is a fight that all of us have to engage in. Put very simply, Joe Biden has completely failed at one of his most basic and important duties as the President. He has failed to protect our borders and protect our people. Not only has he failed at his job, but he's been dishonest about it. He's trying to pass off the idea that somehow he has no ability to do anything to fix it and Congress has to step up, when every single person knows he could make changes and steps right now today to help secure our border and protect our country. Yet he simply refuses to do so. Because of his failures, governor Abbott is having to step up. Governors from across the country are having to step up and do the job of the federal government, because they simply won't.

I'm proud of the fact that we have strong leaders like those that are standing next to and behind me. Because of them, our country will be safer, our people will be better protected. We don't stand with them in football, but I can tell you that Arkansas is most definitely standing with the State of Texas when it comes to protecting our border. There is no fight right now that is more important for us to engage in. It's why we're spending our Sunday afternoons here, because we have to. Because it is absolutely vital to the long-term safety and security of our country.

I'm proud of Governor Abbott's leadership and I'm proud that I get to stand with each of these incredible people as we pledge to support Texas in whatever we can do to help. Arkansas sent National Guard troops here last year, and I can commit today that we'll continue to do that over the course of this year, as much as we can and as much as is needed until the federal government and Joe Biden step up and do their jobs. We're here and we're thankful for your leadership. Governor. With that, I'm going to turn it over to my good friend, governor of Montana, Greg Gianforte.

Governor Greg Gianforte: Thank you, Governor. Let me start by saying Montana stands with Texas in this fight. The governor's here have repeatedly called on the Biden administration to step up and do their job. Most recently, in a joint letter, we asked for the names and identities of people that have crossed illegally into this country. That request was met with silence. It came on top of a letter that shared a ten-point plan to secure the border. That was three years ago. We're still waiting for a response from the White House.

Montana has had our soldiers here on the southern border for most of last year. And Governor Abbott, we're committed to stand with you and continue to provide resources so that we can protect the citizens of the United States and our country.

This is impacting all of our states. In the Northern Rockies where I call home, we've seen a 78% increase in fentanyl just in the last year. We've lost lives and it's broken families apart. We need to secure the border. Our states are being invaded by the people crossing illegally. Our Constitution gives the states the right to self-defense. That's what Governor Abbott is doing and that's why we're here standing with them today. Biden is doing the exact opposite. He's working against the entrances of this country and we are here today to call on him, the federal administration, to do their job. Thank you for calling attention to this issue and Governor Abbott.

Governor Abbott: Thank you. Once again, I want to thank all the governors who join with us today, and all the governors across the entire United States of America who are standing with the right of states to assert self-defense. In furtherance of that self-defense, Texas is the only state in the history of the United States of America to build our own border wall. Texas has deployed our National Guard, who bravely stand guard night and day, and they erect these razor wire barriers. The National Guard has erected more than 100 miles of razor wire barrier that serves effectively to deny illegal entry, and they have ensured that this entire park that we are in right now will not be an area that can be used to pass anymore.

This area we are in right now was at one time not too long ago, an area where there would be 3000, 4000, sometimes 5000 people crossing illegally. Now that we've taken control of this area for the past three days, there's an average of only three people crossing illegally in this area. The point very simply is this, it shows that the state of Texas can do what the federal government is charged to do and has the tools and equipment to do. The president is obligated by laws passed by Congress to actually secure the border and deny illegal entry. Texas has shown that we can reduce it to three people crossing across the border. Joe Biden, it is your turn now, your obligation, your duty to follow the law Congress passed and secure the border just as Texas has. With that, we'll take a few questions.

Press: Governor, the only reason we don't see immigrants right now here [inaudible]. Don't you think it is because Mexico stopped everybody from entering where we are right now and you don't see even nobody there right now? Don't you think is [inaudible]?

Governor Abbott: Let's be clear about something. Don't fool anybody. We know that the people who control the migration across the border are the cartels. The cartels who extort money, who rape the people that they victimize before they come across here. The cartels are losing money trying to come into the state of Texas now. The cartels have rerouted their routes to cross the border because Texas is the only state that's putting up any resistance. Despite the fact that Texas represents more than 60% of the land miles of the border, the overwhelming majority now of people crossing the border are crossing in Arizona and California, two states that are putting up no resistance to illegal immigration. If the United States under President Biden did in Texas, in New Mexico, in California and in Arizona what we're doing here, you would eliminate illegal immigration overnight.

Press: Governor? Governor? Governor? Don't say the border is open. The rationale for denying access to border patrol to this area and 2.5 miles of the [inaudible]?

Governor Abbott: Would you restate the first part of your question again?

Press: Your rationale for denying access to border patrol agents to this area of Shelby Park and 2.5 miles [inaudible]?

Governor Abbott: To be clear, from the very beginning and to this moment, they have access to the boat ramp and they have access to the razor wire area if anybody's life is in danger. On top of that, however, the area where we are is an area where the federal government was using to further criminal activity. They're involved in violating the federal laws of the United States of America on this land. We will not allow this land to be used for illegal purposes.

Priscilla Thompson NBC News: Governor, Priscilla Thompson with NBC News. The Senate is poised to vote on an immigration bill this week. Do you think that that could help you?

Governor Abbott: I have no idea how to answer your question, because I have no idea what's going to be in that Senate bill and I have no idea if the House would agree with it. So, your question actually is filled with unknowns. All I know is this, and that is the open border policies that Joe Biden has allowed can no longer be tolerated. He has the ability as we speak at this very moment to take action to shut down the border and stop illegal immigration. Joe Biden does not need more legislative authority, he just needs a backbone to step up and do his job and secure the border.

Press: Governor Abbott, you're standing in front of a lot of armed men and women, you're here with other governors from many states and military vehicles. You talked about invasion. What do you say to people? We've heard this from Republicans and Democrats who are concerned that there is a civil war or some preclude to some kind of armed conflict between Americans, what would you say to people?

Governor Abbott: It's a false narrative, and really nothing more than a narrative. What we are seeking to do and what we are actually doing, we're actually enforcing the laws of the United States of America. What Americans want, whether it be the border or whether it be carjackings in Washington DC or police officers being beat up in New York City, what Americans want, they want law and order. They want the laws of our country enforced. All we're doing is enforcing the laws of the United States of America.

Press: Governor, how long will the park be under state control?

Governor Abbott: It is going stay under control as long as it takes to maintain security and to eliminate crossings. I'll be honest with you, we could relinquish control of it tomorrow if Joe Biden were to step up and do exactly what we are doing here and stop people from crossing the border illegally. We have seen a president and his predecessor do exactly that. Joe Biden has every tool in his toolbox to make sure that he reduces illegal immigration, as much as Texas was able to reduce it right here. In the meantime, let me add this. As we speak right now, the Texas National Guard, they're undertaking operations to expand this effort. We're not going to contain ourselves just to this park, we are expanding to further areas to make sure that we will expand our level of deterrence and denial of illegal entry into the United States.

Press: Governor, and to all the other governors here. A lot of people have said that things like this in an election year are just a political stunt by Republicans. What do you guys all say to that?

Governor Abbott: Say that to the average American. The average American is angry. The number one issue in the United States of America is the broken border and the illegal immigration that Joe Biden has created. We don't have time to wait until November; we've got lives on the line every single day. Say that to the parents who have lost a child to deadly fentanyl that's growing a number across the country. There are lives at risk every single day. It's like every police officer in every city, in our great state, that understands that they have a daily duty to make sure that their communities are safe regardless of when elections take place. We as governors have that responsibility, to make sure that our states and our country are going to be safe from the illegal immigration crossing.

Governor Kemp: Governor?

Governor Abbott: Go ahead.

Governor Kemp: I would just remind you too, that many of the governors here were here. When was that?

Governor Abbott: Right.

Governor Kemp: A year ago. Way before the campaign started, on the same issue, writing letters to Joe Biden about how to fix the border and the executive action that he could take. So this is not a campaign tactic, this is something that this group and the Republican governors have been concerned with for many, many months and years.

Governor Abbott: Right.

Press: Governor, there are Americans living here on the border who say that sovereignty has been lost and that they're walking around in fear, and they feel that the federal government has failed them. What about you governors? Are you going to be able to step up to protect their sovereignty and give them the right to be free citizens here in their own state?

136   U.S. Issues

Governor Abbott: You're talking about the local residents in this area?

Press: Yes.

Governor Abbott: So, first of all, I think the local residents around here are angry and rightfully so. Their area, their neighborhoods, their golf courses, their shopping areas, all have been invaded. But I cannot tell you the number of ranchers and homeowners who live, whether it be here or in Del Rio or up and down this entire area, who cry and complain about the ranches being ripped apart, their homes being invaded, fearful about the children playing in the streets. All the car chases that are taking place in neighborhoods.

   This has turned into a danger zone for one reason. It was not that way four years ago. Four years ago, this was an area of law and order, a safe area for people to golf and play and enjoy it. And that's because we had a president who was enforcing the immigration laws of the United States. Their property, their land, their safety, and their enjoyment of it can all be restored if we have a president who enforces the laws of the United States as opposed to being hostile to that and being hostile to a state simply trying to enforce the laws of the United States.

Press: Governor, what is the Biden administration, does it take any action to keep standing up with the state of Texas? What are you going to do? Is the declaration of independence the only way? What are you going to do?

Governor Abbott: We will continue to expand our efforts. Our declaration is a declaration of our rights under the United States Constitution, article one, section 10, clause three that guarantees the right of every state that's either invaded or in imminent danger, which we are in imminent danger, to be able to exercise self-defense. Texas will continue to exercise that self-defense and expand the area where we are using that self-defense to make sure we are able to better protect our communities.

Press: [inaudible] state law says illegally as invaders?

Governor Abbott: Say that again now.

Press: Why brand mothers and children civilians crossing between points of entry illegally as invaders?

Governor Abbott: So, I can't understand the details of your question, I'm going to answer the best I can. The fact of the matter is if you look behind you, there are people crossing right now, and they're crossing that bridge. A couple of things about that. One is that whether it be here, El Paso, Brownsville or parts in between, there are thousands of people who cross back and forth every single day for work purposes, for visiting purposes, for tourism purposes, whatever the case may be. That's perfectly fine.

What is completely illegal is for people to enter between a port of entry. Think about this astonishing fact, under Joe Biden a record number of people have died in this river right behind us, and they die in that river because they try crossing in that river. Why in the world don't they just go up a few steps and cross across that bridge, which is an official port of entry? Texas has 28 ports of entry. Get this fact: No one has ever drowned crossing a bridge. If Joe Biden cared about the safety of these migrants that he seems to have empathy for, he would have them cross a bridge as opposed to crossing a river and paying the money that goes to the cartels to cross the river.

Press: Governor, invasion-type rhetoric historically has encouraged vigilante activity. They run around in camo and they cosplay as police. What is your response to that? Will you denounce border vigilantism?

Governor Abbott: Law and order needs to be left to states, to law enforcement, to authorized entities. We don't want anybody taking any type of vigilante action. We believe in public safety, and that means the safety of everybody. The lives of everybody are important and we don't want anybody to be harmed in any way. All that we want is to enforce the immigration laws of the United States. Thank you.

Print Citations

CMS: Abbott, Greg. "Texas Governor Speaks to Republican Governors at the US-Mexico Border." Press Conference at the US-Mexico border, Eagle Pass, TX, February 4, 2024. In *The Reference Shelf: Representative American Speeches, 2023–2024,* edited by Micah L. Issitt, 129–137. Amenia, NY: Grey House Publishing, 2024.

MLA: Abbott, Greg. "Texas Governor Speaks to Republican Governors at the US-Mexico Border." US-Mexico border, 4 February 2024, Eagle Pass, TX. Press Conference. *The Reference Shelf: Representative American Speeches, 2023–2024,* edited by Micah L. Issitt, Grey House Publishing, 2024, pp. 129–137.

APA: Abbott, G. (2024). Texas governor speaks to Republican governors at the US-Mexico border [Press conference]. US-Mexico border, Eagle Pass, TX. In Micah L. Issitt (Ed.), *The reference shelf: Representative American speeches, 2023–2024* (pp. 129–137). Grey House Publishing. (Original work published 2024)

Former President Speaks at the Southern Border

By Donald Trump

"And we have a Marxist that's running and this country is not ready for a Marxist president. She will never build the wall. She doesn't want to build the wall." Republican presidential candidate Donald Trump visited Cochise County, Arizona to give a speech on border security. Trump claimed that his former administration had the migration problem solved, but that the Biden-Harris administration eliminated much of this progress. Trump also repeated false claims about Biden administration economic accomplishments and claimed that migrant crime is expanding around the country.

Donald Trump: So thank you very much, everybody. It's a very sad time for this country in many ways. You had a candidate, I was no fan of Joe Biden, but the way he was taken out was a coup, he got 14 million votes and the person running now got none. She was disgraced, she was figured out by the Democrat voters. She never made it to Iowa. She was the first one out of approximately 22 people that were running for the Democrat nomination, she never even made it to Iowa. Beautiful place, Iowa, but she didn't. Plenty of people did. And Biden got 14 million votes, she got no votes, and now she's running against us. The good news is I think we're winning in the polls based on what I'm seeing. And after the debate, we were winning by many points, as you know, against Biden. They went to see him, they said, you're losing. You're not going to win. You can't win. We're going to get you out. It was a coup of an American president, and it was done with anger, and he's more angry than anybody.

And again, I'm no fan of his. I think he was perhaps the worst president. He was the worst president, largely because of what's happened at the border. He is allowed, in my opinion and in the opinion of the gentlemen behind me who know this better than anybody, much more than 20 million people into our country, many from prisons and jails, many from mental institutions, insane asylums, and many terrorists, and this was when I left. This is a very famous chart now because this chart probably saved my life, but this chart, the arrow on the bottom shows that this was the lowest ... this was the last week in office for me because of a horrible, horrible election where I got many millions more votes than I got the first time, but didn't quite make it, just a little bit short. We've got to clean up our borders, we have to clean up our elections, or we're not going to have a country,

---

Delivered on August 22, 2024 at the US-Mexico border, Cochise County, AZ.

but that's my last week. The arrow on the bottom, you see, as the gentlemen we're talking, that's the lowest point in the recorded history of the border.

This was done by border patrol. This wasn't done by Trump. This was done by border patrol working with ICE and law enforcement. And that's what we're going to do. Again, if you take a look, interestingly, at all of the wall that's laying on its side, that could have been put up in a matter of weeks. It was all set to go, it was all cut out. And if you look at the top of the mountain behind us, it was all shaped, all ready to go, could have been put up in a few weeks. Much of it's been sold for 5 cents on the dollar. It's very expensive. I worked with border patrol very closely, we worked Brandon, we worked with all of your people, and we wanted to design something that worked. And we actually had mountain climbers, we even had drug climbers. They call them drug climbers. They can get over a wall, it's so incredible, with 75 pounds of drugs on their back. They can climb up things.

And we designed this after looking at a lot of different designs and that's an anti-climb paddle that makes it very tough for somebody to climb. This was the one that they wanted, a little more expensive version, but this is the one that's a very important paddle on top and it's called anti-climb. And this was put in here just to shade us because there's a lot of rough people on the other side. So I figured you're the media, you want to be shaded. This gets taken off. This is just temporary to shade us from potential hazards. We know about hazards. But all of this wall was built at great expense and all it had to be erected, we just had to be stood up on its end, concrete on the bottom, goes down six feet. It also went down and shielded from tunnels because we went down about as far as it's practical for them to go down. They build tunnels under walls. We went down pretty deep. We'd go down a lot deeper than the wall. Made it very tough for them.

And we stopped that and we stopped people from coming over. I built hundreds of miles of this, by the way, as far as the eye can see. You look at the other direction, as far as the eye can see, and then I'd hear people say, oh, he didn't build the wall. We built the wall. We built much more than I was anticipated to build and we were going to build an extra 200 miles, much of this is that, which is much more than I said I was going to do, because as we built it, they would go around the edges, so we were going further and further out. And it worked. We had the best numbers ever, and we had them largely because of the wall, and also because the Mexican military helped us, which they never helped. At any time, they never helped. And we were very proud of it. So we went from the best numbers in recorded history to the worst numbers in recorded history or any other history.

And we have a Marxist that's running and this country is not ready for a Marxist president. She will never build the wall. She doesn't want to build the wall. If she changes her mind, it's only because she wants to get elected, because who wouldn't want to have a strong border? You need strong borders and strong elections, and we have neither, but we're going to have very strong borders and we're going to have very strong elections soon. The people are fed up. It's common sense, the people are just fed up. And you saw it, everybody coming from the airport saw the thousands and thousands of people lined up. It looked like Lindbergh coming in from what he did at the time, Broadway. It was amazing when you see all those people, it was a long drive from the airport, and so many thousands and thousands of people. The people in my car said, "I've never seen anything like that." We were in the middle of an area that's not well populated and have thousands of people like that is pretty unbelievable. I hope you got to see it.

And I hope the press writes this story fairly because it's a story of disgrace. We had a border czar who was the border czar. She loved the title, but she didn't want to do the work because she's lazy and, probably more importantly than being lazy, she wants to have an open border. And you say, who would want an open border where criminals can pour into our country? And all you have to do is walk up there, if you have the courage to do it, and go to that open section, stand there for a little while. You'll be running back here very quickly. You really have to write this fairly, this story, because you people don't want to talk about the border, you don't want to talk about the bad things that are going on in our country. We're going to end up not having a country. You're not going to have any media. We don't have media. They don't have media. They do their own media. They don't need media. But you really should cover this story fairly.

Before I begin, I have some, I think, very good words on the border, what to do and how to solve the problem. We had it solved. All they had to do is leave it. Leave it. Just leave it. But before I begin, I want to address the fake job numbers on top of everything else, fellas. Fake jobs. The fake job numbers that the Harris-Biden administration has been reporting for the last year, thanks to a leaker yesterday, meaning probably, in this case, a patriot, they were forced to release numbers. They claimed falsely that they created 818,000 jobs. So they said they did almost a million jobs, 818, 000 jobs that actually didn't exist. They were phantom jobs. They're called phantom jobs. The reason they did that is because I was even a little surprised their job numbers look better because I know the economy's lousy. Everyone here knows it, it's lousy. These people behind me know it's lousy. We have the worst inflation, I believe, in the history of our country and that's absolutely killing people, but it's 818,000 jobs, almost a million. And these are just the jobs we found out about. There's a lot of other false things that now are being looked at. That number will increase. So they reported false numbers and this isn't a revision, there's never been anything like this, this is a fraud put out by Harris and by Biden. And they were going to release the real numbers, it's called a revision, after the election, but it got found out before the election. And I hope you're going to write about it, but it's a big story, and it's a story that's going to be going very far. There's people very upset about it, including government officials are very upset about it. Even people that are Democrats are, because it's a pure fraud. When you have a revision, you have a few jobs one way or the other, and they get it straight at the end of the month, but this one was sheltered for a long time and they wanted to release it after November 5th, I wonder why, when it didn't really matter too much, but even then it mattered.

But so I hope you're going to report it. Almost a million jobs were phantom jobs. They were fake jobs, just like a lot of reporting is fake, and I hope you're going to report it because people have to hear it. They didn't want these numbers to come out and they did come out, and the whistleblower or whoever it was that got them to have to do it, somebody today, a high official said, "well, we don't really believe those numbers because Trump gave them." I didn't give them. I got them from the administration, from the Labor Bureau, and these are the stats that were just let out officially. I mean, they just came out. They were officially released. Those are official numbers. Has nothing to do with me. I just happened to be playing the role of a reporter for a change, but I hope you're going to do something with it because I think it's a serious thing. But it's the same as everything else. And I'm so glad that we decided to do this.

It's a little dangerous to do. I hate to tell you, you guys are in danger with the kind of weaponry that we have, but I felt it was important to do. And this kind of stuff that they put up to shield us, I'm going to make you feel not so good, it doesn't mean a thing compared to what comes through there, but at least they can't see you, but it's dangerous territory. And these people have unbelievable courage, the border patrol, ICE, the police, local law enforcement, unbelievable. I don't even know how they do it. They talk about I was courageous, these people are courageous. They go through this every day, and the amount of horrible injuries sustained in fights and shootings are just incredible. Not reported but incredible. We're here today on the southern border in Arizona, where Comrade Kamala Harris ... I call her Comrade because she is a radical left Marxist.

She wants open borders. I don't understand why anybody would want it, but she wants our country to be open to the world's criminals so they can come in and rape, and pillage, and do whatever they have to do. But she's the most radical left person who has ever run for high political office in our country's history. And by the way, the governor who's done a poor job as governor, Minnesota, Walz, he's done a poor job, very poor job. His numbers are horrible. People are fleeing his state. I love his state. We should have won his state twice, but a lot of hanky-panky goes on there. Hasn't been won since 1972. Richard Nixon was the last one to win it. But every time I go in there, we have massive crowds and everything's good, but nobody seems to be able to win it, so I know why we didn't win it. People don't like to talk about I., but he's a horrible governor, has bad job numbers, bad numbers for leaving, a lot of people leaving the state.

And he's insisted he put a bill, I'm sure the sheriffs would be very happy when they hear this, he signed a bill fairly recently where boys' bathrooms have to have tampons. Tampons in boys' bathrooms. I don't even like to bring the subject up, but it's a subject you have to hear about. That's what he wants. He's a radical left guy who lied like hell last night, and she'll lie tonight. We're doing a review of her tonight on truth because she'll lie, just like the rest of them lie. They talked about what I said about soldiers. I never said anything. I love our soldiers. They made the story up. It was fiction. We had 26 people countering it, but nobody cares. They made up everything. So many different stories. They made up about Project

25. They've been told officially, legally, in every way that we have nothing to do with Project 25. They know it, but they bring it up anyway.

They bring up every single thing that you can bring up, every one of them was false. He brought them up. But they've unleashed a deadly plague of migrant crime on our country by not doing their job. And all of that plank and all of that very expensive wall, it's also got tremendous electronic capability inside, it's got wires for cameras and everything else that you can have. It's the Rolls Royce of walls, I can tell you. It's very hardened steel outside, 7,000 pound concrete inside, and rebar inside of the concrete, all different, all very hard to get through. And it's sad to see it sitting here. We have crime going on up the road. In this direction, it's as far as you can see is wall, we have no problem there, but they come in where they refuse to put it up. That was when I first realized that they want open borders. I thought nobody could be so foolish or stupid to want open borders and have the world's criminal population pour into our country. That's what's happening.

But it shattered so many families' lives and stolen so many incredible young lives. And it's also really badly hurt our Black population and our Hispanic population because these people are taking their jobs. The jobs now are way down for the Black population and the Hispanic population because we have millions of illegal aliens that have poured into our country. They've taken the jobs of African-Americans and Hispanics, and that was obvious to me. Next is going to be unions, you watch. The unions are going to start going well because those jobs are going to be taken to. We're honored to really be here with these incredible people and in particular with some grieving families. And this is a group of people that I've gotten to know, they're incredible people, they've lost a loved one, and thousands of thousands of others are out there, and they are grieving also, but they're not out with you and sitting in this hot sun. I will say this, that at least it gives us a good reason. We're doing something for those incredible people that we'll be talking about very shortly, because we can't let it happen to other people. We can't let what you're going through happen to other families and you know what you're going through, as we discussed, nobody's ever seen anything like it. All for no reason whatsoever. And these are hardened, hardened criminals pouring into our country.

And then they always say, Sheriff, "Oh, the illegal immigrants don't commit crimes like people that live here." It's so wrong. They don't report them, but it's so wrong. They make our criminals look like babies. They make our criminals look like babies. That's about the only thing good. Our criminals all of a sudden don't look so tough to us. These are the roughest people and they're the roughest people from all over the world.

Their jails are being emptied from all over the world. Their criminals are being taken from their cities. And by the way, their crime rates are way down. Their crime rates came way down. Venezuela, all of these countries, their crime rates are down. Their prison population's down. Soon they won't have any prison population because a hundred percent of it will be in our country with the statement,

"If you ever come back, we will kill you." That's the statement they tell them. If you ever come back to Venezuela, and other countries, we will kill you. But it's all over the world. The Congo in Africa, many prisoners let go from the Congo in Africa. Rough prisoners. All over Europe they come, from all over, rough sections, the jails. You have to see jail populations are way down.

So we've done a lot of trips to the border over the years and told a lot of stories about border victims, including the stories of the amazing Angel Moms who have never been appreciated. They're incredible women what they've gone through. They're going through a similar thing. And many of them, I asked about time, but this time because many of them, this took place a long time ago with borders and horrible people coming in, and I don't have to tell you about the crimes, but the level of viciousness of the crime is unbelievable. But they said, "Time doesn't heal." The expression, time heals all wounds. It doesn't. I spoke to some people, they say they're worse now than they were 15 years ago.

And this started largely during Obama, and then we stopped it. We had it stopped. And then the first day in, they just said, "We are not doing anything. We're not doing anything." And all they had to do is let our people that we had in place, the best people, the best people. I was listening to people like Tom Homan, who is just an incredible patriot, tough, smart, gets it. Good man, but he's tough. I've been listening to all these people. They've been friends of mine for a long time. They know it better than anybody. But the level of criminality is unbelievable. It's an onslaught of violence at a level that nobody's ever seen before.

For nearly four years, as border czar, Comrade Kamala has overseen a nation-wrecking border invasion. This is nation-wrecking. This isn't just like, oh, we're going to fix it a little bit later. Gets to a point where you can't fix it. She's allowed at least 20 million people, all illegal aliens into our country, including millions and millions of unvetted fighting-age men from over 158 different countries, 158. Most people didn't realize you had that many countries.

Just recently, Kamala let in the head of a Peruvian gang who was wanted for 23 murders. Welcome to the United States of America. On her orders, Border Patrol is being forced to free tens of thousands of illegal aliens from custody week after week after week. And these are very violent criminals too. These are the most violent criminals that you'll ever see. Every day brings another story about innocent Americans being tortured, raped, murdered, and massacred by illegal aliens that Kamala Harris has set free in our country. "Don't hold them," they're told. "Don't hold them. Let them free. They'll behave." Well, he killed 20 people. Oh, but over here it's different.

Since Comrade Harris took over the border, there has been a 43% nationwide increase in violent crime and a 60% increase in rape. And the FBI should be ashamed of themselves when they report numbers because, in order to keep the violence numbers down, they didn't report some of the worst cities in the country like Chicago and others. What a disgrace. The FBI did that.

In New York, this June, an illegal alien released into our country by Kamala approached two thirteen-year-old children with a machete in broad daylight in front of other people, forced them into the woods, tied them together by the wrist and raped them over and over again. Over and over again. Two Kamala migrants were just arrested for the rape of a forty-six-year-old woman in Coney Island. I know Coney Island very well. That's where I sort of started. My office was out there, Brooklyn, throwing her to the ground and raping her with a knife to her throat. One of them had previously been arrested for raping another woman, but instead of being deported, he was released into our country and told to enjoy your life.

In Fort Wayne, Indiana, a woman who was offered a ride home by two illegal aliens was instead kidnapped, held down and raped, then driven around while the illegals discussed how they planned to kill her. They wanted to kill her. They didn't want to have a witness. And she miraculously escaped by throwing herself out of a rapidly moving car. Was badly hurt, but she escaped at least. Those people came from another country and they were very violent with an unbelievably violent background, violence like you've never seen.

In the Bronx recently, an illegal alien who Kamala set loose into the country, approached a 36-year-old woman while pretending to ask for directions before he wrapped his arms around her throat, pinned her down on a park bench and raped her publicly on a park bench. And she said he wasn't trying to rape me, he was trying to kill me.

In Michigan, earlier this year, an illegal alien broke into a residence and sexually assaulted two young girls, doing tremendous damage to these two young, beautiful girls.

In Virginia a few weeks ago, a 54-year-old mother of four was leaving a convenience store when she noticed an illegal alien trying to steal her car. When she tried to stop him, he ran her down, ran her over, and left her dead on the ground. She was dead. And her family is devastated.

In Texas last month, a Venezuelan illegal alien criminal let in by Comrade Kamala shot a female police officer multiple times with a rifle and she'll never be the same, and that's being nice about it.

A few months ago, I met with the devastated family of Laken Riley, a 22-year-old nursing student who was out for a jog on the campus of the University of Georgia when she was assaulted, beaten, and horrifically murdered. Kamala Harris let in the illegal alien animal who murdered Laken. This monster was in Border Patrol custody under very strong custody. They didn't want to let him go. But under Kamala's policies, he was set free to kill, and that's what he did. Kamala let this bloodthirsty killer go free, and then he murdered beautiful Laken, number one in her class, nursing school. Everybody aspired to be like her. She was the best student, the best everything. Beautiful girl.

Then there's the heartbreaking story of Rachel Morin. . . . Rachel was a cherished thirty-seven-year-old mom, beautiful woman of five incredible children who adored their mother more than anything in the world. They loved their mom.

Earlier this year, while Rachel was out on a run, she wants to keep herself in good shape and she ends up getting killed. In her neighborhood, she was brutally raped and murdered by an illegal alien who was let into America by Kamala Harris and her policies of stupidity. Savage person who committed this heinous crime first killed another woman in El Salvador before walking across our open border. Just walked right in. They didn't have this then.

He then attacked a nine-year-old girl and her mother in a home invasion in Los Angeles where they were very badly hurt before murdering Rachel in the area where Rachel lived in a very different part of this country. It was cold-blooded murder. . .

We had Remain in Mexico. The greatest policy, Remain in Mexico. How good was that? Everybody remained in Mexico until they were checked out, and either they came in or not. Most of them didn't qualify. Title 42, Safe Third Agreements, and 500 miles of border wall that was very, very difficult to even think about getting over, around, or under. The final gaps of the wall were about to be sealed, then Kamala came in and dismantled every single Trump border policy and halted all wall construction. And there it says, but much of it's been so. This is just a small example of what it was, what it is before they lifted up. So you can see on the ground behind me, the sections of wall that taxpayers paid for a lot of money, but Kamala refused to put up. Just refused. She wouldn't do it. Everybody called. I even made some calls. I said, "You got to put it up. You got to put it up."

But she didn't want it open. She wanted a wide open border. What Biden and Kamala have done to the families here with me and so many others, thousands and thousands of others, not only killed, also really badly hurt. Badly hurt to a point where they'll never lead a normal life again. It's shameful and it's evil. Every year under Harris, a new all time record of illegal immigration has been set. Every single year, our great borders are... She'll blow away. Biden's reputation as being the worst president. She'll be a president that'll make him look good just like Biden made Jimmy Carter look good. To get illegals into America as fast as possible, Harris has flown hundreds of thousands by airplane. Then they say, "Oh, well, we didn't want them to go." But then we found out a few months ago that they're flying them in over the border by airplanes to all over our country. Well, that means they do want them to come in and fly in some very dangerous people. . . . .

And I give great credit to the Supreme Court. They have great courage in doing what they're doing. It's not easy. But that was one that everybody was hoping for. A vast majority of people agree with that. It's a very small amount of people that don't. Who would want that? So thank you very much. And she's really provided, Harris, deportation immunity to the vast majority of criminal aliens living inside the United States. They've got immunity. They really have immunity. And importing MS-13 directly into our cities. MS-13 is the most vicious gang, we feel. If I ask the sheriffs behind me, I think probably considered the most vicious gangs in the world, wouldn't you say, Brandon? Never seen anything like it. It's not even believable. I won't tell you about it. It's not even believable. As the DA of San Francisco, Kamala Harris was the godmother of a deadly sanctuary city. She was considered the godmother. All they're doing is protecting criminals which set loose illegal alien criminals rather than hand them over to ICE, who were doing an incredible job. Under a program Kamala set up, an illegal alien arrested on drug charges in 2008 was set free to enjoy job training. A short time later, that same illegal alien attacked a 29-year-old, beautiful young woman, Amanda Kiefer. Stealing her purse and fracturing Amanda's skull. It was vicious and horrible. . . .

Donald Trump: Story after story. Kamala has called for the abolishing of ICE, the closing of every ICE detention facility, and the releasing of some of the most vicious criminals anywhere in the world by doing so. She supports free healthcare for illegal immigrants and has promised to give illegals mass amnesty and citizenship, which will obliterate social security. Oh, social security is going to be obliterated by all of these millions of people that she wants to put on. And also, Medicare will be obliterated. I'm going to save social security. Not going to touch it. We're going to make our country strong. But they're going to obliterate it. She also feels extremely strongly about defund the police. She wants to defund the police. And anytime somebody wants to defund the police, you're never going to get them back to being normal. The police have to be taken care of. They're the best thing we have going to protect us.

They know exactly what's going. When we do deportation, they know every person out there and they know the middle name and they know everything about them and they know all of the bad ones. They know the really bad ones. They'll be a great help. We have to get the criminals out of our country immediately. Kamala is always going to have open borders. If Comrade Harris has the chance, she will allow more than 100 million illegal aliens into our country. Our country will be overrun, and essentially, it won't be a country. It will be not governable. . . .

The choice is simple. Kamala's mass amnesty of criminals or President Trump's mass deportation of criminals. I think that's pretty easy. In addition to all of the other things, there are many other things, that are equally as bad but not as obvious. With your vote, we will seal the border, stop the invasion and launch the largest deportation effort in American history. We will impose tough new sentences on illegal alien criminals. These include ten-year mandatory minimum sentence for anyone guilty of human smuggling, a guaranteed life sentence for anyone guilty of child trafficking, and a death penalty for anyone guilty of child or woman sex trafficking. We'll also impose the death penalty on major drug dealers and traffickers in other countries on their immigration papers. There is a statement that says, "Death for drug traffickers." Big letters, big bold letters, 10 times the size of everything else on the page. I saw it this morning. And those are the countries where they have no problem with drugs. Many of them actually.

We will also impose the death penalty for anyone killing our police, sheriffs, Border Patrol, ICE or law enforcement officials. The death penalty with a quicker trial, not a trial that lasts for 15 years and everybody gets exhausted. We will liberate our country from the illegal alien, drug dealers, robbers, murderers, gang members and child predators, and we will make America safe again for our citizens and make it greater, stronger, better, more beautiful than ever before. And I want to thank you all and especially four very special people, four very special people. And sheriffs and law enforcement, I want to thank you so much because this job is so dangerous. . . .

So we have to stop it. We have to bring our country back. We have to use common sense. You don't have to be conservative, a liberal, a progressive as they like to say now. They don't like the term liberal. Republican, Democrat, it doesn't matter. We have to have strong protection in our country or our country's going to wither away and die. We need a military. We need our great police to be loved and respected and they will be again. Right now, if somebody does something that's a little bit on the tough side to stop something that's very bad, they end up losing their pension, their life, their car, their house. They lose their job, they lose everything. We're going to give immunity to many, many people so that they can do the law.

But again, I want to thank you. I want to thank the media for being here. I hope you can report this story the way it is. It's a very sad moment for our country. We have some very bad people trying to get into office, and if we don't stop them, our country has no chance of greatness. Thank you very much. Thank you. . . .

Print Citations

CMS: Trump, Donald. "Former President Speaks at the Southern Border." Press conference at the US-Mexico border, Cochise County, AZ, August 22, 2024. In *The Reference Shelf: Representative American Speeches, 2023–2024,* edited by Micah L. Issitt, 138–147. Amenia, NY: Grey House Publishing, 2024.

MLA: Trump, Donald. "Former President Speaks at the Southern Border." US-Mexico border, 22 August 2024, Cochise County, AZ. Press conference. *The Reference Shelf: Representative American Speeches, 2023–2024,* edited by Micah L. Issitt, Grey House Publishing, 2024, pp. 138–147.

APA: Trump, D. (2024). Former president speaks at the southern border [Press conference]. US-Mexico border, Cochise County, AZ. In Micah L. Issitt (Ed.), *The reference shelf: Representative American speeches, 2023–2024* (pp. 138–147). Grey House Publishing. (Original work published 2024)

President Unveils New Border Plans

By Joe Biden

"Frankly, I would've preferred to address this issue through a bipartisan legislation because that's the only way to actually get the kind of system we have now that's broken, fixed, to hire more border patrol agents, more asylum officers, more judges. But Republicans have left me no choice." After the failure of bipartisan border control legislation, President Joe Biden gave a public address on border security and reform. He announced the decision to revoke asylum status for those who come into the United States outside of authorized channels and stated that expanding border control will be the best way to manage border security moving forward.

Good afternoon. I've come here today to do what the Republicans in Congress refuse to do, take the necessary steps to secure our border. Four months ago, after weeks of intense negotiation between my staff and Democrats and Republicans, we came to a clear bipartisan deal. It was the strongest border security agreement in decades. But then Republicans in Congress, not all but walked away from it. Why? Because Donald Trump told them to. He told the Republicans, it has been published widely by many of you, that he didn't want to fix the issue. He wanted to use it to attack me. That's what he wanted to do. It was an extremely cynical political move and a complete disservice to the American people who are looking for us, not to weaponize the border, but to fix it. Today I'm joined by a bipartisan group of governors, members of Congress, mayors, law enforcement officials, most of whom live and work along the southern border.

They know the border is not a political issue to be weaponized. The responsibility we have to share to do something about it. They don't have time for the games played in Washington and neither do the American people. So today I'm moving past Republican obstruction and using the executive authorities available to me as president to do what I can on my own to address the border. Frankly, I would've preferred to address this issue through a bipartisan legislation because that's the only way to actually get the kind of system we have now that's broken, fixed, to hire more border patrol agents, more asylum officers, more judges. But Republicans have left me no choice. Today I'm announcing actions to bar migrants who cross our southern border unlawfully from receiving asylum. Migrants will be restricted from receiving asylum at our southern border unless they seek it after entering through an established lawful process.

And those who seek come to the United States legally, for example, by making an appointment and coming to a port of entry, asylum will still be available to

---

Delivered on June 4, 2024 at the White House, Washington, DC.

them, still available. But if an individual chooses not to use our legal pathways, if they choose to come without permission and against the law, they'll be restricted from receiving asylum and staying in the United States. This action will help us gain control of our border, restore order into the process. This ban will remain in place until the number of people trying to enter illegally is reduced to a level that our system can effectively manage. We'll carry out this order consistent with all our responsibilities under international law, every one of them. In addition to this action, we recently made important reforms in our asylum system, more efficient and more secure reforms. The goal is to deliver decisions on asylum as quickly possible.

The quicker decision means that a migrant is less likely to pay a criminal smuggler thousands of dollars to take him on a dangerous journey, knowing that if in fact they move in the wrong direction, they'll be turned around quickly. And two weeks ago, the Department of Justice started a new docket in the immigration courts to address cases where people who've recently crossed the border and can they make a decision within six months rather than six years, because that's what happens now. Additionally, the Department of Homeland Security has proposed new rules to allow federal law enforcement to more quickly remove asylum seekers that have criminal convictions and remove them from the United States. My administration has also recently launched new efforts to go after criminal networks that profit from smuggling migrants to our border. And incentivize people to give tips to law enforcement, provide information that brings smugglers to justice.

We're also sending additional federal prosecutors to hotspots along the border and prosecute individuals who break our immigration laws. One other critical step that we will be taking, and that has made a huge difference, we continue to work closely with our Mexican neighbors instead of attacking Mexico. And it's worked and we've built a strong partnership of trust between the Mexican President López Obrador. And I'm going to do the same with the Mexican Elect President, who I spoke with yesterday. We've chosen to work together with Mexico as an equal partner. And the facts are clear, due to the arrangements that I've reached with President Obrador, with the number of migrants coming to our shared border unlawfully in recent months has dropped dramatically.

But while these steps are important, they're not enough. To truly secure the border, we have to change our laws and Congress needs to provide the necessary funding to hire 1,500 more border security agents. 100 more immigration judges to help tackle the backlog of cases, more than 2 million of them. 4,300 more asylum officers to make decisions in less than six months instead of six years, which is what it takes now. And around 100 more high tech detection machines to significantly increase the ability to screen and stop fentanyl being smuggled into the United States.

These investments being were one of the primary reasons that the Border Patrol Union endorsed the bipartisan deal in the first place. And these investments are essential. They remain essential. As far as I'm concerned, if you're not

U.S. Issues

willing to spend the money to hire more border patrol agents, more asylum officers, more judges, more high tech machinery, you're just not serious about protecting our border. It's as simple as that. I believe that immigration has always been a lifeblood of America. We're constantly renewed by an infusion of people and new talent. The Statue of Liberty is not some relic of American history. It stands for who we are as the United States. So I will never demonize immigrants. I'll never refer to immigrants as poisoning the blood of a country. And further, I'll never separate children from their families at the border. I will not ban people from this country because of their religious beliefs.

I will not use the US military to go into neighborhoods all across the country to pull millions of people out of their homes and away from their families to put into detention camps while awaiting deportation, as my predecessor says he will do if he occupies this office again. On my very first day as president, I introduced a comprehensive immigration reform plan to fix our broken system, secure our border, provide a pathway for citizens, for dreamers, and a lot more. And I'm still fighting to get that done. But we must face a simple truth. To protect America as a land that welcomes immigrants, we must first secure the border and secure it now. The simple truth is there is a worldwide migrant crisis and if the United States doesn't secure our border, there's no limit to the number of people who may try to come here. Because there's no better place in the planet than the United States of America.

For those that say the steps I've taken are too strict, I say to you that be patient. And goodwill of American people are going to be wearing thin right now. Doing nothing is not an option. We have to act. We must act consistent with both our law and our values, our values as Americans. I'll take these steps today, not to walk away from who we are as Americans, but to make sure we preserve who we are for future generations to come. Today, I've spoken about what we need to do to secure the border. In the weeks ahead, and I mean the weeks ahead, I'll speak to how we can make our immigration system more fair and more just. Let's fix the problem and stop fighting about it. I'm doing my part. We're doing our part. Congressional Republicans should do their part. Thank you very much.

Print Citations

CMS: Biden, Joe. "President Unveils New Border Plans." Speech at the White House, Washington, DC, June 4, 2024. In *The Reference Shelf: Representative American Speeches, 2023–2024,* edited by Micah L. Issitt, 148–150. Amenia, NY: Grey House Publishing, 2024.

MLA: Biden, Joe. "President Unveils New Border Plans." The White House, 4 June 2024, Washington, DC. Speech. *The Reference Shelf: Representative American Speeches, 2023–2024,* edited by Micah L. Issitt, Grey House Publishing, 2024, pp. 148–150.

APA: Biden, J. (2024). President unveils new border plans [Speech]. The White House, Washington, DC. In Micah L. Issitt (Ed.), *The reference shelf: Representative American speeches, 2023–2024* (pp. 148–150). Grey House Publishing. (Original work published 2024)

Remarks on the CHIPS and Science Act

By Joe Biden

President Joe Biden discussed the significance of the Creating Helpful Incentives to Produce Semiconductors (CHIPS) and Science Act to an audience at the Milton J. Rubenstein Museum of Science and Technology in Syracuse, New York, noting that this investment in domestic production of semiconductor chips—an essential component of computers, mobile phones, auto technologies, and the internet—will reduce our dependence on foreign imports for something that has become indispensable in the global economy. Moving production back to the United States will also create jobs. Additional funds for technology and other scientific education and research will help keep the United States competitive and self-reliant when it comes to products that are vital to our daily lives and national security.

Hello, hello, hello. It's good to be back in Syracuse. I fell in love with this place, but I fell in love with a girl before I did that. Come—please, all, have a seat.

Shannon, thanks for that introduction and thank you for your brothers and sisters in the building trades, what they're doing to help build a future here in Syracuse.

You know, before I start, I want to take a moment to honor two officers who have already been mentioned—two fallen heroes who were killed in the line of duty this month: Lieutenant Michael Hoosock and—County Sheriff Department—and Syracuse Police Officer Michael Jensen.

We pray for their loved ones, whose hearts have been broken. You know, every time a police officer puts on that shield every morning, their husband or wife, whatever it is, their child worries about will they get that phone call. I got one of those phone calls in a different circumstance—find out you've lost part of your soul, lost part of your heart. For the entire Syracuse community is grieving, and we're grieving with you.

You know, to the men and women in law enforcement here and across the country, you represent the best of us. You really do. It's one of the toughest jobs in America—one of the toughest jobs. And to the families, who I hope to get to meet shortly, I say, "My heart goes out to you." Thank you. And God bless you all.

Folks, I want to thank Governor Hochul for having us here today and for her partnership. And thanks to Chuck Schumer, a relentless advocate for this project we're here to talk about today.

Delivered on April 25, 2024 at the Milton J. Rubenstein Museum of Science and Technology, Syracuse, NY.

152   U.S. Issues

County Executive McMahon, it's good to be back in a place that meant so much to me in my life. I also want to thank Governor Little of Idaho and Boise Mayor McLean for joining us.

Micron's CEO, Sanjay, thank you for your leadership and investment in America. We tried to entice you a little bit with a couple hundred—you know, billions of dollars, but you came. It seemed to work.

And to all the union leaders here, including Randi Weingarten, the American Federation of Teachers, thank you for showing the world that we can do big things again in America.

And all—folks, all over the years I've asked business leaders like Sanjay—because the other team kept criticizing me for wanting to make these investments, you know, things like the infrastructure bill, which was over a trillion dollars. And we're going to have an Infrastructure Decade coming. The last guy had Infrastructure Week and never showed up.

But, you know, I asked him—I was told that, you know, "This is a government intervention." I said, "Sure in the hell is."

I ask every business leader I know—not a joke—"When the federal government makes a multi-billion-dollar investment in something, does that encourage you or discourage you from getting engaged?" Well, guess what? Every single solitary leader said, overwhelmingly, yes, it encourages them to get engaged. And so, that's why we're here today.

You know, during the pandemic, folks, everyone learned about supply chains. You may remember we had a global shortage of semiconductors—smaller than the tip of your finger, and now it's even smaller than that—that would help power everything in our lives from smartphones to cars to dishwashers, satellites.

We invented those chips here in America. We invented them. We made them move. We modernized them. But over time, we stopped—we used to have 40 percent of this market. And over time, we stopped making them.

So, when the pandemic shut down the chips factories overseas, prices of everything went up at—here at home. That semiconductor shortage drove one third of the surge in inflation in 2021, caused long wait lines of all kinds of products.

Folks, I determined that I'm never going to let us be vulnerable to wait lines again. If it's essential, we're going to make it here in America.

And together—and, by the way, that's not hyperbole; that's literal. Together with Schumer, Leader and I, we took action to make sure these chips are made in America again, creating tens of thousands—and I mean tens of thousands—of good-paying jobs, bringing prices down for everyone.

In 2022, together with Leader Schumer, we wrote the Creating Helpful Incentives to Produce Semiconductors (CHIPS) and Science Act. We used to invest significant amounts of money in research and development. We stopped doing it, but I was determined we were going to do it again. It's one of the most significant science and technology investments in our history.

And two months later, I came to Syracuse to celebrate Micron's historic plan to build the biggest semiconductor manufacturing site in all of America, one of the biggest in the world.

As was mentioned, it's the size of—going to be the size of 40 football fields—40—big enough to fit four Carrier Domes inside and still have space leftover.

Today, I'm pleased to announce we're building on that commitment with a landmark preliminary agreement between my administration and Micron, a major chip manufacturer, which is building these fabs here in Upstate New York: $6.1 billion in chips funding paired with $125 billion from Micron to build these facilities here in New York and near Micron headquarters in Idaho.

And I—you know, by the way—it's been mentioned before, it's the single-biggest private investment ever in the history of these two states—Idaho and, you know, New York.

So far from—not far from here, in Clay, New York, it's going to help build two to four manufacturing facilities planned by Micron's mega-fabs.

In Boise, it's going to help build new high-volume manufacturing fabs as well.

In all, it's going to create over 70,000 jobs across both states, at least 9,000 of which are construction jobs, 11,000 manufacturing jobs, tens of thousands more up and down the supply chain. And it includes 9,000 permanent Micron manufacturing jobs right here in Clay—not here, but near, in Clay, little bit from here—many of them paying—catch this—$100,000 a year. And it doesn't require a college degree.

These projects are governed by the largest Project Labor Agreement in the state's history. It makes one of the—and it makes sure that work is done on time with the highest quality and most significant safety standards. And I'm pleased that Micron is planning to sit down with unions to discuss the labor piece.

Look, that's not all. And, by the way, I know I get criticized for being the most pro-union president in American history, but guess what? The middle class built this country, and unions built the middle class.

These brand new facilities are going to produce the most sophisticated, powerful, leading-edge memory chips in the entire world. Each one has—has trillion—not billions, not millions—trillions of tiny features, each 40,000 times thinner than a single hair on your head. And I've got some very thin hair on my head.

They require manufacturing precision down to the size of an atom. They process enormous amounts of information at lightning speed. And they're critical to the emerging technology that will power tomorrow's economy, like artificial intelligence and advanced communications. They'll make everyday things faster, lighter, smaller, and more reliable. And it's about time.

Even though America invented these advanced chips, we don't make any of them today—zero, zero. All manufacturing of leading-edge chips moved to Asia years ago. That's why, today, this is such a big deal. And it is a big deal.

We're bringing advanced chips manufacturing back to America after 40 years. And it's going to transform our semiconductor industry, a pillar of a modern economy. And it's going to create an entirely new ecosystem in research, design, manufacturing of advanced chips here in America.

Folks, where is it written—when I said we were going to become the manufacturing capital of the world again when I got elected, they looked at me, some of my friends, and said, "You're crazy." Well, where the heck is it written that American manufacturing will not be the capital of the world again? It's going to be.

We've already created nearly 800,000 new manufacturing jobs since I took office. And, we're just getting started. And that's a fact. We're just getting started.

It isn't just about investing in America. It's about investing in the American people as well. And that includes training folks for these high-paying jobs—highly skilled new jobs that we're creating. To do that, we're bringing employers, unions, community colleges, high schools together and workforce hubs where folks can learn the skills hands-on.

My wife, Jill, cares a lot about this as well. She's teaching at a community college right now. Last year, she announced our first five workforce hubs in the United States in Pittsburgh; Phoenix; Baltimore; Columbus, Ohio; and Augusta, Georgia. Thousands of workers will be trained in these facilities.

And today, I'm pleased to announce four new hub programs. One hub in Detroit and Lansing, Michigan, folks will make electric cars. Another hub in Philadelphia, one in Milwaukee will train workers that'll replace every poisonous lead pipe in America within the decade. And here in Syracuse—the Syracuse region, a new hub is going to train semiconductor workers for the future.

And I know that Micron is also partnering with the American Federation of Teachers to develop a technology curriculum for high schools in New York state. Think about it, those of you who are as young as me, 40 (laughter)—in your 40s or so. How many schools still have shop in them? How many folks have—where you learn how to work with your hands?

A significant number of public schools did away with it. So many young people who are qualified and want to and are capable who are going to never know that they had that capacity.

Well, I want to thank Randi and Sanjay for their work and Micron's leadership in workforce development, because it's going to make a big difference.

In all—so far, my Investing in America agenda has attracted more than $825 billion—$825 billion in private-sector investment, not a penny of which existed before I got elected. It ignited a manufacturing boom, a clean-energy boom, a semiconductor boom nationwide. And it's clear we have the strongest economy in the world, and that's a fact.

Fifteen million new jobs created in three and half years. Unemployment hasn't been this low for this long for 50 years. Wages are rising. Instead of importing foreign products, we're exporting American jobs, we're exporting American products and creating American jobs—here in America where they belong.

And, folks, my predecessor and his MAGA Republican friends have a very different view. They oppose the CHIPS and Science Act that's powering this growth today. In fact, your congressman, Brandon Williams, called it "corporate welfare."

Bless me, Father. (The President makes the sign of the cross.) (Laughter.)

And Elise Stefanik, a few counties over, called the CHIPS Act—she said it was, "Washington at its worst," end of quote. I guess they're not going to be here today to celebrate.

But now, conversion is wonderful, isn't it? Now they've seen the massive surge in investment and jobs that we've mobilized, and they're singing a different tune now. Now they say this is "critical." You got that? Stefanik said this is "critical."

Now they say what we're doing will, quote, "lead to a more prosperous, secure, and innovative America." Well, there's nothing, I said, like conversion. I agree. Welcome, welcome, welcome.

Folks, look, we got to stop this division. I promised to be a president for all of America, whether you voted for me or not. Today's investment helps Americans everywhere, in red states and blue states, and proof that we have—we leave no one behind.

Of the infrastructure jobs and proposals, we have more of them in red states than in blue states. It's about America.

Let me close with this. The past few years, I've talked to folks all across America, in their communities and at their kitchen tables. They often tell me, back in 2020, they were down. They had lost their business.

How many—did you know somebody who worked at Carrier or another facility and a whole generation that worked there? And you're sitting there as a parent and—a mom—and the kid that comes home, well-educated, says, "I can't live here anymore. There's no job for me. I got to move. I got to move." They lost faith.

Syracuse is a good example. For decades it was a manufacturing boomtown full of good-paying jobs and a solid path to the middle class. I know; I lived here. I went to law school here. I married a wonderful woman from Lake Skaneateles who I came—that's why I came to Syracuse Law School. I felt it.

But over the years, trickle-down economics swept it all away. Under my predecessor, manufacturers left. Factories like BCS Automotive over in Auburn, where her family lived, shut down. Twenty-two thousand local jobs disappeared in the Syracuse region.

That's a story seen in community after community nationwide: hollowed out, robbed of hope. But not on my watch, thanks to investing we're making in America and the partnerships we've formed.

American manufacturing is back. New factories are going up all across the country. And communities like Syracuse are writing a great American comeback story—that's what it is: a comeback story—creating new jobs, new businesses, new hope.

Today, folks, when folks see shovels in the ground on these projects, people going back to work, I hope they feel the pride that I feel—pride in their hometown that's making a comeback, pride in America, pride in knowing we can get big things done when we work together.

That's why I've never been more optimistic about this nation's future. We just have to remember who we are, for God's sake. We're the United States of

156   U.S. Issues

America. And there is nothing—nothing, nothing—beyond our capacity to get done when we work together.

God bless you all. And may God protect our troops. This is a big deal day. Congratulations, Syracuse. Congratulations. Thank you.

Print Citations

CMS: Biden, Joe. "Remarks on the CHIPS and Science Act." Speech at the Milton J. Rubenstein Museum of Science and Technology, Syracuse, NY, April 25, 2024. In *The Reference Shelf: Representative American Speeches, 2023–2024,* edited by Micah L. Issitt, 151–156. Amenia, NY: Grey House Publishing, 2024.

MLA: Biden, Joe. "Remarks on the CHIPS and Science Act." Milton J. Rubenstein Museum of Science and Technology, 25 April 2024, Syracuse, NY. Speech. *The Reference Shelf: Representative American Speeches, 2023–2024,* edited by Micah L. Issitt, Grey House Publishing, 2024, pp. 151–156.

APA: Biden, J. (2024). Remarks on the CHIPS and Science Act [Speech]. Milton J. Rubenstein Museum of Science and Technology, Syracuse, NY. In Micah L. Issitt (Ed.), *The reference shelf: Representative American speeches, 2023–2024* (pp. 151–156). Grey House Publishing. (Original work published 2024)

Remarks on the Third Anniversary of the January 6th Attack and on Defending the Sacred Cause of American Democracy

By Joe Biden

"Trump's mob wasn't a peaceful protest. It was a violent assault. They were insurrectionists, not patriots. They weren't there to uphold the Constitution. They were there to destroy the Constitution." On the anniversary of the January 6, 2020 insurrection in Washington, DC, President Joe Biden gave a speech on democracy and accused Donald Trump of inspiring, encouraging, and supporting the attack on the American government that occurred after Trump lost the 2020 election.

Thank you. Please. Thank you. Please, thank you very, very much. Today the topic of my speech today is deadly serious, and I think it needs to be made at the outset of this campaign. In the winter of 1777, it was harsh and cold as the Continental army marched to Valley Forge. General George Washington knew he faced the most daunting of tasks, to fight an winter war against the most powerful empire that existed in the world at the time. His mission was clear, liberty, not conquest, freedom, not domination, national independence, not individual glory. America made a vow. Never again would we bow down to a king. The months ahead would be incredibly difficult, but General Washington knew something in his bones, something about the spirit of the troops he was leading. Something about the soul of the nation. He was struggling to be born. In his general order he predicted, and I quote "With one heart and one mind, with fortitude and with patience." They would overcome every difficulty the troops he was leading. And they did. They did.

This army that lacked blankets and food, clothes and shoes. This army whose march left bloody bare footprints of the snow, this ragtag army made up of ordinary people, their mission, George Washington declared was nothing less than a sacred cause. That was the phrase he used. A sacred cause. Freedom, liberty, democracy, American democracy. I just visited the grounds of Valley Forge. I've been there a number of times from the time I was a boy scout years ago.

It's the very site that I think every American should visit because it tells a story of the pain and the suffering and the true patriotism it took to make America. Today, we gather in a new year, some 246 years later. Just one day before January 6th, a date forever shared in our memory because it was on that day that

---

Delivered on January 6, 2024 at Montgomery County Community College, Blue Bell, PA.

we nearly lost America. Lost it all. Today, we're here to answer the most important of questions. Is democracy still America's sacred cause? I mean it.

This is not rhetorical, academic or hypothetical, but that democracy is still America's sacred cause is the most urgent question of our time, and it's what the 2024 election is all about. The choice is clear. Donald Trump's campaign is about him. Not America, not you. Donald Trump's campaign is obsessed with the past, not the future. He's willing to sacrifice our democracy, put himself in power. Our campaign is different. For me and Kamala, our campaign is about America. It's about you. It's about every age and background that occupy this country. It's about the future we're going to continue to build together. And our campaign is about preserving and strengthening our American democracy. Three years ago tomorrow we saw with our own eyes, the violent mob storm the United States Capitol. It was almost in disbelief as you first turned on the television.

For the first time in our history, insurrectionists had come to stop the peaceful transfer of power in America. First time. Smashing windows, shattering doors, attacking the police. Outside gallows were erected. As the MAGA crowd chanted "Hang Mike Pence." Inside, they hunted for Speaker Pelosi. The house was chanting as they marched through and smashed windows, "Where's Nancy?" Over 140 police officers were injured. Jill and I attended the funeral of police officers who died as a result of the events of that day. Because of Donald Trump's lies, they died because these lies brought a mob to Washington. He promised it would be wild, and it was. He told the crowd to fight like hell and all hell was unleashed. He promised he would right them, right them. Everything they did, he would be side-by-side with them. Then as usual, he left the dirty work to others. He retreated to the White House. As America was attacked from within, Donald Trump watched on TV in the private small dining room off the Oval Office.

The entire nation watched in horror. The whole world watched in disbelief and Trump did nothing. Members of his staff, members of his family, Republican leaders who were under attack at that very moment, pled with him, act, call off the mob. Imagine had he gone out and said, stop. And still Trump did nothing. It was among the worst derelictions of duty by a president in American history. An attempt to overturn a free and fair election by force and violence. A record 81 million people voted for my candidacy and to end his presidency. Trump lost the popular vote by 7 million. Trump's claims about the 2020 election never could stand up in court. Trump lost 60 court cases. 60. Trump lost the Republican-controlled states. Trump lost before a Trump-appointed judge, and then judges. And Trump lost before the United States Supreme Court. All of it, he lost. Trump lost recount after recount after recount and state after state. But in desperation and weakness, Trump and his MAGA followers went after election officials who ensured your power as a citizen would be heard. These public servants had their lives forever upended by attacks and death threats for simply doing their jobs. In Atlanta, Georgia, a brave Black mother and her daughter, Ruby Freeman and Shaye Moss, were doing their jobs as election workers until Donald Trump and his MAGA followers targeted and threatening them, forcing them from their homes, unleashing racist vitriol on them. Trump's personal lawyer, Rudy Giuliani, was just hit with $148 million judgment for cruelty and defamation that he inflicted against them. Other state and local elected officials across the country faced similar personal attacks. In addition, Fox News agreed to pay a record $787 million for the lies they told about voter fraud.

Let's be clear about the 2020 election. Trump exhausted every legal avenue available to him to overturn the election. Every one. But the legal path just took Trump back to the truth that I'd won the election and he was a loser. Well, so knowing how his mind works now, he had one act left, one desperate act available to him. The violence of January the 6th. And since that day, more than 1,200 people have been charged with assault on the Capitol. Nearly 900 of them have been convicted or pled guilty. Collectively to date they have been sentenced to more than 840 years in prison. What's Trump done? Instead of calling them criminals, he's called these insurrectionists patriots. They're patriots. And he promised to pardon them if he returns to office.

Trump said that there was a lot of love on January the 6th. The rest of the nation, including law enforcement, saw a lot of hate and violence. One Capitol police officer called it a medieval battle. That same officer was called vile, racist names. He said he was more afraid in the Capitol of the United States of America, in the chambers, than when he was fighting as a soldier in the war in Iraq. He said he was more afraid inside the halls of Congress than fighting in the war in Iraq. In trying to rewrite the facts of January 6th, Trump was trying to steal history the same way he tried to steal the election. But we knew the truth because we saw it with our own eyes. It wasn't like something, a story being told. It was on television repeatedly. We saw it with our own eyes. Trump's mob wasn't a peaceful protest. It was a violent assault. They were insurrectionists, not patriots. They weren't there to uphold the Constitution. They were there to destroy the Constitution. Trump won't do what an American president must do. He refuses to denounce political violence. So hear me clearly. I'll say what Donald Trump won't. Political violence is never, ever acceptable in the United States political system. Never, never, never. It has no place in a democracy. None. You can't be pro-insurrectionist and pro-American. Trump and his MAGA supporters not only embrace political violence, but they laugh about it.

At his rally, he jokes about an intruder whipped up by the big Trump lie, taking a hammer to Paul Pelosi's skull and echoing the very same words used on January 6th. "Where's Nancy?" And he thinks that's funny. He laughed about it. What a sick... My God. I think it's despicable, seriously. Not just for a president, for any person to say that, but to say it to the whole world listening. When I was overseas... Anyway. Trump's assault on democracy isn't just part of his past. It's what he's promising for the future. He's being straightforward. He's not hiding the ball. His first rally for the 2024 campaign opened with a choir of January 6th insurrectionists singing from prison on a cell phone while images of the January 6th riot played on a big screen behind him at his rally.

Can you believe that? This is like something out of a fairytale. A bad fairytale. Trump began his 2024 campaign by glorifying the failed violent insurrectionist insurrection on our Capitol. The guy who claims law and order sows lawlessness and disorder. Trump's not concerned about your future, I promise you. Trump is now promising a full-scale campaign of revenge and retribution, his words, for some years to come. They were his words, not mine. He went on to say he'd be a dictator on day one. I mean, if I were writing a book of fiction and I said, "An American president said that," and not in jest. He called, and I quote... This is a quote. "The termination of all the rules, regulation and articles, even those found in the U.S. Constitution, should be terminated," if it fits his will.

It's really kind of hard to believe. Even found in the Constitution, he could terminate? He's threatened the former chairman of the Joint Chiefs of Staff with the death penalty. He says he should be put to death because the chairman put his oath to the Constitution ahead of his personal loyalty to Trump. This coming from a president who called, when he visited his cemetery, called dead soldiers "suckers and losers." Remember that? Sometimes I'm really happy the Irish in me can't be seen. It was right around the time I was at Beau's grave, Tommy. How dare he? Who in God's name does he think he is?

With former aides, Trump plans to invoke the Insurrection Act, which will allow him to deploy... He's not allowed to do it in ordinary circumstances, allow him to deploy U.S. military forces on the streets of America. He said it. He calls those who oppose him "vermin". He talks about the blood of America is being poisoned, echoing the same exact language used in Nazi Germany. He proudly posts on social media the words that best describe his 2024 campaign, "Revenge, power, and dictatorship." There's no confusion about who Trump is, what he intends to do. I placed my hand in our family Bible and I swore an oath on the very same steps of the Capitol, just 14 days after the attack on January the 6th.

As I looked out over the capital city whose streets were lined with National Guard to prevent another attack, I saw an American that had been pushed to the brink, an America that had been pushed to the brink. But I felt enormous pride, not in winning. I felt enormous pride in America because American democracy had been tested. American democracy had held together. And when Trump had seen weakness in our democracy and continued to talk about it, I saw strength. Your strength. It's not hyperbole. Your strength. Your integrity. American strength and integrity. Ordinary citizens, state election officials, the American judicial system, had put the Constitution first and sometimes at their peril. At their peril. Because of them, because of you, the will of the people prevailed, not the anger of the mob or the appetites of one man.

When the attack on January 6th happened, there was no doubt about the truth. At the time, even Republican members of Congress and Fox News commentators publicly and privately condemned the attack. As one Republican senator said, "Trump's behavior was embarrassing and humiliating for the country." But now, that same senator and those same people have changed their tune. As time has gone on, politics, fear, money, all have intervened. Now these MAGA voices who know the truth about Trump on January 6th have abandoned the truth and abandoned democracy. They made their choice. Now the rest of us, Democrats, Independents, mainstream Republicans, we have to make our choice. I know mine, and I believe I know America's. We'll defend the truth, not give in to the Big Lie. We'll embrace the Constitution and the Declaration, not abandon it. We'll honor the sacred cause of democracy, not walk away from it. Today, I make this sacred pledge to you. The defense, protection, and preservation of American democracy will remain, as it has been, the central cause of my presidency.

America, as we begin this election year, we must be clear: Democracy is on the ballot. Your freedom is on the ballot. Yes, we'll be voting on many issues: on the freedom to vote and have your vote counted, on the freedom of choice, the freedom to have a fair shot, the freedom from fear. We'll debate and disagree. Without democracy, no progress is impossible. Think about it. The alternative to democracy is dictatorship: the rule of one, not the rule of We the People. That's what the soldiers of Valley Forge understood. So was me, we have to understand it as well.

We've been blessed so long with a strong, stable democracy. It's easy to forget why so many before us risked their lives and strengthened democracy, what our lives would be without it. Democracy means having the freedom to speak your mind, to be who you are, to be who you want to be. Democracy is about being able to bring about peaceful change. Democracy. Democracy is how we've opened the doors of opportunity wider and wider with each successive generation, notwithstanding our mistakes. But if democracy falls, we'll lose that freedom. We'll lose the power of We the People to shape our destiny.

If you doubt me, look around the world. Travel with me as I meet with other heads of state throughout the world. Look at the authoritarian leaders and dictators Trump says he admires, he out loud says he admires. I won't go through them all. It'd take too long. Look, remember when he refers to what he calls love letter exchanges between he and the dictator of North Korea? Those women and men out there in the audience who have ever fought for the American military, would you ever believe you'd hear a president say something like that? His admiration for Putin. I could go on. Look at what these autocrats are doing to limit freedom in their countries. They're limiting freedom of speech, freedom of press, freedom to assemble, women's rights, LGBTQ rights, people are going to jail, so much more.

It's true. The push and pull of American history is not a fairy tale. Every stride forward in America is met with a ferocious backlash many times from those who fear progress and those who exploit that fear for their own personal gain; from those who traffic in lies told for power and profit; for those who are driven by grievance and grift, consumed by conspiracy and victimhood; from those who seek to bury history and ban books. Did you ever think you'd be at a political event talking about book banning in a presidential election?

162 U.S. Issues

The choice and contest between those forces, those competing forces, between solidarity and division is perennial. But this time, it's so different. You can't have a contest, you can't have a contest if you see politics as an all-out war instead of a peaceful way to resolve our differences. All-out war is what Trump wants.

That's why he doesn't understand the most fundamental truth about this country. Unlike other nations on Earth, America is not built on ethnicity, religion, geography. We're the only nation in the history of the world built on an idea, not hyperbole, built on an idea: "We hold these truths to be self-evident, that all men and women are created equal." It's an idea declared in the Declaration, created in a way that viewed everybody as equal and should be treated equal throughout their lives. We've never fully lived up to that. We have a long way to go. But we've never walked away from the idea. We've never walked away from it before. But I promise you, I will not let Donald Trump and the MAGA Republicans force us to walk away now.

We're living in an era where a determined minority is doing everything in its power to try to destroy our democracy for their own agenda. The American people know it, and they're standing bravely in the breach. Remember, after 2020, January 6th insurrection to undo the election in which more Americans had voted than any other in American history? America saw the threat posed to the country, and they voted him out. In 2022, historic midterm election, in state after state, election after election, the election deniers were defeated. Now, in 2024, Trump is running as the denier-in-chief, the election denier-in-chief. Once again, he's saying he won't honor the results of the election if he loses. Trump says he doesn't understand. Well, he still doesn't understand the basic truth. That is, you can't love your country only when you win. You can't love your country only when you win.

So I'll keep my commitment to be president for all of America, whether you voted for me or not. I've done it for the last three years, and I'll continue to do it. Together, we can keep proving that America is still a country that believes in decency, dignity, honesty, honor, truth. We still believe that no one, not even the President, is above the law. We still believe. The vast majority of us still believe that everyone deserves a fair shot at making it.

We're still a nation that gives hate no safe harbor. I tell you from my experience working with leaders around the world, and I mean this sincerely, not a joke, that America is still viewed as the beacon of democracy for the world. I can't tell you how many world leaders, and I know all of them, virtually all of them, grab my arm in private and say, "He can't win. Tell me. No, my country will be at risk." Think of how many countries, Tommy, you know, that are on the edge. Imagine. We still believe in We the People, and that includes all of us, not some of us.

Let me close with this. In that cold winter of 1777, George Washington and his American troops at Valley Forge waged a battle on behalf of a revolutionary idea, that everyday people, like where I come from and the vast majority of you, not a king or a dictator, that everyday people can govern themselves without a king or a dictator. In fact, in the rotunda of the Capitol, there's a giant painting of General George Washington, not President Washington, and he's resigning his commission as Commander-in-Chief of the Continental Army. A European king at the time said after he won the revolution, now's the time for him to declare his kingship. But instead, the mob that attacked the Capitol waving Trump flags and Confederate flags stormed right past that portrait. That image of George Washington gave them no pause, but it should have. The artist who painted that portrait memorialized that moment because he said it was "One of the highest moral lessons ever given to the world." George Washington was at the height of his power, having just defeated the most powerful empire on Earth. Could have held on the power as long as he wanted. He could have made himself not a future president, but a future monarch in effect. And by the way, when he got elected President, he could have stayed for 2, 3, 4 or 5 terms till he died. But that wasn't the America, he and the American troops of Valley Forge had fought for.

In America, genuine leaders, democratic leaders with a small d don't hold onto power relentlessly. Our leaders return power to the people, and they do it willingly because that's the deal. You do your duty, you serve your country, and ours is a country worthy of service as many Republican presidents and Democratic presidents have shown over the years. We're not perfect, but at our best, we face head on the good, the bad, the truth of who we are. We look in the mirror and ultimately never pretend we're something we're not. That's what great nations do, and we're a great nation. We're the greatest nation on the face of the Earth. We really are.

That's the America I see in our future. We get up, we carry on, we never bow, we never bend, we speak of possibilities, not carnage. We're not weighed down by grievances. We don't foster fear. We don't walk around as victims. We take charge of our destiny. We get our job done with help of the people we find in America, who find their place in a changing world and dream and build a future that not only they, but all people deserve a shot at. We don't believe, none of you believe America's failing. We know America's winning. That's American patriotism. It's not winning because of Joe Biden. It's winning. This is the first national election since January 6th, insurrection placed the dagger at the throat of American democracy since that moment. We all know who Donald Trump is. The question we have to answer is, who are we? That's what's at stake. Who are we?

In the year ahead as you talk to your family and friends, cast your ballots, the power is in your hands. After all we've been through in our history, from independence to civil war, to two world wars, to a pandemic, to insurrection, I refuse to believe that in 2024, we Americans will choose to walk away from what's made us the greatest nation in the history of the world. Freedom, liberty, democracy is still a sacred cause, and there's no country in the world better positioned to lead the world than America.

I've said it many times, that's why I've never been more optimistic about our future, and I've been doing this a hell of a long time. Just remember who we are with patience and fortitude, with one heart. We are the United States of America for God's sake. I mean it. I believe with every fiber, there's nothing beyond our capacity if we act together and decently with one another. Nothing. Nothing. Nothing. I mean it. We're the only nation in the world that's come out of every crisis stronger than we went into that crisis. That was true yesterday, it is true today, and I guarantee you, will be true tomorrow. God bless you all and may God protect our troops. Thank you. I understand power. Thank you all much. Thank you. Thank you. Thank you.

Print Citations

CMS: Biden, Joe. "Remarks on the Third Anniversary of the January 6th Attack: Defending the Sacred Cause of American Democracy." Speech at Montgomery County Community College, Blue Bell, PA, January 6, 2024. In *The Reference Shelf: Representative American Speeches, 2023–2024,* edited by Micah L. Issitt, 157–164. Amenia, NY: Grey House Publishing, 2024.

MLA: Biden, Joe. "Remarks on the Third Anniversary of the January 6th Attack: Defending the Sacred Cause of American Democracy." Montgomery County Community College, 6 January 2024, Blue Bell, PA. Speech. *The Reference Shelf: Representative American Speeches, 2023–2024,* edited by Micah L. Issitt, Grey House Publishing, 2024, pp. 157–164.

APA: Biden, J. (2024). Remarks on the third anniversary of the January 6th attack: Defending the sacred cause of American democracy [Speech]. Montgomery County Community College, Blue Bell, PA. In Micah L. Issitt (Ed.), *The reference shelf: Representative American speeches, 2023–2024* (pp. 157–164). Grey House Publishing. (Original work published 2024)

When Labor Unions Are Strong, America Is Strong

By Kamala Harris

"Divided we can beg, united we can demand." Vice President Kamala Harris spoke at a campaign event in Detroit, Michigan. She commemorated Labor Day by speaking about the history of union labor in the United States and the benefits of unionization for the working class and the economy.

Hi, everyone. Good afternoon, Detroit. Oh, it's good to be in the house of labor.

Can we hear it for Tyrese [West]? Tyrese, I want to thank you for your extraordinary leadership and all of your words and the heart and soul that you put into your work, like I know all the members of Laborers' International Union of North America (LIUNA) and everyone here does every day, because we love our country and we know what is at stake. Thank you, Tyrese. Thank you.

So, it is so good to be with so many incredible leaders and elected officials who are here. Governor [Gretchen] Whitmer was here earlier; Senator [Debbie] Stabenow; your next United States senator, Representative Elissa Slotkin. And I always want to thank Representatives [Debbie] Dingell—where is she? There she is . . . [Haley] Stevens, [Shri] Thanedar, all of you for the work that you do every day.

And to all the labor leaders who are here, I thank you all for your extraordinary work. Don't we love Labor Day? We love Labor Day.

It's always been that way, right? The way we celebrate Labor Day is we know that hard work is good work. We know that when we organize, when we bring everyone together, it's a joyful moment where we are committed to doing the hard work of lifting up America's families.

And I want to thank everyone here for that work and the way you do it every day, including General President [Brent] Booker of the Laborers'; President [Shawn] Fain of the United Auto Workers (UAW); President [Becky] Pringle of National Education Association (NEA); President [James] Slevin of the Utility Workers; and President [Randi] Weingarten of the American Federation of Teachers (AFT).

And thank you to all of the union members who are here this afternoon.

So, on Labor Day and every day, we celebrate the dignity of work. We celebrate unions, because unions helped build America and unions helped build America's middle class.

Delivered on September 2, 2024 at Northwestern High School, Detroit, MI.

166 U.S. Issues

It is true across our nation, and it is true here in Detroit. Nearly 140 years ago, in this very city, 10,000 people marched in one of our nation's first Labor Day parades. Many held signs that read "Divided, we can beg. United, we can demand."

For generations, in Detroit and across our nation, the brothers and sisters of labor have stood together to righteously demand fair pay, better benefits, and safe working conditions. And let me say, every person in our nation has benefited from that work.

Everywhere I go, I tell people: Look, you may not be a union member. You better thank a union member—for the five-day workweek. You better thank a union member for sick leave. You better thank a union member for paid leave. You better thank a union member for vacation time.

Because what we know is when union wages go up, everybody's wages go up. When union workplaces are safer, every workplace is safer. When unions are strong, America is strong.

We know what we're talking about. The labor movement has always understood the power of the collective and the power of unity.

And while we are fighting so much nonsense that is about trying to divide our country, trying to pull us apart, look to what the history and the present of labor tells us about the power of the collective and unity—the spirit of that work, as much as the product of that work. It's very telling and gives us really good lessons about what creates strength.

And, you know, many of you know, my parents met while they were active in the Civil Rights Movement. So, when I was young, my parents—because I see some young leaders here today—when I was young, my parents would take me to the meetings and take me to the marches. I was in a stroller.

And from a very young age, I learned that when people stand together, when we join voices, knowing that the vast majority of us have so much more in common than what separates us—when we join those voices, we can drive extraordinary change, which is why I believe in my heart and soul no one should ever be made to fight alone. We are all in this together. We are all in this together.

But I'll tell you, I think that there has been a certain backward-thinking approach over the last several years, which is to suggest that the measure of the strength of a leader is based on who you beat down instead of what we know: The true measure of the strength of a leader is based on who you lift up—who you lift up. That's the measure of the strength of a leader. Let's stop with the nonsense.

And in this election, we all here know there are two very different visions for our nation. Ours is focused on the future; and theirs is focused on the past. And we fight for the future. We fight for a future where all people receive dignity and respect and opportunity for—not just for some but for all. That's what we are fighting for.

And so, we are sixty-four days out from the election day. And in Michigan, mail-in absentee voting starts in twenty-four days.

So, this election—this election and our fight is a fight for the promise of America, a promise—

And ours is a fight for the promise—the promise of America—a promise of freedom, of opportunity, and justice not just for some but for all.

But what we know is, as we fight to move our nation forward, Donald Trump intends to pull us back to the past.

But we're not going back. We are not going back. So we know what that would look like, right? So, intends to pull us back, including back to a time before workers had the freedom to organize.

As president, we will always remember Donald Trump blocked overtime benefits for millions of workers—Tyrese talked a bit about this—and opposed efforts to raise the minimum wage. He appointed union busters to the National Labor Relations Board. And he supported so-called right-to-work laws. And, here's the thing. We have a choice here, right? And we're not going back, because we also know that if Donald Trump were reelected, he intends to give tax cuts to billionaires and big corporations. He intends to cut Social Security and Medicare.

He wants to impose what in effect is a national sales tax on everyday products and basic necessities that will cost—and economists have said this—that will cost a typical American family almost $4,000 a year.

He wants to repeal the Affordable Care Act and take us back to a time in our country which most of us remember, when insurance companies, you remember, had the power to deny people—children who had asthma, a survivor of breast cancer, a grandparent with diabetes.

Look, America has tried those failed policies before. And they are failed policies. And we are not going back. We are not going back. We are not going back.

And instead—and instead, we fight for a future—a future where no person has to go broke just because they got sick.

And so, when I am president, we will continue to strengthen the Affordable Care Act. We will bring down the cost of prescription drugs not only for some but for all Americans. We fight for a future where every worker has the freedom to organize. And so, when I am president, we will pass the PRO Act and end union busting once and for all.

And I'll remind everybody, on all these bills, we got to elect a Congress who supports that—to be able to actually get that work done.

We fight for a future where every person has the opportunity not just to get by but to get ahead. And so, when I am president, we will continue to build what I call an "opportunity economy" so that every American has an opportunity to own a home, to start a business, to build intergenerational wealth for their family.

We fight for a future where every senior can retire with dignity. And so, when I am president, we will continue to defend Social Security, Medicare, and pensions, just like we have done.

Sixty-four days—sixty-four days—the most important election of our lives and probably one of the most important in the life of our nation.

And here's what I'd say to all the brothers and sisters assembled: We know this is going to be a very tight race to the very end. And I got your back. But I'm telling you, we know how they play. We know what they do.

So, let's not pay too much attention to the polls. Let's know, like labor always does: We are out here running like we are the underdog in this race, because we know what we are fighting for. We know what we stand for, and that's why we know what we fight for.

And we got some hard work ahead of us. But, again, we all like hard work, because hard work is good work. And to do that hard work, I'm going to count on everyone here, all the leaders here, for your work, for your organizing, knocking on doors, and getting folks to the polls.

Because, put bluntly, Michigan, y'all know how to win. You know how to win. You know how to win.

So, today, I ask: Detroit, Michigan, are you ready to have your voices heard? Do we believe in freedom? Do we believe in opportunity? Do we believe in the promise of America? And are we ready to fight for it?

And when we fight—we win. God bless you.

Print Citations

CMS: Harris, Kamala. "When Labor Unions Are Strong, America Is Strong." Speech at Northwestern High School, Detroit, MI, September 2, 2024. In *The Reference Shelf: Representative American Speeches, 2023–2024,* edited by Micah L. Issitt, 165–168. Amenia, NY: Grey House Publishing, 2024.

MLA: Harris, Kamala. "When Labor Unions Are Strong, America Is Strong." Northwestern High School, 2 September 2024, Detroit, MI. Speech. *The Reference Shelf: Representative American Speeches, 2023–2024,* edited by Micah L. Issitt, Grey House Publishing, 2024, pp. 165–168.

APA: Harris, K. (2024). When labor unions are strong, America is strong [Speech]. Northwestern High School, Detroit, MI. In Micah L. Issitt (Ed.), *The reference shelf: Representative American speeches, 2023–2024* (pp. 165–168). Grey House Publishing. (Original work published 2024)

4
International Issues

Netanyahu speaking at a joint session of Congress in July 2024. House Speaker Mike Johnson (left) and Senator Ben Cardin (right) are in the background. Photo by Office of Speaker Mike Johnson, via Wikimedia. [Public Domain.]

An Update on the Crisis in the Middle East

By Joe Biden

"It's time for this war to end and for the day after to begin." President Joe Biden addressed the Israel Crisis in May of 2024. He discussed a ceasefire and peace proposal that had been proposed by the United States with the support of Israeli politicians. By September, Israeli and Hamas leaders had not yet been able to agree on a ceasefire agreement, but US efforts continued, working alongside officials from Egypt and Qatar.

I want to give an update on my efforts to end the crisis in Gaza.

For the past several months, my negotiators of foreign policy, intelligence community, and the like have been relentlessly focused not just on a ceasefire that would inevitably be fragile and temporary but on a durable end to the war. That's been the focus: a durable end to this war.

One that brings all the hostages home, ensures Israel's security, creates a better "day after" in Gaza without Hamas in power, and sets the stage for a political settlement that provides a better future for Israelis and Palestinians alike.

Now, after intensive diplomacy carried out by my team and my many conversations with leaders of Israel, Qatar, and Egypt and other Middle Eastern countries, Israel has now offered a comprehensive new proposal.

It's a roadmap to an enduring ceasefire and the release of all hostages. This proposal has been transmitted by Qatar to Hamas.

Today, I want to lay out its terms for the American citizens and for the world. This new proposal has three phases.

The first phase would last for six weeks. Here's what it would include: a full and complete ceasefire; a withdrawal of Israeli forces from all populated areas of Gaza; a release of a number of hostages—including women, the elderly, the wounded—in exchange for the release of hundreds of Palestinian prisoners. There are American hostages who would be released at this stage, and we want them home.

Additional, some remains of hostages who have been killed would be returned to their families, bringing some degree of closure to their terrible grief.

Palestinians—civilians—would return to their homes and neighborhoods in all areas of Gaza, including in the north.

Delivered on May 31, 2024 at the White House, Washington, DC.

172 International Issues

Humanitarian assistance would surge with 600 trucks carrying aid into Gaza every single day.

With a ceasefire, that aid could be safely and effectively distributed to all who need it. Hundreds of thousands of temporary shelters, including housing units, would be delivered by the international community.

All of that and more would begin immediately.

During the six weeks of phase one, Israel and Hamas would negotiate the necessary arrangements to get to phase two, which is a permanent end to hostilities.

Now, I'll be straight with you. There are a number of details to negotiate to move from phase one to phase two. Israel will want to make sure its interests are protected.

But the proposal says if the negotiations take longer than six weeks for phase one, the ceasefire will still continue as long as negotiations continue.

And the United States, Egypt, and Qatar would work to ensure negotiations keep going—all agreements—until all the agreements are reached and phase two is able to begin.

Then phase two: There would be an exchange for the release of all remaining living hostages, including male soldiers; Israeli forces would withdraw from Gaza; and as long as Hamas lives up to its commitments, a temporary ceasefire would become, in the words of the Israeli proposal, "the cessation of hostilities permanently," end of quote. "Cessation of hostilities permanently."

Finally, in phase three, a major reconstruction plan for Gaza would commence. And any final remains of hostages who have been killed would be returned to their families.

That's the offer that's now on the table and what we've been asking for. It's what we need.

The people of Israel should know they can make this offer without any further risk to their own security because they've devastated Hamas forces over the past eight months. At this point, Hamas no longer is capable of carrying out another October 7th, which [is] one of the Israelis' main objective in this war and, quite frankly, a righteous one.

I know there are those in Israel who will not agree with this plan and will call for the war to continue indefinitely. Some are even in the government coalition. And they've made it clear: They want to occupy Gaza, they want to keep fighting for years, and the hostages are not a priority to them.

Well, I've urged the leadership in Israel to stand behind this deal, despite whatever pressure comes.

And to the people of Israel, let me say this. As someone whose had a lifelong commitment to Israel, as the only American president who has ever gone to Israel in a time of war, as someone who just sent the U.S. forces to directly defend Israel when it was attacked by Iran, I ask you to take a step back and think what will happen if this moment is lost.

We can't lose this moment. Indefinite war in pursuit of an unidentified notion of "total victory" will not bring Israel in—will only bog down Israel in Gaza, draining the economic, military, and human resources, and furthering Israel's isolation in the world.

That will not bring hostages home. That will not bring an enduring defeat of Hamas. That will not bring Israel lasting security.

But a comprehensive approach that starts with this deal will bring hostages home and will lead to a more secure Israel. And once a ceasefire and hostage deal is concluded, it unlocks the possibility of a great deal more progress, including calm along Israel's northern border with Lebanon.

The United States will help forge a diplomatic resolution, one that ensures Israel's security and allows people to safely return to their homes without fear of being attacked.

With a deal, a rebuilding of Gaza will begin [with] Arab nations and the international community, along with Palestinian and Israeli leaders, to get it done in a manner that does not allow Hamas to re-arm.

And the United States will work with our partners to rebuild homes, schools, and hospitals in Gaza to help repair communities that were destroyed in the chaos of war.

And with this deal, Israel could become more deeply integrated into the region, including—it's no surprise to you all—a potential historic normalization agreement with Saudi Arabia. Israel could be part of a regional security network to counter the threat posed by Iran.

All of this progress would make Israel more secure, with Israeli families no longer living in the shadow of a terrorist attack.

And all of this would create the conditions for a different future and a better future for the Palestinian people, one of self-determination, dignity, security, and freedom. This path is available once the deal is struck.

Israel will always have the right to defend itself against the threats to its security and to bring those responsible for October 7th to justice. And the United States will always ensure that Israel has what it needs to defend itself.

If Hamas fails to fulfill its commitments under the deal, Israel can resume military operations. But Egypt and Qatar have assured me and they are continuing to work to ensure that Hamas doesn't do that. And the United States will help ensure that Israel lives up to their obligations as well.

That's what this deal says. That's what it says. And we'll do our part.

This is truly a decisive moment. Israel has made their proposal. Hamas says it wants a ceasefire. This deal is an opportunity to prove whether they really mean it.

Hamas needs to take the deal.

For months, people all over the world have called for a ceasefire. Now it's time to raise your voices and to demand that Hamas come to the table, agrees to this deal, and ends this war that they began.

Of course, there will be differences on the specific details that need to be worked out. That's natural. If Hamas comes to negotiate ready to deal, then Israel negotiations must be given a mandate, the necessary flexibility to close that deal.

The past eight months have marked heartbreaking pain: pain of those whose loved ones were slaughtered by Hamas terrorists on October 7th; hostages and their families waiting in anguish; ordinary Israelis whose lives were forever marked by the shattering event of Hamas's sexual violence and ruthless brutality.

And the Palestinian people have endured sheer hell in this war. Too many innocent people have been killed, including thousands of children. Far too many have been badly wounded.

We all saw the terrible images from the deadly fire in Rafah earlier this week following an Israeli strike targeting Hamas. And even as we work to surge assistance to Gaza, with 1,800 trucks delivering supplies these last five days the humanitarian crisis still remains.

I know this is a subject on which people in this country feel deep, passionate convictions. And so do I. This has been one of the hardest, most complicated problems in the world. There's nothing easy about this—nothing easy about it.

Through it all, though, the United States has worked relentlessly to support Israelis' security, to get humanitarian supplies into Gaza, and to get a ceasefire and a hostage deal to bring this war to an end.

Yesterday, with this new initiative, we've taken an important step in that direction.

And I want to level with you today as to where we are and what might be possible. But I need your help. Everyone who wants peace now must raise their voices and let the leaders know they should take this deal; work to make it real, make it lasting; and forge a better future out of the tragic terror attack and war.

It's time to begin this new stage, for the hostages to come home, for Israel to be secure, for the suffering to stop. It's time for this war to end and for the day after to begin.

Thank you very much.

Print Citations

CMS: Biden, Joe. "An Update on the Crisis in the Middle East." Speech at the White House, Washington, DC, May 31, 2024. In *The Reference Shelf: Representative American Speeches, 2023–2024*, edited by Micah L. Issitt, 171–174. Amenia, NY: Grey House Publishing, 2024.

MLA: Biden, Joe. "An Update on the Crisis in the Middle East." The White House, 31 May 2024, Washington, DC. Speech. *The Reference Shelf: Representative American Speeches, 2023–2024*, edited by Micah L. Issitt, Grey House Publishing, 2024, pp. 171–174.

APA: Biden, J. (2024). An update on the crisis in the Middle East [Speech]. The White House, Washington, DC. In Micah L. Issitt (Ed.), *The reference shelf: Representative American speeches, 2023–2024* (pp. 171–174). Grey House Publishing. (Original work published 2024)

Remarks Following a Meeting with Prime Minister Benjamin Netanyahu of Israel

By Kamala Harris

"Let us all condemn terrorism and violence. Let us all do what we can to prevent the suffering of innocent civilians. And let us condemn antisemitism, Islamophobia, and hate of any kind." Vice President Kamala Harris gave a public address in July of 2024 after meeting with Israeli Prime Minister Benjamin Netanyahu. Harris noted the level of suffering in Gaza due to the Israeli occupation, but also claimed that the United States would continue to ensure Israeli security.

All right. Good afternoon, everybody. Okay. So, I just had a frank and constructive meeting with Prime Minister Netanyahu. I told him that I will always ensure that Israel is able to defend itself, including from Iran and Iran-backed militias, such as Hamas and Hezbollah.

From when I was a young girl collecting funds to plant trees for Israel to my time in the United States Senate and now at the White House, I've had an unwavering commitment to the existence of the state of Israel, to its security, and to the people of Israel.

I've said it many times, but it bears repeating: Israel has a right to defend itself, and how it does so matters.

Hamas is a brutal terrorist organization. On October 7, Hamas triggered this war when it massacred 1,200 innocent people, including 44 Americans. Hamas has committed horrific acts of sexual violence and took 250 hostages.

There are American citizens who remain captive in Gaza: Sagui Dekel-Chen, Hersh Goldberg-Polin, Edan Alexander, Keith Siegel, Omer Neutra. And the remains of American citizens Judy Weinstein, Gad Haggai, and Itay Chen are still being held in Gaza.

I have met with the families of these American hostages multiple times now. And I've told them each time, they are not alone and I stand with them. And President Biden and I are working every day to bring them home.

I also expressed with the prime minister my serious concern about the scale of human suffering in Gaza, including the death of far too many innocent civilians. And I made clear my serious concern about the dire humanitarian situation there, with over 2 million people facing high levels of food insecurity and half a million people facing catastrophic levels of acute food insecurity.

Delivered on July 25, 2024 at the Executive Office Building, Washington, DC.

International Issues

What has happened in Gaza over the past nine months is devastating—the images of dead children and desperate, hungry people fleeing for safety, sometimes displaced for the second, third, or fourth time. We cannot look away in the face of these tragedies. We cannot allow ourselves to become numb to the suffering. And I will not be silent.

Thanks to the leadership of our president, Joe Biden, there is a deal on the table for a ceasefire and a hostage deal. And it is important that we recall what the deal involves.

The first phase of the deal would bring about a full ceasefire, including a withdrawal of the Israeli military from population centers in Gaza. In the second phase, the Israeli military would withdraw from Gaza entirely, and it would lead to a permanent end to the hostilities.

It is time for this war to end and end in a way where Israel is secure, all the hostages are released, the suffering of Palestinians in Gaza ends, and the Palestinian people can exercise their right to freedom, dignity, and self-determination.

There has been hopeful movement in the talks to secure an agreement on this deal. And as I just told Prime Minister Netanyahu, it is time to get this deal done.

So, to everyone who has been calling for a ceasefire and to everyone who yearns for peace, I see you and I hear you.

Let's get the deal done so we can get a ceasefire to end the war. Let's bring the hostages home. And let's provide much-needed relief to the Palestinian people.

And ultimately, I remain committed to a path forward that can lead to a two-state solution. And I know right now it is hard to conceive of that prospect, but a two-state solution is the only path that ensures Israel remains a secure, Jewish, and democratic state and one that ensures Palestinians can finally realize the freedom, security, and prosperity that they rightly deserve.

And I will close with this, then. It is important for the American people to remember the war in Gaza is not a binary issue. However, too often the conversation is binary, when the reality is anything but.

So, I ask my fellow Americans to help encourage efforts to acknowledge the complexity, the nuance, and the history of the region.

Let us all condemn terrorism and violence. Let us all do what we can to prevent the suffering of innocent civilians. And let us condemn antisemitism, Islamophobia, and hate of any kind. And let us work to unite our country. I thank you.

Print Citations

CMS: Harris, Kamala. "Remarks Following a Meeting with Prime Minister Benjamin Netanyahu of Israel." Speech at the Executive Office Building, Washington, DC, July 25, 2024. In *The Reference Shelf: Representative American Speeches, 2023–2024,* edited by Micah L. Issitt, 175–177. Amenia, NY: Grey House Publishing, 2024.

MLA: Harris, Kamala. "Remarks Following a Meeting with Prime Minister Benjamin Netanyahu of Israel." Executive Office Building, 25 July 2024, Washington, DC. Speech. *The Reference Shelf: Representative American Speeches, 2023–2024,* edited by Micah L. Issitt, Grey House Publishing, 2024, pp. 175–177.

APA: Harris, K. (2024). Remarks following a meeting with Prime Minister Benjamin Netanyahu of Israel [Speech]. Executive Office Building, Washington, DC. In Micah L. Issitt (Ed.), *The reference shelf: Representative American speeches, 2023–2024* (pp. 175–177). Grey House Publishing. (Original work published 2024)

We Must Summon the Courage to Stand Up to Wealth and Power and Deliver Justice for People at Home and Abroad

By Bernie Sanders

Bernie Sanders, former presidential candidate and senator for the state of Vermont gave a speech at the 2024 Democratic National Convention in Chicago. Sanders endorsed Kamala Harris, explored the successes of the Biden administration, and called for voters and politicians to address income inequality and injustice.

Thank you. Thank you. My fellow Americans, it is an honor.

It is an honor to be with you tonight because we're laying the groundwork for Kamala Harris to become our next president. And let me tell you why that is so important. I want you all to remember where we were three and a half years ago. We were in the midst of the worst public health crisis in a hundred years and the worst economic downturn since the Great Depression. 3,000 Americans were dying every day and our hospitals were overwhelmed with COVID patients. All across the country, businesses were shutting down. Unemployment was soaring. Workers were losing their health insurance. Schools were closing, state and city budgets were running out of money. People were being evicted from their homes. Children in America were going hungry. That was the reality the Biden-Harris administration faced as they entered the Oval Office, a nation suffering, a nation frightened, and people looking to their government for support and within two months of taking office, our government did respond.

We passed the American Rescue Plan, which provided $1,400 for every man, woman, and child in the working class. We extended and expanded benefits for the unemployed. We provided emergency assistance for small businesses to stay open. We guaranteed healthcare coverage to tens of millions of Americans through one of the largest expansions of Medicaid in history. We provided rent relief and mortgage assistance, which prevented tenants and homeowners from being evicted. We established emergency food programs for hungry children and the elderly, and protected the pensions of millions of union workers and retirees from being slashed by up to 65%. Oh, and by the way, we cut childhood poverty by over 40% through an expanded Childhood Tax Credit. Thank you, President Biden. Thank you, vice President Harris. Thank you, Democratic Congress.

Delivered on August 20, 2024 at the Democratic National Convention, Chicago, IL.

We Must Summon the Courage to Stand Up to Wealth and Power   **179**

Now, I say all of this not to relive that difficult moment, but to make one simple point, when the political will is there, government can effectively deliver for the people of our country. And now we need to summon that will again, because too many of our fellow Americans are struggling every day to just get by, to put food on the table, to pay the rent, and to get the healthcare they need. Brothers and sisters, bottom line, we need an economy that works for all of us, not just the billionaire class. My fellow Americans, when 60% of our people live paycheck to paycheck, the top 1% have never ever had it so good. And these oligarchs, these oligarchs tell us we shouldn't tax the rich, the oligarchs tell us we shouldn't take on price gouging, we shouldn't expand Medicare to cover dental, hearing and vision, and we shouldn't. Social security benefits for struggling seniors.

Well, I've got some bad news for them. That is precisely what we are going to do. And we're going to win this struggle because this is precisely what the American people want from their government. And my friends, at the very top of that to-do list is the need to get big money out of our political process. Billionaires in both parties should not be able to buy elections, including primary elections. For the sake of our democracy, we must overturn the disastrous Citizens United Supreme Court decision and move toward public funding of elections. And let me tell you what else we must do, we need to join the rest of the industrialized world and guarantee healthcare to all people as a human right, not a privilege.

We need to raise the minimum wage to a living wage. We need to pass the PRO Act so that workers can organize an union and gain the decent pay and benefits they deserve. We need to strengthen public education, raise teachers' salaries, and make sure that every American, regardless of income, receives the higher education he or she needs. We need to take on big Pharma and cut our prescription drug cost in half so that we no longer pay any more than other countries. Joe and Kamala made sure that no senior in America pays over $35 a month for insulin. We need to make sure that reality is true for every American. I look forward to working with Kamala and Tim to pass this agenda.

And let us be very clear, this is not a radical agenda. But let me tell you what a radical agenda is, and that is Trump's Project 2025. At a time of massive income and wealth inequality, giving more tax breaks to billionaires is radical. Putting forth budgets to cut Social Security, Medicare, and Medicaid is radical. Letting polluters destroy our planet is radical. And my friends, we won't let that happen.

Fellow Americans, in the last three and a half years working together we have accomplished more than any government since FDR, but much, much more remains to be done. We must summon the courage to stand up to wealth and power and deliver justice for people at home and abroad. Abroad, we must end this horrific war in Gaza, bring home the hostages and demand an immediate ceasefire. At home right here, we must take on big Pharma, big oil, big ag, big tech, and all the other corporate monopolists whose greed is denying progress for working people. On November 5th, let us elect Kamala Harris as our president and let us go forward to create the nation we know we can become. Thank you all very much.

Print Citations

CMS: Sanders, Bernie. "We Must Summon the Courage to Stand Up to Wealth and Power and Deliver Justice to People at Home and Abroad." Speech at the Democratic National Convention, Chicago, IL, August 20, 2024. In *The Reference Shelf: Representative American Speeches, 2023–2024,* edited by Micah L. Issitt, 178–180. Amenia, NY: Grey House Publishing, 2024.

MLA: Sanders, Bernie. "We Must Summon the Courage to Stand Up to Wealth and Power and Deliver Justice to People at Home and Abroad." Democratic National Convention, 20 August 2024, Chicago, IL. Speech. *The Reference Shelf: Representative American Speeches, 2023–2024,* edited by Micah L. Issitt, Grey House Publishing, 2024, pp. 178–180.

APA: Sanders, B. (2024). We must summon the courage to stand up to wealth and power and deliver justice to people at home and abroad [Speech]. Democratic National Convention, Chicago, IL. In Micah L. Issitt (Ed.), *The reference shelf: Representative American speeches, 2023–2024* (pp. 178–180). Grey House Publishing. (Original work published 2024)

Address to the United Nations: On the Cusp of an Historic Saudi-Israel Peace

By Benjamin Netanyahu

"We face such a choice today. It will determine whether we enjoy the blessings of a historic peace of boundless prosperity and hope or suffer the curse of a horrific war, of terrorism and despair." Israeli Prime Minister Benjamin Netanyahu spoke to the United Nations General Assembly in September of 2024. Netanyahu claimed to want peace with the Palestinian people, claimed responsibility for peace agreements with the United Arab Emirates (UAE), Bahrain, Sudan, and Morocco, and said that peace required the Palestinian people to "reconcile themselves" to the Jewish state.

Ladies and gentlemen, over three millennia ago, our great leader Moses addressed the people of Israel as they were about to enter the Promised Land. He said they would find there two mountains facing one another: Mount Gerizim, the site on which a great blessing would be proclaimed, and Mount Ebal, the site of a great curse. Moses said the people's fate would be determined by the choice they made between the blessing and the curse.

That same choice has echoed down the ages not just for the people of Israel but for all humanity.

We face such a choice today. It will determine whether we enjoy the blessings of a historic peace of boundless prosperity and hope or suffer the curse of a horrific war, of terrorism and despair.

When I last spoke at this podium five years ago, I warned about the tyrants of Tehran. They have been nothing but a curse. A curse to their own people, to our region, to the entire world. But at that time, I also spoke about a great blessing that I could see on the horizon.

Here's what I said. Quote: "The common threat of Iran has brought Israel and many Arab states closer than ever before in a friendship that I have not seen in my lifetime."

I said: "The day would soon arrive when Israel would be able to expand peace beyond Egypt and Jordan to other Arab neighbors." End quote.

Now, in countless meetings with world leaders, I made the case that Israel and the Arab states shared many common interests, and that I believed that these many common interests could facilitate a breakthrough for a broader peace in our region.

Delivered on September 22, 2024 at the United Nations General Assembly, New York, NY.

You applaud now, but at the time, many dismissed my optimism as wishful thinking.

Their pessimism was based on a quarter-century of good intentions and failed peacemaking.

Why were these good intentions, why did they always meet failure? Because they were based on one false idea, that unless we first concluded a peace agreement with the Palestinians, no other Arab state would normalize its relations with Israel.

I've long sought to make peace with the Palestinians. But I also believe that we must not give the Palestinians a veto over new peace treaties with Arab states.

The Palestinians could greatly benefit from a broader peace. They should be part of the process, but they should not have a veto over the process. And I also believe that making peace with more Arab states would actually increase the prospects of making peace between Israel and the Palestinians.

See, the Palestinians are only 2% of the Arab world. As long as they believe that the other 98% will remain in a war-like state with Israel, that larger mass, that larger Arab world could eventually choke, dissolve, destroy the Jewish state.

So when the Palestinians see that most of the Arab world has reconciled itself to the Jewish state, they too will be more likely to abandon the fantasy of destroying Israel and finally embrace a path of genuine peace with it.

For years, my approach to peace was rejected by the so-called experts. Well, they were wrong. Under their approach, we didn't forge a single peace treaty for a quarter century.

Yet in 2020, under the approach that I advocated, we tried something different, and in no time we achieved a remarkable breakthrough. We achieved four peace treaties working with the United States. Israel forged four peace agreements in four months with four Arab states: the United Arab Emirates, Bahrain, Sudan and Morocco.

The Abraham Accords were a pivot of history. And today, we all see the blessings of those accords.

Trade and investment with our new peace partners are booming. Our nations cooperate in commerce, energy, water, agriculture, medicine, climate and many, many, other fields.

Close to a million Israelis have visited the United Arab Emirates in the past three years. Every day, Israelis save time and money by doing something they couldn't do for 70 years. They fly over the Arabian Peninsula to destinations in the Gulf, India, the Far East, Australia.

The Abraham Accords ushered in another dramatic change. It brought Arabs and Jews closer together.

We see it in the frequent Jewish weddings in Dubai, in the dedication of a Torah scroll in a synagogue in Bahrain, in the visitors flocking to the museum of Moroccan Judaism in Casablanca. We see it in lessons that are given to Arab students about the Holocaust in the UAE. There's no question, the Abraham Accords heralded the dawn of a new age of peace.

But I believe that we are at the cusp of an even more dramatic breakthrough: an historic peace with Saudi Arabia.

Such a peace will go a long way to ending the Arab-Israeli conflict. It will encourage other Arab states to normalize relations with Israel. It will enhance the prospects of peace with the Palestinians. It will encourage a broader reconciliation between Judaism and Islam, between Jerusalem and Mecca, between the descendants of Isaac and the descendants of Ishmael.

All these are tremendous blessings.

Two weeks ago, we saw another blessing already in sight. In the G20 Conference, President Biden, Prime Minister Modi, and European and Arab leaders announced plans for a visionary corridor that will stretch across the Arabian Peninsula and Israel. It will connect India to Europe with maritime links, rail links, energy pipelines, fiber-optic cables.

This corridor will bypass maritime chokepoints and dramatically lower the costs of goods, communication and energy for over two billion people.

What a historic change for my country! You see, the Land of Israel is situated on the crossroads between Africa, Asia and Europe. And for centuries, my country was repeatedly invaded by empires passing through it in their campaigns of plunder and conquest elsewhere. But today, as we tear down walls of enmity, Israel can become a bridge of peace and prosperity between these continents.

Peace between Israel and Saudi Arabia will truly create a new Middle East.

So understand the magnitude of the transformation that we seek to advance. Let me show you a map of the Middle East in 1948, the year Israel was established.

Here is Israel in 1948. It's a tiny country, isolated, surrounded by a hostile Arab world.

In our first 70 years we made peace with Egypt and Jordan. And then in 2020, we made the Abraham Accords, peace with another four Arab states. Now look at what happens when we make peace between Israel and Saudi Arabia.

The whole Middle East changes. We tear down the walls of enmity. We bring the possibility of peace to this entire region. But we do something else.

You know, a few years ago I stood here with a red marker to show the curse, a great curse, the curse of a nuclear Iran. But today, I bring this marker to show a great blessing. The blessing of a new Middle East, between Israel, Saudi Arabia and our other neighbors.

We will not only bring down barriers between Israel and our neighbors. We'll build a new corridor of peace and prosperity that connects Asia through the UAE, Saudi Arabia, Jordan, Israel, to Europe. This is an extraordinary change, a monumental change, another pivot of history.

As the circle of peace expands, I believe that a real path towards a genuine peace with our Palestinian neighbors can finally be achieved.

But there's a caveat. It has to be said here forcefully. Peace can only be achieved if it is based on truth. It cannot be based on lies. It cannot be based on endless vilification of the Jewish people.

Palestinian leader Mahmoud Abbas must stop spreading the horrible antisemitic conspiracies against the Jewish people and the Jewish state. He recently said that Hitler wasn't an antisemite. You can't make this up. But he did. He said that.

The Palestinian Authority must stop glorifying terrorists. They must stop its ghoulish pay-to-slay policy of giving money to Palestinian terrorists for the murder of Jews. This is all outrageous. It must stop for peace to prevail.

Antisemitism must be rejected wherever it appears, whether on the left or on the right, whether in the halls of universities or in the halls of the United Nations.

For peace to prevail the Palestinians must stop spewing Jew-hatred and finally reconcile themselves to the Jewish state. By that I mean not only to the existence of the Jewish state but to the right of the Jewish people to have a state of their own in their historic homeland, the Land of Israel.

And let me tell you, the people of Israel yearn for a genuine peace. I yearn for such a peace.

As a young soldier over half a century ago, my comrades and I in Israel's Special Forces faced mortal danger on many fronts, on many battlefields. From the warm waters of the Suez Canal to the frozen slopes of Mount Hermon, from the banks of the Jordan River to the tarmac of Beirut airport.

These experiences and other experiences taught me the cost of war.

A fellow soldier was killed next to me. Another died in my arms. I buried my older brother.

Those who have personally suffered the curse of war can best appreciate the blessing of peace. There are many hurdles on the path of peace. There are many hurdles on the extraordinary path to peace that I've just described.

But I am committed to doing everything I can to overcome those hurdles, to forge a better future for Israel and all the peoples in our region.

Two days ago, I discussed this vision of peace with President Biden. We share the same optimism for what can be achieved. And I deeply appreciate his commitment to seize this historic opportunity.

The United States of America is indispensable in this effort. Just as we achieved the Abraham Accords with the leadership of President Trump, I believe we can achieve peace with Saudi Arabia with the leadership of President Biden.

Working together with the leadership of Crown Prince Muhammed Bin Salman, we can shape a future of great blessings for all our peoples.

Now you know, Ladies and Gentlemen, you know there's a fly in this ointment, because rest assured, the fanatics ruling Iran will do everything they can to thwart this historic peace. Iran continues to spend billions to arm its terror proxies. It continues to extend its terror tentacles in the Middle East, Europe, Asia, South America, even North America. They even tried to assassinate the Secretary of State of the United States of America. They even tried to assassinate the National Security Advisor of the United States of America. This tell you all you need to know about Iran's murderous intentions and Iran's murderous nature.

Iran continues to threaten international shipping lanes, hold foreign nationals for ransom and engage in nuclear blackmail. Over the past year, its murderous goons have killed hundreds and arrested thousands of Iran's brave citizens.

Iran's drones and missile program threaten Israel and our Arab neighbors. And Iran's drones have brought and bring death and destruction to innocent people in the Ukraine.

Yet the regime's aggression is largely met by indifference in the international community.

Eight years ago, the Western powers promised that if Iran violated the nuclear deal, the sanctions would be snapped back.

Well, Iran is violating the deal. But the sanctions have not been snapped back. To stop its nuclear ambitions, this policy must change.

Sanctions must be snapped back and above all, Iran must face a credible military threat. (*Note: Netanyahu's office clarified that he misspoke when delivering his address, erroneously referring to a "credible nuclear threat.")

As long as I am prime minister of Israel, I will do everything in my power to prevent Iran from getting nuclear weapons.

Equally, we should support the brave women and men of Iran who despise this regime and yearn for freedom, who've gone out bravely on the sidewalks of Tehran and Iran's other cities and face death.

It is the people of Iran, not their oppressors, who are our real partners for a better future.

Ladies and gentlemen, whether our future will prove to be a blessing or a curse will also depend on how we address perhaps the most consequential development of our time, the rise of artificial intelligence.

The AI revolution is progressing at lightning speed. It took centuries for humanity to adapt to the agricultural revolution.

It took decades to adapt to the industrial revolution.

We may have but a few years to adapt to the AI revolution.

The perils are great and they are before us: the disruption of democracy, the manipulation of minds, the decimation of jobs, the proliferation of crime and the hacking of all the systems that facilitate modern life. Yet even more disturbing, is the potential eruption of AI-driven wars that could achieve an unimaginable scale.

Behind this perhaps looms an even greater threat, once the stuff of science fiction: that self-taught machines could eventually control humans instead of the other way around.

The world's leading nations, however competitive, must address these dangers. We must do so quickly and we must do so together. We must ensure that the promise of an AI utopia does not turn into an AI dystopia.

We have so much to gain. Imagine the blessings of finally cracking the genetic code, extending human life by decades and dramatically reducing the ravages of aging. Imagine healthcare tailored to each individual's genetic composition and predictive medicine that prevents diseases long before they occur.

Imagine robots helping to care for the elderly. Imagine the end of traffic jams with self-driving vehicles on the ground, below the ground and in the air.

Imagine personalized education that cultivates each person's full potential throughout their lifetime. Imagine a world with boundless clean energy and natural resources for all nations. Imagine precision agriculture and automated factories that yield food and goods in an abundance that ends hunger and want.

I know this sounds like a John Lennon song, but it could all happen. Imagine that we can achieve the end of scarcity, something that eluded humanity for all history. It's all within our reach. And here's something else within our reach. With AI we can explore the heavens as never before and extend humanity beyond our blue planet.

For good or bad, the developments of AI will be spearheaded by a handful of nations. And my country Israel is already among them.

Just as Israel's technological revolution provided the world with breathtaking innovations, I am confident that AI developed by Israel will once again help all humanity.

I call upon world leaders to come together to shape the great changes before us, but to do so in a responsible and ethical way.

Our goal must be to ensure that AI brings more freedom and not less, prevents wars instead of starting them, and ensures that people live longer, healthier, more productive and peaceful lives. It's in our reach.

As we harness the powers of AI, let us always remember the irreplaceable value of human intuition and wisdom. Let us cherish and preserve the human capacity for empathy which no machine can replace.

Thousands of years ago, Moses presented the children of Israel with a timeless and universal choice, "Behold, I set before you this day a blessing and a curse." May we choose wisely between the curse and the blessings that stand before us this day. Let us harness our resolve and our courage to stop the curse of a nuclear Iran and roll back its fanaticism and aggression.

Let us bring forth the blessings of a new Middle East that will transform lands once ridden with conflict and chaos into fields of prosperity and peace.

And may we avoid the perils of AI by combining the forces of human and machine intelligence to usher in a brilliant future for our world, in our time and for all time.

Print Citations

CMS: Netanyahu, Benjamin. "Address to the United Nations: On the Cusp of an Historic Saudi-Israel Peace." Speech at the United Nations General Assembly, New York, NY, September 22, 2024. In *The Reference Shelf: Representative American Speeches, 2023–2024*, edited by Micah L. Issitt, 181–187. Amenia, NY: Grey House Publishing, 2024.

MLA: Netanyahu, Benjamin. "Address to the United Nations: On the Cusp of an Historic Saudi-Israel Peace." United Nations General Assembly, 22 September 2024, New York, NY. Speech. *The Reference Shelf: Representative American Speeches, 2023–2024*, edited by Micah L. Issitt, Grey House Publishing, 2024, pp. 181–187.

APA: Netanyahu, B. (2024). Address to the United Nations: On the cusp of an historic Saudi-Israel peace [Speech]. United Nations General Assembly, New York, NY. In Micah L. Issitt (Ed.), *The reference shelf: Representative American speeches, 2023–2024* (pp. 181–187). Grey House Publishing. (Original work published 2024)

Speech to the European Parliament on the Houthi Attacks in the Red Sea

By Josep Borrell

"We are now here to discuss the repeated and unacceptable Houthi attacks on commercial ships in the Red Sea, which violate international law, threaten maritime security and peace in the region, and disrupt global trade." The Commissioner for Jobs and Social rights for the European Union gives a speech to the Diplomatic Service in January of 2024 speaking about Houthi rebel pirates launching attacks on the Red Sea in support of Palestinians during the Israeli occupation.

Madam President, Honourable Members [of the European Parliament],

We are now here to discuss the repeated and unacceptable Houthi attacks on commercial ships in the Red Sea, which violate international law, threaten maritime security and peace in the region, and disrupt global trade. Until today, 28 attacks were carried out by the Houthis since mid-November. The Houthis are presenting their repeated attacks as a support to the Palestinian people, and they have launched some missiles toward Israel. The Houthis, together with Hezbollah and some Iraqi and Syrian militias, are aligned with Hamas.

The EU has continuously condemned those acts and underlined that they must stop, notably through the EU Spokesperson' Statements of 5 and 13 December and through our latest EU27 Statement of 12 January. The EU also called for the immediate release of the "Galaxy Leader" vessel and its 25-member crew, illegally seized on 19 November.

EU services are also following closely the joint military response of the United Kingdom and the United States, members of the 'Prosperity Guardian' Operation, to repeated Houthi attacks against maritime vessels. The United States and the United Kingdom have carried out joint strikes on 11 and 12 January on over 60 targets at 16 sites in Yemen, with the support of Australia, Bahrain, Canada and the Netherlands, as a response to repeated and escalating Houthi attacks in the Red Sea, notably the complex attack of 9 January following repeated messages from the international community.

The EU continues actively engaging and coordinating with partners in all diplomatic fora, to counter the Houthi threats to commercial vessels and find effective solutions. The High Representative, on behalf of the EU and its Member States, issued a joint statement, published last Friday welcoming the 10 January UN Security Council resolution 2722. The UN Security [Council] resolution

---

Delivered on January 15, 2024 at the European Parliament, Strasbourg, France.

recognises that States are entitled to defend themselves against the attacks against their vessels—[that are] in perfect contradiction, by the way, of international law.

The EUNAVFOR Operation Atalanta shares maritime awareness with the multi-nation Operation "Prosperity Guardian" from its operations in the Red Sea and the Gulf of Aden. Further options will be discussed at the level of the European Council concerning the EU maritime response.

However, it is unlikely that the Houthis will be deterred immediately given the international visibility they have enjoyed with these actions. Houthi leaders have already indicated they will continue their attacks as long as the situation in Gaza remains. They have already resumed attacks with a missile fired towards US forces on 14 January.

The last point of concern is the impact these developments in the Red Sea can have on peace efforts in Yemen which had reached a new positive phase on 23 December with the UN's takeover of the peace process following a year of Saudi-Houthi backchannel talks.

Closing Remarks

The debate today illustrates the importance and the complexity of the situation in the Red Sea and the Gulf region, as a whole, and the challenges that the European Union faces indeed in relation to this conflict but also to other conflicts.

The European Union is actively working on solutions to restore maritime security in the Red Sea.

This is an international problem that requires an international solution and coordination.

As you asked me about what the European Union is preparing in relation to the EUNAVFOR Operation Atalanta, further options concerning the European Union's maritime response will be discussed at Council level based on proposals presented by the High Representative.

The European Union is engaging with partners in different diplomatic fora. To protect navigational freedoms and maritime security, the European Union considers ways to enhance its presence, assets, and capacity of actions in the Red Sea and beyond.

It is too early to evaluate the impact of the Houthis attacks and United States/United Kingdom retaliation on the discussions concerning an internal cease-fire in Yemen. The European Union will continue to support UN Special Envoy [for Yemen, Hans] Grundberg's work and the UN-steered peace process leading to a final comprehensive and inclusive peace deal, including a permanent nation-wide ceasefire.

And just one personal remark: I am a bit surprised that those who are bombing every night civilians, killing civilians, destroying infrastructures, houses, apartments, that they are in the full front to condemn what finally is a military operation against terrorist attacks against the peaceful vessels.

Thank you.

190 International Issues

Print Citations

CMS: Borrell, Josep. "Houthi Attacks in the Red Sea." Speech at the European Parliament, Strasbourg, France, January 15, 2024. In *The Reference Shelf: Representative American Speeches, 2023–2024,* edited by Micah L. Issitt, 188–190. Amenia, NY: Grey House Publishing, 2024.

MLA: Borrell, Josep. "Houthi Attacks in the Red Sea." European Parliament, 15 January 2024, Strasbourg, France. Speech. *The Reference Shelf: Representative American Speeches, 2023–2024,* edited by Micah L. Issitt, Grey House Publishing, 2024, pp. 188–190.

APA: Borrell, J. (2024). Houthi attacks in the Red Sea [Speech]. European Parliament, Strasbourg, France. In Micah L. Issitt (Ed.), *The reference shelf: Representative American speeches, 2023–2024* (pp. 188–190). Grey House Publishing. (Original work published 2024)

NATO Secretary Warns China That It Must Stop Financially Supporting Russia's Invasion of Ukraine

By Jens Stoltenberg

"What happens in Ukraine, in Europe matters for Asia and what happens in Asia matters for Europe." North Atlantic Treaty Organization (NATO) Secretary-General Jens Stoltenberg spoke at a NATO summit about the role of other authoritarian governments supporting Russia's invasion of Ukraine. Stoltenberg labeled China and North Korea as "decisive enablers" of Russia's Ukraine invasion and highlighted the importance of Ukrainian independence to global security.

Speaker 1: Secretary, great to sit down with you. Thank you so much. I want to ask you first of all about this piece of news that we saw that Russian President Vladimir Putin, is going to travel to North Korea for a two-day visit. And a Kremlin aide has been quoted as saying that the visit would include a partnership agreement which would need to include security issues. What do you make of this?

Jens Stoltenberg: It demonstrates how Russia now is aligning more and more with authoritarian leaders, Iran, Beijing, but also with North Korea. And North Korea has delivered more than 1 million shells for artillery to Russia. North Korea is helping Russia to conduct a war of aggression against Ukraine. And in return, Russia is delivering technology for their missile and nuclear programs.

Speaker 1: Will there be a specific NATO response to whatever this agreement looks like?

Jens Stoltenberg: Well, our response has been clear all the way that this just shows how dependent Russia now is on other authoritarian powers, but also how Russia is violating UN Security Council agreements on not supporting North Korea's missile and nuclear programs. It shows that security is not regional. What happens in Ukraine, in Europe matters for Asia and what happens in Asia matters for Europe.

Speaker 1: On that, you spoke to The Telegraph over the weekend about NATO's nuclear posture. I know that it hasn't broadly changed, but you did say it's important to "communicate the direct message that we of course are a nuclear

---

Delivered on June 17, 2024 at the Wilson Center Auditorium, Ronald Reagan Building and International Trade Center, Washington, DC.

alliance." Is there a specific threat here that you were referring to that you believe NATO needs to counter?

Jens Stoltenberg: Now this is a general message that NATO remains a nuclear alliance. That's our ultimate deterrence. The purpose of NATO is not to fight the war. The purpose of NATO is to prevent the war, to ensure that any potential adversary knows that an attack on NATO will trigger a response from the whole alliance. And therefore we need also the ultimate security guarantees that the nuclear weapons provide.

Speaker 1: Regardless of Kremlin, the spokesperson, Dmitry Peskov, said your words were "nothing else but an escalation." What's your response?

Jens Stoltenberg: Well, this is nothing new. NATO has had a nuclear deterrent since we were founded and we are transparent about this. There are no changes. This is a—

Speaker 1: It's not an escalation?

Jens Stoltenberg: Not at all. It is Russia that is escalating by partly having a lot of dangerous nuclear rhetoric, but also by actually threatening to use nuclear weapons in Ukraine. Nuclear weapons shall never be used in a nuclear war, should never be fought and can never be won. And that has to be fully understood in Moscow.

Speaker 1: I want to ask you about something you mentioned in your comments today. You said allies need to impose a cost on China unless its support for Russia stops. What do you think that cost should look like?

Jens Stoltenberg: Well, that's a bit too early to say, but the reality is that China is trying to get it both ways. China's propping up the Russian war economy. They are sharing a lot of technologies, microelectronics, which are key for Russia to build missiles, weapons they use against Ukraine. But at the same time, China tries to maintain normal economic relationships with European and NATO allies.

Speaker 1: You think there should be sanctions perhaps?

Jens Stoltenberg: At some stage we should consider some kind of economic cost if China doesn't change their behavior because now China is the main supporter of Russia's war effort, war aggression against Ukraine, the biggest war in Europe since the Second World War. And at the same time, they're trying to have normal relationship with European allies and this cannot work in the long run.

Speaker 1: A quick follow up on that. Have you spoke to NATO member states about possible sanctions, what that cost could look like?

Jens Stoltenberg: Well, this is an ongoing conversation among NATO allies on how to deal with the security consequences or the fact that China is propping up Russia's war effort in Ukraine. It's not for NATO to make decisions on sanctions as that's for individual allies, the European and US. But of course, the discussion about what are the consequences for China if they continue to provide support, that's something that goes on among NATO allies.

Speaker 1: Another point of news from NATO. On Friday, NATO agreed to play a bigger role in coordinating weapons deliveries. And you said it would put "our support for Ukraine on a firmer footing for years to come." Is this a direct response to concerns about a change in the White House after November?

Jens Stoltenberg: Well, what we have seen is that NATO allies have provided unprecedented support Ukraine, but at the same time, this winter we saw serious delays and gaps in our support. And we need to do whatever we can to ensure that we prevent those kind of gaps in the future. Because we know that the stronger our support to Ukraine, the sooner the war can end because the quicker President Putin will understand that he cannot wait us out. And therefore, I hope that allies can agree a more long-term pledge supported to Ukraine and also to give NATO a stronger role in providing that support.

Speaker 1: But Donald Trump, the former president, doesn't agree. And he said over the weekend that the scale of US support for Ukraine is too much. And he called President Zelenskyy the greatest salesman of all time. And he said, "He just left four days ago with $60 billion and he gets home and he announces that he needs another 60 billion. It never ends." Do you have a response to that?

Jens Stoltenberg: Well, I strongly believe that it will not be in the security interest of the United States if President Putin wins in Ukraine because that will send a message to him. But also to President Xi that when they violate a national law, when they invade another country, they get what they want. This is not only about Ukraine, it's also about sending a message to President Xi that he shouldn't use military force against Taiwan or in any way in the Asia-Pacific. Therefore, it is in the US security interest to ensure that Ukraine prevails. We have to remember that European allies are really matching what the US is doing. It's not the US doing this alone. European allies are providing as much military support to Ukraine as to United States.

Speaker 1: You also said in your remarks today that NATO will continue to bring Ukraine closer to membership so when the time is right, it can join without delay. Is there any indication of when that time would be? Because Ukraine is interested obviously in joining the alliance as soon as possible.

Jens Stoltenberg: I'm not able to say when that decision will be taken because to be invited to NATO, we need not the majority of NATO allies to agree, but we

194 International Issues

need all allies. We need consensus. But in the meantime, we are building a bridge. We are moving Ukraine closer to a membership, not least by providing them military support to ensure that they have the NATO standards, the NATO doctrines. And are more and more what we call interoperable with NATO so when the time is right, we can make Ukraine a member of the alliance straight away.

Speaker 1: Looking ahead to the summit that will be held here in Washington in July, what are you hoping will be reached at this summit?

Jens Stoltenberg: That we are sending a very clear message to Moscow that we are supporting Ukraine for long haul and also that we agree a long-term pledge support, but also a stronger NATO role in providing the support because that will help to convince Moscow that they have to sit down and agree just a peaceful solution to this war that ensures that Ukraine can continue as a sovereign independent nation in Europe.

Speaker 1: Moscow has given no indication it's willing to sit down or even interested in that?

Jens Stoltenberg: No, and that's the problem because Moscow believes that if they just wait a year or two, then they will wait us out and then they will get what they want. We need to convey to them that they cannot wait us out. We had to convey a very long-term commitment. And by conveying a long-term commitment to Ukraine that can help to end this war soon. The paradox is the longer we can commit the stronger support to Ukraine, the sooner we can have an end to the war.

Speaker 1: Mr. Secretary, thank you so much for the conversation.

Jens Stoltenberg: Thanks so much for having me.

Print Citations

CMS: Stoltenberg, Jens. "NATO Secretary Says West Must 'Impose a Cost' on China for Financially Supporting Russia's Invasion of Ukraine." Press conference at the Wilson Center Auditorium, Ronald Reagan Building and International Trade Center, Washington, DC, June 17, 2024. In *The Reference Shelf: Representative American Speeches, 2023–2024*, edited by Micah L. Issitt, 191–194. Amenia, NY: Grey House Publishing, 2024.

MLA: Stoltenberg, Jens. "NATO Secretary Says West Must 'Impose a Cost' on China for Financially Supporting Russia's Invasion of Ukraine." The Wilson Center Auditorium, Ronald Reagan Building and International Trade Center, 17 June 2024, Washington, DC. Press conference. *The Reference Shelf: Representative American Speeches, 2023–2024*, edited by Micah L. Issitt, Grey House Publishing, 2024, pp. 191–194.

APA: Stoltenberg, J. (2024). NATO secretary says West must "impose a cost" on China for financially supporting Russia's invasion of Ukraine [Press conference]. The Wilson Center Auditorium, Ronald Reagan Building and International Trade Center, Washington, DC. In Micah L. Issitt (Ed.), *The reference shelf: Representative American speeches, 2023–2024* (pp. 191–194). Grey House Publishing. (Original work published 2024)

Statement on Russia's Aerial Assault on Ukraine's Energy Grid

By Joe Biden

"Let me be clear: Russia will never succeed in Ukraine, and the spirit of the Ukrainian people will never be broken." President Joe Biden delivered a public address in August of 2024 after Russian aerial attacks targeted Ukraine infrastructure and the Ukrainian power system. Biden detailed some of the history of the Russian invasion of Ukraine and discussed the US commitment to protecting Ukraine against continued Russian hostility.

Earlier today, Russia launched waves of missiles and drones against Ukrainian cities and energy infrastructure. Ukrainian officials report that this outrageous attack resulted in the deaths of Ukrainian civilians and targeted more than two dozen critical energy sites. I condemn, in the strongest possible terms, Russia's continued war against Ukraine and its efforts to plunge the Ukrainian people into darkness. Let me be clear: Russia will never succeed in Ukraine, and the spirit of the Ukrainian people will never be broken.

The United States will continue to lead a coalition of more than 50 countries in support of Ukraine. This coalition is providing Ukraine with critically needed military equipment, including air defense systems and interceptors. As I announced at the NATO Summit in July, the United States and our allies have provided Ukraine with the equipment for five additional strategic air defense systems, and I have re-prioritized U.S. air defense exports so they are sent to Ukraine first. The United States also is surging energy equipment to Ukraine to repair its systems and strengthen the resilience of Ukraine's energy grid.

As I told President Zelenskyy on August 23, U.S. support for Ukraine is unshakable. Since February 2022, the people of Ukraine have courageously defended against Russia's invasion, retaking more than half the territory Russian forces seized in the initial days of the war. Ukraine remains a free, sovereign and independent nation, and Ukrainian forces are fighting every day to defend their homeland and their freedom. The United States will stand with the people of Ukraine until they prevail.

Delivered on August 26, 2024 at the White House, Washington, DC.

196 International Issues

Print Citations

CMS: Biden, Joe. "Statement on Russia's Aerial Assault on Ukraine's Energy Grid." Speech at the White House, Washington, DC, August 26, 2024. In *The Reference Shelf: Representative American Speeches, 2023–2024,* edited by Micah L. Issitt, 195–196. Amenia, NY: Grey House Publishing, 2024.

MLA: Biden, Joe. "Statement on Russia's Aerial Assault on Ukraine's Energy Grid." The White House, 26 August 2024, Washington, DC. Speech. *The Reference Shelf: Representative American Speeches, 2023–2024,* edited by Micah L. Issitt, Grey House Publishing, 2024, pp. 195–196.

APA: Biden J. (2024). Statement on Russia's aerial assault on Ukraine's energy grid [Speech]. The White House, Washington, DC. In Micah L. Issitt (Ed.), *The reference shelf: Representative American speeches, 2023–2024* (pp. 195–196). Grey House Publishing. (Original work published 2024)

Address on Attempted Assassination of Trump: We Cannot Go Down This Road

By Joe Biden

"While we may disagree, we are not enemies, we're neighbors, we're friends, coworkers, citizens, and most importantly, we're fellow Americans. We must stand together." President Joe Biden delivered a national address from the White House on July 14, 2024, after the attempted assassination of Donald Trump. Biden called on all Americans to abandon caustic divisions and to come together to oppose violence and gave information on the crime available at the time.

My fellow Americans. I want to speak to you tonight about the need for us to lower the temperature in our politics and to remember while we may disagree, we are not enemies, we're neighbors, we're friends, coworkers, citizens, and most importantly, we're fellow Americans. We must stand together. Yesterday's shooting at Donald Trump's rally in Pennsylvania calls on all of us to take a step back, take stock of where we are, how we go forward from here. Thankfully, former Trump is not seriously injured. I spoke with him last night and I'm grateful he's doing well and Jill and I keep him and his family in our prayers. We also extend our deepest condolences to the family of the victims who was killed. Corey was a husband, a father, a volunteer firefighter, a hero, sheltering his family from those bullets, we should all hold his family and all those injured in our prayers.

Earlier today, I spoke about an ongoing investigation. We do not know the motive of the shooter yet. We don't know his opinions or affiliations. We don't know whether he had help or support or if he communicated with anyone else. Law enforcement professionals, as I speak, are investigating those questions. Tonight, I want to speak to what we do know. A former president was shot, an American citizen killed while simply exercising his freedom to support the candidate of his choosing. We cannot, we must not go down this road in America. We've traveled before throughout our history, violence has never been the answer. Whether it's with members of Congress and both parties being targeted and shot, or a violent mob attacking the capitol on January 6th, or brutal attack on the spouse of former speaker of the house, Nancy Pelosi, or information and intimidation on election officials, or the kidnapping plot against the sitting governor or an attempted assassination on Donald Trump, there's no place in America for this kind of violence or for any violence ever, period. No exceptions.

Delivered on July 14, 2024 at the White House, Washington, DC.

We can't allow this violence to be normalized. The political record in this country has gotten very heated. It's time to cool it down. We all have a responsibility to do that. Yes, we have deeply felt strong disagreements. The stakes in this election are enormously high. I've said it many times that the choice that we make in this election is going to shape the future of America and the world for decades to come. I believe that with all my soul, I know that millions of my fellow Americans believe it as well, and some have a different view as to the direction our country should take. Disagreement is inevitable in American democracy. It's part of human nature, but politics must never be a little battlefield and God forbid, a killing field.

I believe politics ought to be an arena for peaceful debate, to pursue justice, to make decisions guided by the Declaration of Independence in our constitution. We stand for an America not of extremism and fury, but of decency and grace. All of us now face the time of testing as the election approaches and the higher the stakes, the more fervent the passions become. This places an added burden on each of us to ensure that no matter how strong our convictions, we must never descend into violence. Republican convention will start tomorrow. I have no doubt they'll criticize my record and offer their own vision for this country. I'll be traveling this week making the case for our record and the vision, my vision of the country, our vision. I'll continue to speak out strongly for our democracy, stand up for our constitution and the rule of law to call for action at the battle box, no violence on our streets. That's how democracy should work. We debate and disagree. We compare and contrast the character of the candidates, the records, the issues, the agenda, the vision for America.

But in America, we resolve our difference at the battle box. That's how we do it at the battle box, not with bullets. The power to change America should always rest in the hands of the people not in the hands of a would-be assassin. The path forward through a competing visions of the campaign should always be resolved peacefully, not through acts of violence. We're blessed to live in the greatest country on earth, and I believe that with every soul, every power of my being. So tonight I'm asking every American to recommit to make America... Think about it, what's made America so special. Here in America, everyone wants to be treated with dignity and respect and hate must have no safe harbor. Here in America. We need to get out of our silos where we only listen to those with whom we agree, we're misinformation is rampant, where foreign actors fan the flames of our division to shape the outcomes consistent with their interests, not ours. Let's remember here in America, our unity is the most elusive of goals right now.

Nothing is more important for us now than standing together. We can do this. From the beginning. Our founders understood the power of passion, so they created a democracy that gave reason and balance a chance to prevail over a brute force. That's the America we must be. An American democracy where arguments are made in good faith. An American democracy, where the rule of law is respected. An American democracy where decency, dignity, fair play aren't just quaint notions, but living, breathing realities. We owe that to those who come before us, to those who gave their lives in this country. We owe that to ourselves. We owe it to our children and our grandchildren. Look, let's never lose sight of who we are. Let's remember, we are the United States of America. There is nothing, nothing, nothing beyond our capacity when we do it together. God bless you all and may God protect our troops.

Print Citations

CMS: Biden, Joe. "Address on the Attempted Assassination of Trump: We Cannot Go Down This Road." Speech at the White House, Washington, DC, July 14, 2024. In *The Reference Shelf: Representative American Speeches, 2023–2024,* edited by Micah L. Issitt, 197–199. Amenia, NY: Grey House Publishing, 2024.

MLA: Biden, Joe. "Address on the Attempted Assassination of Trump: We Cannot Go Down This Road." The White House, 14 July 2024, Washington, DC. Speech. *The Reference Shelf: Representative American Speeches, 2023–2024,* edited by Micah L. Issitt, Grey House Publishing, 2024, pp. 197–199.

APA: Biden, J. (2024). Address on the attempted assassination of Trump: We cannot go down this road [Speech]. The White House, Washington, DC. In Micah L. Issitt (Ed.), *The reference shelf: Representative American speeches, 2023–2024* (pp. 197–199). Grey House Publishing. (Original work published 2024)

5
2024 Commencement Speeches

Biden speaks at a rally in Maryland for gubernatorial candidate Wes Moore, November 7, 2022. Photo by Elvert Barnes, CC BY-SA 2.0, via Wikimedia.

Commencement Speech to the Morehouse College Class of 2024

By Joe Biden

"It's natural to wonder if democracy you hear about actually works for you." President Joe Biden delivered the commencement speech at Morehouse College, a private, historically black university in Atlanta, Georgia. Biden discussed faith, the importance of family support, and the relationship between democracy and racial justice.

Thank you. Thank you, thank you, thank you. President Thomas, faculty, staff, alumni, and a special thanks... I'll ask all the folks who helped you get here. Your mothers, fathers, grandmothers, grandfathers. All those who got you here, all the way in the back, please, parents, grandparents, all who helped, stand up because we owe you a debt of gratitude. All the family.

That is not hyperbole. A lot of you, like my family, had to make significant sacrifices to get your kids to school. It mattered. It mattered a lot. And the friends of Morehouse and the Morehouse men of class of 2024, I got more Morehouse men in the White House telling me what to do than I know what to do. You all think I'm kidding, don't you? You know I'm not. And it's the best thing that's happened to me. Scripture says, "The prayers of a righteous man availeth much." In Augusta, Georgia, a righteous man, once enslaved, set foot for freedom.

The story goes, he feared no evil. He walked through the valley of the shadow of death on his way north to free soil in Philadelphia. A Baptist minister, he walked with faith in his soul, power and the steps of his feet, to glory. But after the Union won the war, he knew his prayers availed him freedom that was not his alone. And so this righteous man, Richard Coulter returned home, his feet weary, his spirit in no ways tired. 157 years ago, you all know the story but the rest of the world doesn't and should. In the basement of a Baptist church in Augusta, he and two other ministers, William Jefferson White and Edmund Turney, planted the seeds of something revolutionary, and it was at the time: a school. A school to help formerly-enslaved men entered in the ministry, where education would be the great equalizer from slavery to freedom. An institution of higher learning that would become Morehouse College.

I don't know any other college in America that has that tradition, that consequence. To the class of 2024, you join, as you know, a sacred tradition. An education makes you free and a Morehouse education makes you fearless. I mean it. Visionary, exceptional. Congratulations. You are Morehouse men. God love you.

Delivered on May 19, 2024 at Morehouse College, Atlanta, GA.

And again, I thank your families and your friends who helped you get here, because they made sacrifices for you as well. This graduation day is a day for generations. A day of joy. A day earned, not given.

We gather on this Sunday morning because if we were in church perhaps we would read this reflection. It would be a reflection about resurrection and redemption. Remember, Jesus was buried on Friday and it was Sunday, on Sunday, he rose again.

But we don't talk enough about Saturday when his disciples felt all hope was lost. In our lives and the lives of the nation, we have those Saturdays to bear witness the day before glory. Seeing people's pain and not looking away. But what work is done on Saturday to move pain to purpose? How can faith get a man, get a nation through what was to come?

Here's what my faith has taught me: I was the first Biden to ever graduate from college, taking out loans, my dad and my... all through school to get me there. My junior year, spring break, I fell in love at first sight, literally. The woman I adored. I graduated from law school in her hometown and I got married and took a job at a law firm in my hometown, Wilmington, Delaware. But then everything changed.

One of my heroes, and he was my hero, a Baptist minister, a Morehouse man, Dr. Martin Luther King. In April of my law school graduation year, he was murdered, my city of Wilmington, and we were, to our great shame, a slave state and we were segregated. Delaware erupted into flames when he was assassinated, literally. We're the only city in America where the National Guard patrolled every street corner for nine full months with drawn bayonets. The longest stretch of any American city since the Civil War. Dr. King's legacy had a profound impact on me and my generation, whether you're black or white.

I left the fancy law firm. I had just joined and decided to become a public defender and then a county councilman, working to change our state's politics, to embrace the cause of civil rights. The Democratic Party in Delaware was a southern Democratic Party at the time. We wanted to change it to become a northeastern Democratic Party. Then we were trying to get someone to run for the United States Senate, the year Nixon ran. I was 29 years of age. I had no notion of running.

I loved reading about, everybody knew I was going to run. I didn't know I was going to run. When a group of senior members of the Democratic Party came to me, they couldn't find anybody to run and said, "You should run." Nixon won my state by 60% of the vote. We won by 3,100 votes. We won by the thinnest of margins, but with a broad coalition, including students from the best HBCU in America, Delaware State University. You guys are good but they got me elected. All y'all think I'm kidding. I'm not kidding.

But by Christmas I was a newly-elected senator hiring staff in Washington D.C. when I got a call from the first responders, my fire department in my hometown, that forever altered my life. They put a young woman first responder on the line to say, "There's an automobile accident. A tractor trailer hit your wife's car

Commencement Speech to the Morehouse College Class of 2024 **205**

while she was Christmas shopping with your three children." And poor woman, she just blurted out, she said, "Your wife and daughter are killed." My 13-month-old daughter. "They're dead. And your almost three-year-old and four-year-old sons are badly injured. We're not sure they're going to make it, either." I rushed from Washington to their bedside. I wanted to pray but I was so angry. I was angry at God. I was angry at the world.

I had the same pain 43 years later when that four-year-old boy who survived was a grown man and a father himself lying in another hospital bed at Walter Reed Hospital having contracted stage four glioblastoma because he was a year in Iraq as a major and won the Bronze star living next to a burn pit. Cancer took his last breath. In this walk of life you can understand, you come to understand that we don't know where or what fate will bring you, or when.

We also know we don't walk alone. When you've been a beneficiary of the compassion of your family, your friends, even strangers, you know how much the compassion matters. I've learned there was no easy optimism but by faith, by faith we can find redemption. I was a single father for five years. No man deserves one great love, let alone two. My youngest brother was a hell of an athlete. Did a great thing. He introduced me to a classmate of his. Said, "You'll love her. She doesn't like politics."

But all kidding aside, until I met Jill, who healed the family in all the broken places. Our family became my redemption. Many of you have gone through similar and even worse things, but you lean on others, they lean on you, and together you keep the faith in a better day tomorrow, but it's not easy. I know four years ago, as some of your speakers have already mentioned, it felt like one of those Saturdays. The pandemic robbed you of so much. Some of you lost loved ones, mothers, fathers, brothers, sisters who aren't able to be here to celebrate with you today. You missed your high school graduation. You started college just as George Floyd was murdered, and there was a reckoning on race.

It's natural to wonder if democracy you hear about actually works for you. What is democracy? If black men are being killed in the street, what is democracy? The trail of broken promises still leave black communities behind. What is democracy if you have to be 10 times better than anyone else to get a fair shot? And most of all, what does it mean, as we've heard before, to be a black man who loves his country even if it doesn't love him back in equal measure?

When I sit behind the Resolute desk in the Oval Office in front of the fireplace across from my desk I have two busts, one of Dr. King and one of Bobby Kennedy. And I often find myself looking at those busts, making decisions. I ask myself, are we living up to what we say we are as a nation? To end racism and poverty, to deliver jobs and justice, to restore our leadership in the world? I look down and see the rosary on my wrist that was that of my late sun, that he had on him when he died at Walter Reed, and I was with him.

And I ask myself, "What would he say?" I know the answer because he told me in his last days. My son knew the days were numbered. The last conversation was, "Dad, I'm not afraid but I'm worried. I'm worried you're going to give up when I go. You're going to give up." We have an expression in the Biden family. When you want someone to know, give your word, you say, "Look at me." He was lying and he said, "Look at me, dad. Look at me." He said, "Give me your word. Give me your word as my father that you will not quit. That you will stay engaged. Promise me, dad. Stay engaged. Promise me. Promise me." I wrote a book called Promise Me, Dad not for the public at large, although a lot of people would end up buying it. It's for my grandchildren or great-grandchildren to know who Bo Biden was.

The rosary on my wrist, the busts in my office remind me that faith asks you to hold onto hope, to move heaven and earth to make better days. Well, that's my commitment to you. To show you democracy, democracy, democracy is still the way. If black men are being killed in the street, we bear witness. For me, that means to call out the poison of white supremacy, to root out systemic racism. I stood up for George Floyd's family to help create a country where we don't need to have that talk with your son or grandson as they get pulled over.

Instead of a trail of broken promises, we're investing more money than ever in black families and black communities. We're reconnecting black neighborhoods cut off by old highways and decades of disinvestment when no one cared about the community. We've delivered checks in pockets to reduce black child poverty. The lowest rate in history. Removing every lead pipe in America so every child can drink clean water without fear of brain damage, and they can't afford to remove the lead pipes themselves. We're delivering affordable high-speed internet so no child has to sit in their parent's car or do their homework in a parking lot outside of McDonald's.

Instead of forcing you to prove you're 10 times better, we're breaking down doors so you have 100 times more opportunities. Good-paying jobs you can raise a family on in your neighborhood. Capital to start small business and loans to buy homes. Health insurance, prescription drugs, housing that's more affordable and accessible. I've walked the picket line in defense of the rights of workers.

I'm relieving the burden of student debt, many of you have already had the benefit of it, so I can chase your dream and grow the economy. And the Supreme Court told me I couldn't. I found two other ways to do it.

And we're able to do it because it grows the economy. And I, In addition to the original $7 billion investment in HBCUs, I'm investing $16 billion more dollars more in our history, because you're vital to our nation. Most HBCUs don't have the endowments. The jobs of the future require sophisticated laboratories, sophisticated opportunities on campus. We're opening doors so you can walk into a life of generational wealth, to be providers and leaders of your families and communities.

Today, record numbers of black Americans have jobs, health insurance and, more than ever, democracy is also about hearing and heeding your generation's call to a community free of gun violence and a planet free of climate crisis, and showing your power to change the world. But I also know some of you ask, what is democracy? We can't stop wars that break out and break our hearts. In a democracy we debate and dissent about America's role in the world.

I want to say this very clearly: I support peaceful, nonviolent protest. Your voices should be heard, and I promise you I hear them. I determine to make my administration look like America. I have more African-Americans in high places, including on the court, than any president in American history because I need the input. What's happening in Gaza and Israel is heartbreaking. Hamas is vicious, attacking Israel, killing innocent lives and holding people hostage. I was there nine days after, was sent pictures of tying a mother and a daughter with a rope, pouring kerosene on them, burning them. Watching as they die. Innocent Palestinians caught in the middle of all this. Men, women, and children killed or displaced, in desperate need of water, food, and medicine. It's a humanitarian crisis in Gaza. That's why I've called for an immediate ceasefire. An immediate ceasefire. Stop the fighting. Bring the hostages home. And I've been working on a deal as we speak. Working around the clock to lead an international effort to get more aid into Gaza, rebuild Gaza.

I'm also working around the clock for more than just one ceasefire. I'm working to bring the region together. I'm working to build a lasting, durable peace because the question is, and you see what's going on in Israel today, what after? What after Hamas? What happens then? What happens in Gaza? What rights do the Palestinian people have? I'm working to make sure we finally get a two-state solution. The only solution. The two people live in peace with security and dignity.

This is one of the hardest, most complicated problems in the world, and there's nothing easy about it. I know it angers and frustrates many of you, including my family, but most of all I know it breaks your heart. It breaks mine as well. Leadership is about fighting through the most intractable problems. It's about challenging anger, frustration, and heartbreak to find a solution. It's about doing what you believe is right even when it's hard and lonely.

You're all future leaders. Every one of you graduating today, and that's not hyperbole. You're future leaders, all of you. You'll face complicated, tough moments. In these moments, you'll listen to others but you'll have to decide guided by knowledge, conviction, principle, and your own moral compass. The desire to know what freedom is, what it can be is the heart and soul of why this college is founded in the first place.

Proving that a free nation is born in the hearts of men, spellbound by freedom. That's the magic of Morehouse. That's the magic of America. But let's be clear, what happens to you and your family when old ghosts and new garments seize power? Extremists come for the freedoms you thought belonged to you and everyone. Today in Georgia they won't allow water to be available to you while you wait in line to vote in an election. What in the hell is that all about?

I'm serious. Think about it. And then the constant attacks on black election workers who count your vote. Insurrectionists who storm the Capitol with Confederate flags are called patriots by some. Not in my house. Black police officers, black veterans protecting the Capitol were called another word, as you'll recall. They also say out loud, these other groups, "Immigrants poison the blood of our country," Like the grand wizard and fascists said in the past. But you know and I know we all bleed the color. In America we're all created equal.

Extremists close the doors of opportunity, strike down affirmative action, attack the values of diversity, equality, and inclusion. I never thought, when I was graduating in 1968 as your honoree just was, we talked about, I never thought I'd be a president in a time when there's a national effort to ban books. Not to write history but to erase history. They don't see you in the future of America, but they're wrong. To me we make history, not erase it. We know black history is American history.

Many of you graduates don't know me, but check my records. You'll know what I'm saying. I mean from my gut. We know black men are going to help lead us to the future. Black men from this class in this university.

And graduates, this is what we're up against: extremist forces aligned against the meaning and message of Morehouse. And they peddle a fiction, a caricature of what being a man is about. Tough talk, using power, bigotry. Their idea of being a man is toxic. I ran them all the time when I was younger. I don't want to get started.

But that's not you, it's not us. You all know and demonstrate what it really means to be a man. Being a man is about strength, of respect and dignity. It's about showing up, because it's too late if you have to ask. It's about giving hate no safe harbor and leaving no one behind, and defending freedoms. It's about standing up to the abuse of power, whether physical, economic, or psychological. It's about knowing faith without works is dead.

Look, you're doing the work. Today I look out at all you graduates and I see the next generation of Morehouse men who are doctors and researchers curing cancer, artists shaping our culture, fearless journalists and intellectuals challenging convention. I see preachers and advocates who might even join another Morehouse man in the United States Senate. You can clap for him. He's a good man.

So I said I'm proud to have the most diverse administration in history, to tap into the full talents of our nation. I'm also proud to put in the first black woman on the United States Supreme Court.

And I have no doubt one day a Morehouse man will be on that court as well.

You know it. I've been vice president to the first black president, and become my close friend, and president to the first woman vice president. Why I have no idea, no doubt that a Morehouse man will be president one day just after an AKA from Howard. She's tough, guys.

Look, let me close to this: I know I don't look like I've been around very long, but in my career, for the first 30 years I was told, "You're too young kid." They used to stop me from getting on the Senate elevator when I first got there, for real. Now I'm too old. Whether you're young or old, I know what endures. The strength and wisdom of faith endures.

And my hope for you is, my challenge to you is that you can still keep the faith so long as you can. That cap on your head proves you've earned your crown. The question is now, 25 years from now, 50 years from now when you're asked to stand and address the next generation of Morehouse men, what will you say you did with that power you've earned? What will you say you've done for your family, for your community, your country when it mattered most?

I know what we can do. Together, we're capable of building a democracy worthy of our dreams. A future where every, even more of your brothers and sisters can follow their dreams. A boundless future where your legacies lift us up to show those who follow a bigger, brighter future that proves the American dream is big enough for everyone to succeed. Class of 2024, four years ago it felt probably like Saturday. Four years later you made it to Sunday, to commencement, to the beginning.

And with faith and determination you can push the sun above the horizon once more. You can reveal a light hope, and I'm not kidding, for yourself and for your nation. The prayers of righteous man availeth much. A righteous man, a good man, a Morehouse man. God bless you all. We're expecting a lot from you. Thank you.

Print Citations

CMS: Biden, Joe. "Commencement Speech to the Morehouse College Class of 2024." Speech at Morehouse College, May 19, 2024. In *The Reference Shelf: Representative American Speeches, 2023–2024,* edited by Micah L. Issitt, 203–209. Amenia, NY: Grey House Publishing, 2024.

MLA: Biden, Joe. "Commencement Speech to the Morehouse College Class of 2024." Morehouse College, 19 May 2024, Atlanta, GA. Speech. *The Reference Shelf: Representative American Speeches, 2023–2024,* edited by Micah L. Issitt, Grey House Publishing, 2024, pp. 203–209.

APA: Biden, J. (2024). Commencement speech to the Morehouse College Class of 2024 [Speech]. Morehouse College, Atlanta, GA. In Micah L. Issitt (Ed.), *The reference shelf: Representative American speeches, 2023–2024* (pp. 203–209). Grey House Publishing. (Original work published 2024)

What "Follow Your Dreams" Misses

By Grant Sanderson

"The cliché to follow your dreams overlooks how critical it is that the dreams you have are about something more than just yourself." Grant Sanderson, YouTube celebrity and operator of the 3Blue1Brown channel, gave a commencement address at Harvey Mudd College in Claremont, California. Sanderson discussed the changes in his own career path since college and advised students to be aware of the simplification in being told to follow their dreams.

Thank you, President Nembhard, for that very warm introduction and for inviting me. And thank you to the class of 2024 for including me in such a special day. I had the joy of getting to know many of you last year on this visit, and I distinctly remember coming away with the feeling that a future in your hands is a bright future indeed. For those in the audience who don't know who I am, I focus on making videos about mathematics with an emphasis on visualizations.

It's a weird job. I do love it, though, and it's no exaggeration to describe it as a dream job. And a common cliché is for someone who is lucky enough to land in a dream job to stand confidently in front of a group of fledgling graduates and to compel them to follow their dreams. Frankly, on its own, I don't think this is very good advice.

The Truth Behind Following Your Dreams

To be clear, there is truth behind the cliché. It is true that those who make the biggest ripples are the ones who are fueled by passion. It is true that the life that you live is much more enjoyable if you can find something doing what you love. And it's also true that you shouldn't feel shackled by societal constraints.

But for one thing, not everyone has a pre-baked dream sitting there waiting to be followed.

That's completely okay. And even if you are one of the lucky ones who has a passion that you want to roll into a career, I think there are a few pragmatic concerns that don't always fit very neatly into an inspirational speech that are required to make this actually work. Now I know I'm talking to a very nerdy audience, so I'm tempted to describe my aims here a little bit more mathematically precisely, where in the vector space of all possible advice, if you consider the follow-your-dreams vector, I want to explore its orthogonal subspace.

Delivered on May 12, 2024 at Harvey Mudd College, Claremont, CA.

My Story

Maybe though it's better if I just start with a story. Before I entered college, I was one of those who knew what I wanted to major in. There's no surprises here. It was math.

This was a topic that I had loved for a long time, as long as I can remember. When I was in college, I was plenty seduced by the adjacent field of computer science and programming, and I would spend my summers interning at software startups. But I distinctly remember coming back at the end of each of those summers and thinking, man, you know what I really want to do with my life? Is spend more time doing math.

So I had a passion. It wasn't something I would want to follow, but in hindsight, that passion was a lot more arbitrary and maybe a little more self-centered than I would have liked to admit at the time. Why did I love math? You know, if I'm honest, I think it had its roots in the fact that when I was young, the adults emphasized this is an important topic to learn, and they told me I was good at it.

This makes me spend more time with it. Spending time with something is how you get better at something, and that kicked off a positive feedback loop, in both senses of the word positive feedback. Now, as time went on, I do believe it became less about perceptions. When I was in college, I remember genuinely enjoying the aesthetic delights that beautiful math problem solving has to have.

Shifting Goals After College

But thinking of it as a career ambition, not just a hobby, this has the fatal flaw that I was viewing the world through a lens of what I personally enjoyed, not giving enough weight to a plan for how exactly it would add value to others. I don't know if you felt it yet, but today marks a day in your life when a fundamental goal changes. When you're a student, the fundamental goal is to grow, to learn, to become better. So many institutions and structures around you are there to support you in growing and learning and getting better, and to reward you for doing so.

In life after college, the goal changes a little, and success hinges on how effectively you're able to add value to others. Now, these aren't at odds with each other, in fact, they go hand in hand. You're much better positioned to make a difference if you're armed with an expertise and if you spend your life honing that expertise. But there is a big difference between personal growth being the end in and of itself versus being a means to an end.

A Tale of Two Musicians

By way of comparison, I also loved the violin when I was growing up. And let's take a moment to imagine two distinct music students. I'm going to name them Paganini and Taylor. Both of them are talented, very talented, but Paganini pushes for technical excellence.

He tries to perfect virtuosically challenging pieces. Taylor strives to write music that speaks to people, that resonates with them emotionally. Now in a music school, Paganini is going to get the better grades every time, he's always going to get the better position, but pursuing music careers, Taylor's at the clear advantage.

My first piece of advice, something I would have told myself I could go back in time and be in the seat where you are now, is that if you have a passion that you want to incorporate into a career, take a step back and recognize the fact that this is a passion that grew in a time of your life when the goal was to learn and to grow, but you're transitioning to a period when the primary aim shifts to adding value to others.

Adding Value to Others

The cliché to "follow your dreams" overlooks how critical it is that the dreams you have are about something more than just yourself. Those who excel in their first jobs are the ones who make life easier for everyone around them, even when it involves doing things they don't love. Those who excel in PhD programs are the ones who recognize how their work fits into a broader research community, not just the ones who view it as the next chapter in school. The successful entrepreneurs are the ones who have a relentless focus on making sure that what they have to sell is what people want to buy, not just those who are looking to make something impressive.

Now, for some people, when you hear the words follow your dreams, it falls flat because you don't have a defining passion. Like I said earlier, that's completely okay. If anything, it might put you at an advantage. I think you'll do just as well if you start by seeking out opportunities where the skills that you've developed here intersect with adding values to others, and from there I promise the passion will follow.

Action Precedes Motivation

One of the best pieces of advice I remember receiving from a friend many years ago is that action precedes motivation. This is often useful on a much smaller scale. We feel most awake after getting out of bed, not before. A drive to exercise comes from the habit of exercising, it doesn't go the other way around.

But I think the idea that action precedes motivation applies to this bigger question of finding a career doing what you love. I do love making videos, and I really do love teaching, but when I was finishing college I had no penchant or experience with videos at all, and my interest in teaching was honestly only insofar as it scratched this itch to do more math. It was only by stumbling into a wacky career where I was doing both of them that I came to love them. Now, in my own story, what happened after college involves a fair bit of luck, but luck can come in a lot of different forms, and I think with a little bit of foresight you can actually avoid having to rely on chance in quite the same way.

Survivorship Bias

There's a post I like on the webcomic XKCD that shows a man standing on a stage, and he has bags of cash surrounding him. "'Never stop buying lottery tickets,' he says. 'No matter what people tell you, I failed again and again, but I never gave up, and here I am as proof that if you put in the time, it pays off.'" The caption notes that every inspirational speech should come with a disclaimer about survivorship bias. The obvious way that Follow Your Dreams is susceptible to survivorship bias is that for all of the high-risk, high-reward paths, things like professional athletics, starting a social media company, making a career in the arts, it's only the few who rise to the top who are in a position to give advice at all. ¶But there's also a more subtle way that survivorship bias applies here. It's not just about the odds of winning a particular game, it has to do with whether the game you choose to play meshes well with the way that the future unfolds. If you were a software enthusiast in the late 1980s, you would be well-poised to ride the dot-com boom in the decades that followed. If you were someone with a niche interest in an actor film production, you would find yourself with an unexpected opportunity when YouTube and other film-sharing platforms started to rise in prominence.

My Own Path
When I was finishing my undergrad, one of the ways that I scratched that itch to do more math was to hack together a very rudimentary Python library for making math visualizations, and I used it to make a couple videos about neat proofs and problems that I enjoyed and posting them online. I was not planning for this to be a career. I had an appreciation for how valuable personal projects are, but it didn't go much beyond that. This led to conversations with Khan Academy, a group I had great respect for, and it turned into a job there, making more lessons online.

Lucky Timing and My Own Path
In the meantime, I continued my own channel as a side hobby, and it didn't blow up, but there was a very modest growth of others who enjoyed the same kind of visualizations that I did, and I saw it in just a steady tick up in the audience size. My original plan, I think, was to spend a year or two doing this online education stuff working at Khan Academy and maybe returning to do a PhD.

But as time went on, something between the gratitude that I saw from many students around the planet for the lessons I'd put out and the slow and steady growth on my own channel led me to doubling down and forming a somewhat unorthodox career in online lessons and math visualizations. Now looking back, it would feel very incomplete if I were to somehow ascribe the success that I found, to the extent there was any, to the fact that I was following a dream, pursuing a passion. Passion plays into it.

You can't have good lessons without a teacher who cares, but we can't ignore the other factors at play. I already brought up the biggest one, success is a function of the value you bring to others, so a pursuit equally fueled by love but which did nothing to help or to entertain people just wouldn't have had a chance to work.

But another factor I want to focus on is how I was very lucky with the timing. If I had been born 10 years earlier, I don't think I could have reached the same number of people posting lessons on a much more infant version of the internet, where there was less infrastructure that could have existed to help form a career doing so.

Opportunities in a Less Crowded Landscape
If I had started 10 years later, the space would have been a lot more saturated. So another piece of advice that I'd like to offer, another little ingredient that makes following your dreams a little more likely to work out, is to ask yourself what's possible now that wasn't possible 10 years ago and which might get harder 10 years from now.

There are more opportunities in a less crowded landscape, there are more chances to grow if you're part of a rising tide, but this requires pushing past the inevitable discomfort that comes from following a path that has little to no precedent. I want to take a moment to talk about whose dreams you should be thinking about, because it's not just your own.

When I was visiting Harvey Mudd last year, I had the pleasure of talking to one of the gems in your math department, Talithia Williams, and I asked her, hey, what made you pursue math in the first place? She had a very clear story. She told me she hadn't thought about it very much until one distinct day in her high school calculus class, her teacher, Mr. Dorman, pulled her aside and said, Talithia, you're really good at this.

The Power of Encouragement
You should consider majoring in math. Actually she had never thought about it before, but that one comment was enough to knock over the first in a series of dominoes that led to a very flourishing career in the topic. Over the years, I've asked a lot of mathematicians the same question, and you would be shocked how often I hear a very similar answer, there was this one particular teacher, and one seemingly simple thing that they did that was the beginning in a long series of encouragements. Never underestimate just how much influence you can have on others, especially the ones who are younger than you are.

Getting older is a process of slowly seeing the proportion of people around you who are younger than you are rise inexorably closer to 100%. As this happens, you stand to have as much influence by shaping the dreams of those behind you as you do by following those of your own. And as a very last point, the biggest risk in the follow your dreams cliche is the implication that there's one static target point at all. In the next 10, 20, 30 years, the world around you is going to change a lot.

Expecting Change
And those changes are going to be unpredictable. I hardly need to emphasize this point, you are the class who spent your formative transition from high school to college under a pandemic. But it's not just the world around you. Tonight, when

you're celebrating your graduation, and hopefully remembering to celebrate Mother's Day as well, take a few moments to ask the people who are older than you how they've changed, how their personalities, how their value systems have changed since they were a student.

You'll notice that essentially all of them have an answer, which suggests you have every reason to expect that there's going to be something fundamental about you that changes as well in the coming decades, probably unpredictably. Almost everyone I know has undergone some kind of shift since college. Some came to place more value on having a family than they used to. Some shifted from a trajectory that was oriented towards an academic career to going into industry.

Adaptability Is Key

Some went the other way around and after spending some time in industry, returned to grad school. And so, so many of them have jobs that simply didn't exist at the time of their graduation. So rather than having any one particular goal that defines who you are, you'll take better advantage of whatever the future has to offer you if you remain nimble, and if you're responsive to the changes in the world, and if you anticipate change within yourself. My final piece of advice is to not treat passion as something to follow.

Think of it as an initial velocity vector. It gives a clear direction to point yourself, and loving what you do can have you move quickly. But you should expect and you should even hope that the specific direction that you're moving changes based on the force vectors around you. Now in these unpredictable decades to come, your generation is the one that holds more sway than any other over how it unfolds.

Harvey Mudd Graduates' Potential

And you, the graduating class of Harvey Mudd, represent some of the most talented and thoughtful minds in that generation. Influence is not distributed uniformly in the population, and I for one would feel a lot more comfortable if it was you who were at the helm, guiding this crazy ship that we're all riding. If you step into the next chapter of life with an implacable focus on adding value to others, you're more likely to be the ones at the helm. If you recognize that action precedes motivation, you're more likely to be at the helm.

And if you ask what's possible now that wasn't ten years ago, you're more likely to be at the helm. If you appreciate just how much power you have to shape the lives of the generation that follows you, you're more likely to be at the helm. And if you remain adaptable to a changing world, treating passion not as a destination but as a fuel, following not dreams but opportunities, you're more likely to be at the helm. One final time, would everyone please join me in congratulating the class of 2024 on what they've done to get here, and make some noise to let them know how excited we are to see where they go from here.

Thank you.

216 2024 Commencement Speeches

Print Citations

CMS: Sanderson, Grant. "What 'Follow Your Dreams' Misses." Commencement speech at Harvey Mudd College, Claremont, CA, May 12, 2024. In *The Reference Shelf: Representative American Speeches, 2023–2024,* edited by Micah L. Issitt, 210–216. Amenia, NY: Grey House Publishing, 2024.

MLA: Sanderson, Grant. "What 'Follow Your Dreams' Misses." Harvey Mudd College, 12 May 2024, Claremont, CA. Commencement speech. *The Reference Shelf: Representative American Speeches, 2023–2024,* edited by Micah L. Issitt, Grey House Publishing, 2024, pp. 210–216.

APA: Sanderson, G. (2024). What "follow your dreams" misses [Speech]. Harvey Mudd College, Claremont, CA. In Micah L. Issitt (Ed.), *The reference shelf: Representative American speeches, 2023–2024* (pp. 210–216). Grey House Publishing. (Original work published 2024)

Our World Is on Fire:
Welcome to the Battlefield

By Maria Ressa

"You don't know who you are until you're tested, until you fight for what you believe in. Because that defines who you are." Maria Ressa, a Filipino and American journalist, former CNN investigative journalist, creator of the news organization Rappler, and winner of the Nobel Peace Prize, delivered the commencement speech at Harvard University in 2024. Ressa spoke about the importance of allowing protests, of paying attention to journalism and facts, and the threats of the "outrage economy."

Thank you, President Garber, and thank you, former President Gay, who called me last year to extend this offer. It's an incredible honor to address the distinguished Harvard faculty, the mysterious Harvard Corporation, and the loving friends and family who have traveled far and close to be here with you today. But wait, most of all, despite everything, because you worked really hard, I am so thrilled to congratulate the battle-tested graduates of the class of 2024. Thank you.

This was a harder speech to write than the Nobel lecture, you know, because since 2021, the world has gotten so much worse. We live in a dystopian science fiction world where everything can change in the blink of an eye when you have been forced to turn crisis into opportunity. No one knows this better than the class of 2024.

A pandemic meant no high school graduation. Your first year here in lockdown, wearing masks, afraid of contact, you laid out all of the problems, the existential problems we face today. We were pushed online in the virtual world and that made things worse because the accelerant to conflict and violence to us against them, to wars that have killed tens of thousands sparking historic campus protests, that accelerant is technology.

It turned what once used to be our civilized Harvard thinking slow public discussions into what's become a gladiator's battle to the death. I know this firsthand. The Philippines, America's former colony, 110 million people was social media's Petri dish. For a crucial six years, Filipinos spent the most time online and on social media globally, and we became the testing ground for these American tech companies.

Delivered on May 23, 2024 at Harvard University, Cambridge, MA.

The Spread of Disinformation

Their platform's designs [are] exploited by power and money in information warfare. It became worse when TikTok joined the fray. If the tactics worked on us, it was deployed for you. That's what happened in 2016 when 126 million Americans were targeted by Russian disinformation, and on January 6th in the violence on Capitol Hill, when Silicon Valley sins came home to roost.

Because I accepted your invitation to be here today, I was attacked online and called antisemitic by power and money because they want power and money. While the other side was already attacking me because I had been on stage with Hillary Clinton. Hard to win, right?

But I'd already survived information operations from my own government. Free speech used to pound you to silence, 90 hate messages per hour in 2016. That was eight years ago, fed me death threats for breakfast. They attacked the way I looked, the way I sound, they dehumanized me.

But, you know, the funniest thing, because when you're the target, you just have to laugh, is that I was supposedly both CIA and communist. None of these were true. But the end goal, please know this, is chaos. Break down trust. If you don't have the right information, you can't act.

Attacks on Journalists

That's partly the reason why journalists are on the front lines. The Meta narrative, disinformation network seeded against us, and this is globally, was journalist equals criminal. Then the bottom up attacks in the Philippines against us began on social media. That was followed a year later by the weaponization of the law.

In 2019, I was arrested twice in about a month, posted bail eight times. In about three months, I thought I was gonna have to do a workflow for arrests. But before it all ended, I had 10 arrest warrants. Rappler and I paid more in bail and bonds than our dictator's wife, Imelda Marcos, you remember her shoes? She was convicted for corruption.

But I did nothing wrong except to do my job, to report the facts, to hold power to account. For this I had to be okay with spending the rest of my life in jail. At one point, it was more than a century in jail that I faced. To be here today, I had to ask for permission to travel from our Supreme Court. Anyone else out here on bail? Just me?

It taught me a valuable lesson. These times will hopefully teach you the same lesson I learned. You don't know who you are until you're tested, until you fight for what you believe in. Because that defines who you are. But you're Harvard, you better get your facts right, because now you are being tested.

The Chilling Effect and Campus Protests

The chilling effect means that many are choosing to stay silent because there are consequences to speaking out. I'm shocked at the fear and anger, the paranoia splitting open the major fracture lines of society, the inability to listen. What happened to us in the Philippines, it's here.

The campus protests are testing everyone in America. Protests are healthy. They shouldn't be violent. Protests give voice, they shouldn't be silenced.

But you live in complicated, complex times where I think administrators and students also faced an unacknowledged danger: technology, making everything faster, meaner, more polarized with insidious information operations online that are dividing generations. Rappler will be documenting this and publishing in the next couple of weeks. Maybe Rappler's experience can help you.

After all, we were in hell and now we're in purgatory, right? It can get better. And here are three ways we've learned, right? One, choose your best self. Two, turn crisis into opportunity. And three, it's wonderful to have heard this several times from the stage today, three, be vulnerable.

Choosing Your Best Self

One, choose your best self, set and stay focused on your goals, but know the values you live by. How important is power? How much money will make you happy? Because the only thing you can control in the world is you.

Too often we let ourselves off the hook, refusing to look at our own difficult or ugly truths. We rationalize bad behavior. Remember that character is created in the sum of all the little choices we make. If you're not clear about your values, you may wake up one day and realize you don't like the person you've become. So choose your best self.

You're standing on the rubble of the world that was, recognize it. I said this in the Nobel lecture, an atom bomb exploded in our information ecosystem because social media turned our world upside down, spreading lies faster than facts, while amplifying fear and anger, fueling hatred by design for profit. Whether it's the AI of social media or Generative AI, we don't have integrity of information.

We don't have integrity of facts. And here's three sentences I've said over and over. Without facts, you can't have truth. Without truth, you can't have trust. Without these three, we have no shared reality, no rule of law, no democracy. We can't begin to solve existential problems like climate change.

The Outrage Economy and Online Violence

This outrage economy built on our data, microtargeting us, transformed our world, rewarding the worst of humanity. Online violence is real-world violence. And as you've pointed out, people are dying from genocide in Myanmar, fueled by Facebook according to the UN and Meta itself, to Ukraine, Sudan, Haiti, Armenia, Gaza.

The challenge, the challenge today is whether our international rules-based order still works, does it? The challenge is justice core to our humanity. Too many powerful people are getting away with impunity from countries to companies. And it is dividing us in ways that are literally destroying us, destroying democracy, destroying trust.

In Cambridge Commons, just on the other side of that gate, there's a marker to American patriot William Dawes, who like his more famous friend Paul

Revere, rode through here sounding the alarm, "The British are coming!" Well, today's equivalent, an alarm that's made me feel like Cassandra and Sisyphus combined because I feel like I've been shouting since 2016 when I watched our institutions crumble quickly in the Philippines. And I will say it now, the fascists are coming.

In 2023, the Global Democracy Index fell to its lowest level ever. Today, 71% of the world lives under autocratic rule. We are electing illiberal leaders democratically, and once in power, these autocrats not only crush institutions in their countries, but they form alliances and create Kleptocracy, Inc. This is your challenge. It is our challenge.

Harvard's Role and Zuckerberg's Commencement Speech

And Harvard played a role in getting us here. Seven years ago, Mark Zuckerberg stood at this podium, finally got his degree and said that his life's purpose was to connect the whole world, "Move fast, break things," Facebook said. Well, it broke democracy.

In my book, *How to Stand up to a Dictator*, we were fighting too. I named two, not just Rodrigo Duterte in the Philippines, he's one man who crushed institutions, but even more powerful was Mark Zuckerberg because he, along with tech bros, are controlling the world. Okay, I will shut up.

Enough, right? Because let me bring it to you, the battle to regain trust begins now with all of you. Harvard says it educates the future leaders of the world. Well, if you future leaders don't fight for democracy right now, there will be little left for you to lead.

How do you do this? And this leads to two, turn crisis into opportunity. I think you've lived through this. Accept that crisis is here to stay.

Turning Crisis into Opportunity

In Rappler, my co-founders, and one of them is here, Glenda Gloria, who's a Neiman Fellow from 2018. We learned to embrace the worst scenarios we could imagine. And this happened during our darkest times. Then we workflowed what our company would do. We drilled our team and we prepared for the worst.

We also learned strangely to become punching bags because we didn't want to tear down our judiciary. We didn't want to tear down our government. We knew how potent fear is and we tried to step in, I mean, at some point you get angry when silence is consent. But you understand.

Well, I did have good news. Remember, we put out all of our worst case scenarios. And the reality we lived through was so much better than we could have imagined. Hell, purgatory, right? It didn't mean we weren't afraid. We just made a pact among the four co-founders of Rappler that only one of us could be afraid at any single time. We rotated the fear.

But now, for you, for us, the corruption of our information ecosystem is about to get worse. Because of deep fakes, you can't trust your eyes and ears. Because of chat bots, you can't trust that the person you're communicating with is even human.

The Enshittification of the Internet

After Elon Musk bought Twitter, he fired its trust and safety teams, Meta and Google also cut some of their staff. So as half the world goes to the polls, goes to vote this year, there will be fewer safety measures in place to protect us. Now big tech is choking traffic to new sites, which means you will get less news in your feeds.

How do you know what's real? How do you know what's fact when your emotions are what's manipulated? When our biology is hacked? Instead of the facts, the enshittification, enshittification of the internet is in full bloom, more trash, more propaganda, more information operations that push our emotional buttons. Paris Mayor Anne Hidalgo deleted X last year calling it "a human sewer."

We will have to struggle harder for agency, for independent thought. And it's not just the tech companies that abdicated responsibility for protecting us, it's also democratic governments like the United States, tech is the least regulated industry around the world. That's why the US needs to reform or revoke Section 230 of the 1996 Communications Decency Act.

We need to stop the impunity. We also need to acknowledge our crisis of faith. I've always believed in the goodness of human nature, but that has never been tested as much as it is today, when the incentive structure of the technology that connects us rewards the bad, eliminates the best of who we can be.

Being Vulnerable and Building Trust

So we need to restore our faith in humanity, and that starts with compassion. There's a word that goes beyond empathy in South Africa. I love this word, *ubuntu*. I am because we are.

It's a deeper faith in another person. It's deeper than stepping in someone else's shoes. But in order to get there, to get to ubuntu, we have to lower our shields, which leads us to three, be vulnerable.

You've accomplished a lot to be here today. You might think being vulnerable is weak and it is hard to trust. But in every relationship, in every negotiation, in order to move forward and accomplish anything meaningful, someone lowers their shield first, brings down their ego, the defense mechanism, then others follow.

Let that person be you. Because when you are vulnerable, you create the strongest bonds. You restore trust and the ability to find creative solutions to intractable problems. You become resilient and enable the most inspiring possibilities.

Conclusion

So choose your best self. Turn crisis into opportunity. Be vulnerable. This is it.

222 2024 Commencement Speeches

This time matters. What you do matters. The war isn't just happening in Gaza, in Sudan, in Ukraine. It isn't just out there. It's in your pocket. Each of us is fighting our own battles for facts, for integrity, because the dictator to-be can zoom in and target each of us.

So let me end by reminding you we're standing on the rubble of the world that was, and we, you must have the courage, the foresight to imagine and create the world as it should be. More compassionate, more equal, more sustainable. Your Harvard education gives you the tools. Make it a world that is safe from fascists and tyrants.

Alone, no matter how much of a superstar you are, you will accomplish very little. We will accomplish very little alone. This is about what we can do together to find what binds us together.

Our world on fire needs you. So class of 2024, welcome to the battlefield. Join us.

Print Citations

CMS: Ressa, Maria. "Our World Is on Fire: Welcome to the Battlefield." Commencement address at Harvard University, Cambridge, MA, May 23, 2024. In *The Reference Shelf: Representative American Speeches, 2023–2024,* edited by Micah L. Issitt, 217–222. Amenia, NY: Grey House Publishing, 2024.

MLA: Ressa, Maria. "Our World Is on Fire: Welcome to the Battlefield." Harvard University, 23 May 2024, Cambridge, MA. Commencement address. *The Reference Shelf: Representative American Speeches, 2023–2024,* edited by Micah L. Issitt, Grey House Publishing, 2024, pp. 217–222.

APA: Ressa, M. (2024). Our world is on fire: Welcome to the battlefield [Speech]. Harvard University, Cambridge, MA. In Micah L. Issitt (Ed.), *The reference shelf: Representative American speeches, 2023–2024* (pp. 217–222). Grey House Publishing. (Original work published 2024)

I Cannot Wait to See How You Will Harness the Power of Love

By John Legend

"The power of education is that it empowers you to serve. It empowers you to build. It empowers you to give." Musician, singer, and songwriter John Legend delivered a commencement address at Loyola Marymount University in Los Angeles. Legend talked about the difficulties of obtaining an education during the pandemic and about the importance of working together to move forward through adversity.

Oh my goodness. Y'all sounded so good. I want to hear you sing a little bit more, I mean. That's quite the greeting.

I usually have to like push the audience to sing with me. But you all started before I even had to ask you and I'm very appreciative LMU. Thank you President Snyder, Provost Poon, Executive Vice President Rae, and thank you for that wonderful introduction Chairman Viviano. Thank you—thank you all for the invitation, the introduction, and the very, very, very warm welcome that I feel today.

Hello Loyola Marymount University. To the faculty, staff, and alumni, family, and friends of the graduates, we are all very happy to see you here. I can feel your joy and your pride. Thank you for letting me share in this moment.

And of course, to the stars of the show, the brilliant, radiant LMU class of 2024, y'all did it. Congratulations. I am very honored, grateful, and humbled that I also will forever be a member of the LMU class of '24. Thank you.

Reflections on Graduation

I'm going to go back in ancient history. I remember preparing for my own graduation way, way back in the 20th century, 1999, before most of you were born. And I must admit I was a little cynical about the whole graduation ceremony. The pomp and circumstance felt unnecessary.

But as I sat in those same seats you're sitting right now, as I experienced my commencement in that stadium with all my friends and classmates, sharing in this big rite of passage, the ceremony made me feel something. I was inspired. I was proud. I felt connected to my thousands of fellow graduates.

And since then, through all these years, from all that life gives and all that life takes, I've come to realize that we should savor these moments. Take the time to pause and reflect, to revel in our accomplishments and with our communities. Celebrate with the people we love. So do me a favor, class of 2024.

Delivered on May 4, 2024 at Loyola Marymount University, Los Angeles, CA.

Can we just take a breath and let it soak in? Look at the people around you. Your people. Take a mental snapshot.

Overcoming Challenges

Savor it. Relish it. Remember it. Because that joy you feel right now, that's what this ceremony is really about.

And man, do you all deserve this ceremony today? You have earned it. You have traveled a remarkable journey to this time, to this place. And I don't need to say it because it's already been said.

But if we rewind the clock four years, the spring of 2020, sometimes we want to block out that time, right? We were in a global pandemic. You were robbed of all the traditional milestones. You didn't have a senior prom. You didn't walk across your high school graduation stage. You finished your senior year trapped in a Zoom screen. There's no point in sugarcoating it. It sucked.

Then in the fall of 2020, you began your journey again on Zoom screens and masked and socially distanced. Somehow you juggled your first year seminars with study sessions as you figured out how to adult. You participated, hopefully, in one of the most consequential elections of our lifetime in which democracy was on the ballot. And as you prepared for your second semester, we all watched an attempt to overturn that election insurrection at our nation's capital.

That was all during your first year of college, long before you could partake in a well-deserved drink. You deserve that drink. You deserved it. And yet, class of 2024, your resilience and resolve, the way you powered through with grit and determination and a little bit of fun, sense of humor.

The way you looked out for one another, forged connection with one another amidst an epidemic of isolation and loneliness. The way you advocated for the causes in which you believe, the way you immersed yourselves in the work and play that brings meaning and life. It fills me with so much hope. And hope, hope, that's something we all could use a little more of these days.

The Solidarity Generation

Let's talk about hope, about the faith that you give me for the future, about the optimism I feel when I look into your faces. Why do I have so much hope, class of 2024? It starts with you and your unique education. President Snyder rightfully deemed this class the solidarity generation, a class that recognizes, thanks to the challenges you've overcome, that the most effective way to drive change, to find joy, to survive is by doing it together.

From a once-in-a-century pandemic, like Yinka said, you learned the importance of caring for one another, of putting the needs of your community above your own self-interest. From converging national and global crises, you've learned to march together for accountability and action and justice, to get in good trouble, as the late John Lewis would say. But just as important, from your time here, you learned that the power of an education lies not in just acing the test or landing a fancy management consulting job like I did after college. Yes, I was a consultant for a while, believe it or not.

The power of education is that it empowers you to serve. It empowers you to build. It empowers you to give. And I see your commitment to service reflected in the host of organizations at the heart of campus life here, from the Pam Rector Center for Service and Action, to the coaches and volunteers that put on special games every year.

And I see it in the next chapters many of you will write. I see it in the scholars, doctors, lawyers, teachers, founders, artists, producers, and yes, musicians you are becoming. I see it in the causes this class has championed, on this garden at Alumni Mall, across Los Angeles, and far beyond. I see it in your advocacy for your fellow student-athletes, in your work to address the climate crisis, and to advance justice here in America and around the world.

Purpose and Challenges
I see it in your academic work too, in the effort you've taken across disciplines to better understand our world. All of this education, this service, all of it is a remarkable gift. It will be part of you forever. I can say that with confidence because I know how my college experience shaped my beliefs, my relationships, my career, the music I write, the work that I do.

I know it helped me understand my purpose. I know your experiences at LMU will help you understand your purpose and live your purpose. And we need purpose, especially in those moments of profound challenge. Of course, this is one of those moments.

It's a heated time on our nation's college campuses. We've got roiling crises all around the world. Everything seems to be on fire. Places like Israel and Palestine, Ukraine, Iran, even here at home, where the threat of autocracy continues to gather.

But also in the places that probably deserve more of our attention. Haiti, Myanmar, Sudan. Other areas of conflict around the world. In so many of these painful instances, the patterns are similar. So-called leaders act with malice and apparent impunity. They exploit people's very real fears and anxieties. They inflame ethnic conflicts. They pit people and communities against one another.

They deploy misinformation and disinformation. They exploit inequalities. They peddle grievance and resentment. And they thrive on dehumanization.

Dehumanization and Its Dangers
When you dehumanize someone, when you call them vermin or animals, when you say an immigrant community will poison our blood, you create a permission structure that allows people to harm them one by one or family by family or community by community. This sort of attitude is a dangerous thing. All of history's worst moral catastrophes, from slavery to genocide, are fueled by this sort of dehumanization. And the autocrat's playbook usually involves identifying

someone as an "other" or enemy, dehumanizing them, and then saying, "I alone can fix it."

Or "I alone can impose law and order or dispense with democracy, dispense with checks and balances and the rule of law. You need a strong man. You need to concentrate power with me and take it away from the people where it belongs." Our history books are replete with these types of leaders, replete with the havoc they've wreaked, the injustice they've wrought, the wars they've started, the lives they've destroyed.

And those of us who believe in our shared humanity, in democracy, should be worried that these forces of dehumanization might have their way again in 2024. Our problems are not neat. The solutions are not easy, and I'm not going to suggest that they are. But I believe, and I'm certain your LMU professors do too, that a great education teaches you that your job is to think critically.

To challenge assumptions, to question the status quo, to interrogate the common wisdom. Moral clarity is certainly comfortable. We prefer for everything to be black and white. Social media pushes everyone to pick a side.

Navigating Complexity

And yet, most things happen in those shades of gray. Humanity, life, is filled with nuance and complexity. And I say lean into that nuance. Engage with the complexity.

So how do we do this? How do we do this, class of 2024? How do we engage with complexity? We do it by listening with more humility. Listening with more curiosity. Listening with more intentionality. Listening with more empathy. After all, with the freedom of speech comes the responsibility, the community responsibility, to listen to each other, to give a full and fair hearing.

We engage with complexity by recognizing that in a multiracial, multiethnic, pluralist democracy, we are going to disagree. That's inevitable. The noise and the mess are features, not bugs. At the same time though, diversity and difference need not be synonymous with intractable division.

Even when we disagree, we have no choice but to find ways to tolerate each other, to respect each other, to live with each other. We might start with the assumption that for the most part, most of the time, most people are operating in good faith. So we can extend grace to them and the benefit of the doubt. We might acknowledge that we each are bringing our own histories and experiences and biases to our perceptions, our own legitimate fears and anxieties.

And then we might, each of us, try to see the world through one another's eyes. To do the really hard thing, to genuinely honor one another's humanity, even when we disagree. Because we all are God's children. We all are someone's child or sibling or friend.

Israel and Palestine

And class of '24, we may as well talk about the elephant in the garden. Let's talk for a moment about Israel and Palestine. No doubt, there is staggering, stupefying complexity swirling all around and through this multi-dimensional, multi-generational crisis. The vexing, bedeviling questions have stymied world leaders and ordinary citizens for decades.

But one thing is clear. There has been too much profound human suffering. Millions of innocents, Israeli and Palestinian, Jewish, Muslim, Christian and secular, they yearn for just and lasting peace. They yearn to live with dignity, all of them, like all human beings, with equal rights and equal opportunity.

And yet, they remain trapped in what Dr. Martin Luther King Jr. called a "descending spiral." As you've learned here, there are profound limits to what war can accomplish. War may win territory, but it does not win hearts and minds. War can subjugate, but it cannot unify. War can destroy, but it cannot build. And the ultimate weakness of violence, Dr. King said, is that it only begets more violence. Violence leads only to vengeance and reprisal. Fire to more fire. We know this.

All of human history affirms it. And Dr. King said repeatedly, during another period of national upheaval and campus unrest, that "darkness cannot drive out darkness. Only light can do that. Hate cannot drive out hate. Only love can do that." The same is true of the here and now. Violence will never be a lasting solution to violence. Hate will never be the solution to hate. Instead, we must be the light. We must be the love.

Now, I can imagine what at least a few of you are thinking. All this Kumbaya talk is nice, but thousands of people are dying. How could it be that in the face of war and autocracy and ethnic conflict, after all of the compounding trauma of our recent past, that we should just love more? I can understand the skepticism, but hear me out. I come from a family of preachers.

The Power of Love
Alright. I'm the grandson of a preacher, the great grandson of a preacher, the nephew of several preachers. I grew up going to a lot of church, and I've heard a lot of sermons. And what many of us learned during those Sunday sermons, and I'm sure some of you have learned at this fine Jesuit Marymount University, is that there isn't just one kind of love.

There are at least three. There's *eros*, romantic love, the intoxicating love, the love that burns hottest. You know, the type of love that makes you want to sing. "All of me loves all of you." Hey, I made a career of that kind of love. Then there's *philia*, brotherly and sisterly love. That means love for our family and friends, love for our teammates, love for the places that shape us. It's the love that has you picking up a Mendocino farm sandwich for your buddy or throwing them in Foley Pond on their birthday.

But I want to spend some time on the third kind of love, class of 2024, the type of love that Dr. King called the most powerful, transcendent kind of love. It's called *agape*. Agape is the universal love that's intrinsic to the human heart.

Agape Love

The love that burns the longest. It's bigger than any of us because it resides in all of us. It's not the love of rom-coms or pop songs, nothing against pop songs. Agape is a righteous, rebellious kind of love.

And through our histories, the most powerful tool at our disposal to build social change and social justice. You see, it's easy to love your friend or your lover. Agape emboldens us to love our enemies. It's easy to love the people who share our sense of what's right, the people with whom we agree.

Agape emboldens us to love the people who, at least in our eyes, could not be more wrong. It's easy to love the people who are marching with us. Agape emboldens us to love the people who are marching against us, even the people who try to silence or suppress us. Agape is the love that dares us to believe deeply in our shared humanity and that we can find a way through together.

Growing up, I spent a lot of time at the library, reading about Dr. King and other civil rights icons, Frederick Douglass and Ida B. Wells and James Baldwin and Fannie Lou Hamer. I wasn't into comic books.

Heroes of Love

These were my superheroes. And together, they summoned the power of Agape during other periods of turbulence and transformation to challenge America to live up to its founding aspirations, to challenge all of us to make the American project our own step-by-step, ballot-by-ballot, protest-by-protest, law-by-law. And why am I sharing this with you despite the vitriol all around us, despite the crackdowns, despite the insanity of our politics at this fraught, perilous moment? Because I believe with every fiber of my being that love, that Agape love, is the true path toward the world that we want.

Radical love. Audacious love. Defiant love. Love is how we turn that descending spiral of violence into a virtuous cycle. Love is how we reject anti-Semitism. We reject Islamophobia. We reject bigotry and homophobia. We repudiate the forces of autocracy and avarice.

Love is how we learn from the fullness of our histories, from the pride and the pain of our past, to prevent ourselves from being trapped by history. Love is how we dismantle the pernicious systems of caste, of racial inequality, that trick us into denying that your liberation is bound up with mine, and mine with yours. Love allows us to forgive. And I believe in love because of my own life, because of my own story.

A Personal Story

Allow me to get personal for a moment. I grew up in Springfield, Ohio. Alright. We got Ohioans everywhere. We like to leave Ohio. Springfield is a small, blue-collar city. My idol, my hero, my inspiration was my grandmother, Elmira Lloyd. She was the daughter of a preacher who later became the wife of a preacher.

Like I said, it's something of a family business. In our church, my mother directed the choir, my father played the drums, but my grandmother was the heart of it all, in her seat behind the organ. I remember vividly how after church, we would gather in her house every Sunday. She would cook collard greens, cornbread, chicken, and week after week, month after month, year after year, she would sit with me at the piano and taught me to play gospel music.

When you hear me playing today, you're hearing my grandmother in me. I wouldn't be the musician I am today without Elmira Lloyd. And then we lost her when I was just 10 years old. I was heartbroken, but nobody was more heartbroken, more lost, than my mother.

A Mother's Struggle

They were very close. They led the choir together. And after her mother died, my mother spiraled into depression and addiction. For a decade, she was out of our lives.

I felt cheated and angry. During this time, we were raised by our single father. My three siblings and I took care of each other, picking up whatever chores were necessary to keep the house going. I would cook dinner from the time I was like 12 years old.

Not a hamburger helper. I went to high school, applied to colleges, graduated from both high school and college, all without my mother in my life. And frankly, I didn't want anything to do with her at that time. I blamed her for failing us, for deserting us.

And I thought I had proven that I could succeed without her. And then one day, it hit me like a ton of bricks that my mom did what she did because she was in deep pain. She was alone. She didn't need punishment.

Healing Through Love

She needed love. She needed people to see her humanity, her real human frailty, to help her and give her a second chance. So one day, I looked into the eyes of the person who abandoned her family, my family, who for a decade left me deeply confused and deeply wounded, and I forgave. We had some difficult conversations with my siblings, some confrontations.

We listened. She listened. And together, with love as our North Star, we healed. Today, my relationship with my mother is as strong as ever. She just celebrated her 70th birthday with a big party back in Ohio a few weeks ago. She's a wonderful grandmother. She's living her best life. And it was this experience with my mother, and because of her, because of her encounters with the criminal justice system, because of some of my relatives' encounters with the criminal justice system, I was inspired to create my own organization called Free America.

Reforming the System

I learned about our country's addiction to mass incarceration, how the United States has just 5% of the world's population but 25% of its incarcerated people, how one in three black men will serve prison time, how more black men are under corrective control today than were enslaved on the eve of the Civil War.

And I listened. I met with people currently incarcerated, visited some of the state prisons here in California. I met with their families.

I met with survivors of crime. I met with district attorneys, correction officers, state legislators, civil rights activists. And what then followed was the most challenging, humbling, gratifying work of my life. I saw families forgive people who hurt their loved ones.

I saw some of the very people that perpetuated mass incarceration take steps to reform the system. I saw the people who put up the walls begin to tear them down. This is what love can do. Class of 2024, these are no ordinary times, no question about it.

The Solidarity Generation

But the history through which you lived, the history you've witnessed, the history you're making, all of this has made you extraordinary. And we need extraordinary now more than ever. The crucible of these last few years has forged in you the solidarity generation that resilience and resolve. It's forged strength of mind and character with deeper empathy perhaps than any generation before.

It's forged a conviction that you can change the world and that you must. Too much is at stake for you to fall prey to indifference or to fear or to division. You are prepared to be thinkers and creators, dreamers and doers, leaders for others, for our shared humanity, for justice. And I like to think that these last few years have instilled in you the recognition that love matters most of all.

The kind of love that has defined my life's journey. That radical, audacious, defiant love. Because if love could bring healing and forgiveness to my broken family, if the crime victims I met with can extend love and empathy and grace to the perpetrators who hurt their families, then we all can. In this hour of division, class of '24, this is what we all need.

Love Is the Greatest

As the Scripture says, "faith and hope and love. But the greatest of these is love." Because with love we can listen. With love we can understand. With love we can see ourselves in each other. We can discover our abiding mutuality. With love we can serve. With love we can heal.

We can build. We can do. We can undo. With love we can sing the words of my friend and idol, Stevie Wonder. "Good morning or evening, friends. Here's your friendly announcer. I've got serious news to pass on to everybody. You know that love's in need of love today. Oh, don't delay. Send yours in right away." We need love, LMU. Class of 2024, I'm so proud of you.

I'm so excited for you. I cannot wait to see how you will harness the power of love. I cannot wait to see what you will do for this world and for each other. From the bottom of my heart, I thank you.

I congratulate you. I love you all. And we are all counting on you, so let's go Lions. Thank you so much. God bless you. Thank you.

Print Citations

CMS: Legend, John. "I Cannot Wait to See How You Harness the Power of Love." Commencement speech at Loyola Marymount University, Los Angeles, CA, May 4, 2024. In *The Reference Shelf: Representative American Speeches, 2023–2024,* edited by Micah L. Issitt, 223–231. Amenia, NY: Grey House Publishing, 2024.

MLA: Legend, John. "I Cannot Wait to See How You Harness the Power of Love." Loyola Marymount University, 4 May 2024, Los Angeles, CA. Commencement speech. *The Reference Shelf: Representative American Speeches, 2023–2024,* edited by Micah L. Issitt, Grey House Publishing, 2024, pp. 223–231.

APA: Legend, J. (2024). I cannot wait to see how you harness the power of love [Speech]. Loyola Marymount University, Los Angeles, CA. In Micah L. Issitt (Ed.), *The reference shelf: Representative American speeches, 2023–2024* (pp. 223–231). Grey House Publishing. (Original work published 2024)

Index

1996 Communications Decency Act, 221
3Blue1Brown channel, 210

Abbas, Mahmoud, 184
Abbott, Greg, 81, 129
Affordable Care Act, 21, 28, 38, 167
America First Policy Institute, 82
American Civil War, 98
American democracy, 4, 111, 157, 158, 160, 161, 163, 198
American Federation of Teachers (AFT), 152, 154, 165
American Rescue Plan, 178
AmeriCorps, 50
antisemitism, 175, 176, 184
Army National Guard, 26
Arnold, Benedict, 99
Articles of the Constitution, 96
Arulanandam, Andrew, 81
Assange, Julian, 100
Austin, Lloyd, 113

Baldwin, James, 228
Barr, Bob, 81
Barrett, Amy Coney, 87
Biden, Joe, 3, 9, 10, 18, 23, 24, 26, 35, 36, 42, 47, 56, 59, 66, 82, 83, 84, 85, 87, 88, 89, 90, 91, 92, 96, 97, 100, 106, 107, 110, 111, 112, 113, 117, 120, 123, 129, 130, 131, 132, 133, 134, 135, 136, 137, 138, 140, 145, 148, 151, 157, 163, 171, 175, 176, 178, 183, 184, 195, 197, 203, 204, 206
Big Ag, 108, 118, 179
Big Pharma, 5, 28, 49, 108, 118, 179
Big Tech, 108, 123, 179, 221
Bill of Rights, 20, 96, 97, 98, 99, 100, 101, 102, 103, 104, 105

Bollea, Terry, 93
Booker, Brent, 165
border patrol agents, 134, 148, 150
Border Patrol Union, 149
Bush, George W., 101

Cannon, Aileen, 62
Capone, Al (Alphonse), 85, 86
Carrier Domes, 153
Censorship Project, 111
Chavez, Cesar, 6
Childhood Tax Credit, 178
Civil Rights Movement, 19, 166
Civil War, 5, 41, 98, 163, 204, 229
climate crisis, 4, 23, 206, 225
colonialism, 108
Comperatore, Corey, 61
Confederate flags, 163, 207
Constitutional Convention, 96
constitutional rights, 96, 97, 99, 101, 110
Continental Army, 157, 163
Copenhaver, James, 61
Cotton, Charles, 80
Coulter, Richard, 203
Covey, David, 82
COVID-19, 49, 64, 66, 69, 88, 96, 97, 99, 103, 105, 115, 123, 178
Creating Helpful Incentives to Produce Semiconductors (CHIPS) and Science Act, 151, 152

Dawes, William, 219
Declaration of Independence, 101, 102, 104, 136, 198
Democrat Party, 62
Democratic National Convention, 18, 26, 30, 35, 42, 44, 47, 178
Democratic Party, 3, 37, 109, 110, 111, 112, 204

234 Index

Dettelbach, Steve, 88
Dingell, Debbie, 165
Diplomatic Service, 188
Dixon, Tudor, 124
*Dobbs v. Jackson Women's Health
    Organization*, 7, 13, 15, 16
Doughty, Terry, 111
Douglass, Frederick, 228
Dutch, David, 61
Duterte, Rodrigo, 220

Eisenhower, Dwight D., 73
EUNAVFOR Operation Atalanta, 189
European Union, 188, 189

Facebook, 100, 111, 219, 220
Fain, Shawn, 165
Fallon, Pat, 81
Fifth Amendment, 99
First Amendment, 98, 100, 111
FISA Act, 101
Floyd, George, 205, 206
Founding Fathers, 96
Framers of the Constitution, 96
Freedom to Vote Act, 23
Freeman, Ruby, 158

Gaetz, Matt, 106
gaslighting, 9, 97
Gaza, 4, 23, 24, 42, 54, 171, 172, 173,
    174, 175, 176, 179, 189, 207, 219,
    222
Gianforte, Greg, 132
Giuliani, Rudy, 159
Global Democracy Index, 220
global security, 191
Gloria, Glenda, 220
Google, 100, 221
Gorsuch, Neil, 87
Graham, Billy, 77
Graham, Franklin, 77
Great Depression, 5, 178
Hagenbuch, Brent, 82
Hamas leaders, 171

Hamer, Fannie Lou, 228
Hannity, Sean, 87
Harris, Kamala, 6, 7, 11, 13, 18, 20,
    26, 28, 30, 31, 32, 33, 35, 36, 37,
    39, 41, 42, 43, 44, 46, 47, 49, 53,
    106, 120, 121, 123, 124, 125, 126,
    141, 143, 144, 145, 165, 175, 178,
    179
Harris, Shyamala, 18
Harvard Corporation, 217
Heinlein, Robert, 98
Hidalgo, Anne, 221
homophobia, 228
Hoosock, Michael, 151
House Select Committee on
    Assassinations, 102
Houthi attacks, 188
Houthi rebel pirates, 188
How to Stand up to a Dictator, 220
Hulk Hogan, 93
Huxley, Aldous, 98

imperialism, 108
Instagram, 100
ISIS, 64, 74, 75, 91, 123
Islamophobia, 175, 176, 228
Israel crisis, 23, 24, 66, 74, 76, 171,
    172, 173, 174, 175, 176, 181, 182,
    183, 184, 185, 186, 188, 207, 225,
    226, 227

Jackson, Ketanji Brown, 53
Jackson, Ronny, 81
Jefferson, Thomas, 3, 105
Jensen, Michael, 151
jobs and social rights, 188
John Lewis Voting Rights Act, 23
Johnson, Boris, 113
Jong Un, Kim, 24, 74

Kafka, Franz, 98
Kavanaugh, Brett, 87
Kelly, John, 53
Kemp, Brian, 131

Index   **235**

Kennedy v. Biden, 100
Kennedy, Robert F., 96
Kennedy, Robert F., Jr., 96, 108
Kerwin, Helen, 82
King, Martin Luther, 83, 204, 227
Koestler, Arthur, 98
Korean War, 26
Ku Klux Klan, 48
Kudlow, Larry, 87

Labor Day, 165, 166
Laborers' International Union of North
    America (LIUNA), 165
Lecter, Hannibal, 72
Lee, Bill, 130
Legend, John, 223
Lewis, John, 23, 44, 224
LGBTQ rights, 161
Libertarian National Convention, 96
Libertarian Party, 101, 105
Lincoln, Abraham, 3, 107, 114

Madison, James, 96, 100
Madoff, Bernie, 106
MAGA Republican, 53, 64, 81, 154,
    158, 159, 160, 162
maritime security, 188, 189
Marshall, Thurgood, 19
Mason, George, 96
McCarthy, Joe, 97
Means, Casey, 114
Medicaid, 178, 179
Medicare, 21, 22, 28, 37, 49, 55, 70,
    117, 125, 146, 167, 179
Meta, 218, 219, 221
military adventurism, 113
Minsk agreement, 113
misinformation, 3, 12, 82, 98, 100,
    101, 111, 198, 225
mismanagement, 59
Moss, Shaye, 158
Motley, Constance Baker, 19
Mudd, Harvey, 210, 214, 215
Murthy v. Biden, 100

Musk, Elon, 221

NAFTA, 69, 121
National Education Association
    (NEA), 165
National Guard, 26, 31, 47, 132, 133,
    135, 160, 204
National Labor Relations Board, 167
National Rifle Association (NRA), 80
Nazi Germany, 160
Nazi swastikas, 48
Netanyahu, Benjamin, 175, 181
NIH grants, 117
Nord Stream pipeline, 113
Nordisk, Novo, 117
North Atlantic Treaty Organization
    (NATO), 4, 23, 53, 112, 191, 192,
    193, 194, 195
nuclear weapons, 74, 75, 112, 185,
    192
Nungaray, Jocelyn, 73

Obama, Barack, 34, 35, 44, 71, 74, 75,
    81, 88, 91, 100, 124, 143
Obama, Michelle, 30, 33, 35
Obamacare, 38
Obrador, López, 149
Ocasio-Cortez, Alexandria, 42
online violence, 219
Operation "Prosperity Guardian," 189
Operation Artichoke, 102
Operation Bluebird, 102
Orbán, Viktor, 73, 74
Orwell, George, 98
Ozempic prescription, 117

PAC money, 106
PACT Act, 53
Palestinian Authority, 184
Parks, Rosa, 6
Peace Corps, 50
Pelosi, Nancy, 63, 197
Pence, Mike, 158
Perot, Ross, 110

236 Index

Planned Parenthood, 11, 13
Pringle, Becky, 165
PRO Act, 167, 179
Project Labor Agreement, 153
Putin, Vladimir, 4, 23, 53, 54, 110, 112, 113, 161, 191, 193

racial inequality, 228
racial justice, 47, 203
Rappler, 217, 218, 219, 220
Red Scare, 97
Red Sea, 188, 189
Republican Governor Association, 130
Republican National Convention, 59, 93, 106
Republican Party, 59, 62, 67, 86
Ressa, Maria, 217
Revere, Paul, 219-220
Revolutionary War, 99
Riley, Laken, 73, 144
Robinson, Mark, 83
Roe v. Wade, 7, 8, 9, 10, 13, 16, 52, 55
Rogers, Mike, 123, 124
Rollins, Brooke, 82
Romo, Tony, 82, 83
Roosevelt, Franklin, 3
Russian aerial attacks, 195
Russian disinformation, 218
Russian hostility, 195
Russian invasion of Ukraine, 195

Salman, Muhammed Bin, 184
Sanders, Bernie, 178
Sanders, Sarah Huckabee, 131
Sanderson, Grant, 210
Schoolcraft, Alan, 82
Schumer, Chuck, 151
Second Amendment, 27, 84, 85, 88, 99
Secret Service agents, 60
Slevin, James, 165
Slotkin, Elissa, 165
Snowden, Edward, 100

Social Security, 21, 22, 26, 28, 37, 55, 70, 109, 146, 167, 179
Solzhenitsyn, Alexander, 98
Space Force, 64, 88
Stefanik, Elise, 155
Steube, Greg, 81
Stevens, Haley, 165
Stoltenberg, Jens, 191, 192, 193, 194

Taney, Roger, 98
Texas Department of Public Safety, 129, 130
Texas National Guard, 135
Thanedar, Shri, 165
Thompson, Priscilla, 134
TikTok, 218
totalitarianism, 98
Traxler, Sarah, 11, 13
Trump, Donald, 7, 8, 9, 21, 22, 23, 24, 27, 28, 29, 32, 35, 36, 38, 42, 47, 48, 49, 51, 52, 53, 54, 55, 59, 61, 66, 68, 69, 70, 71, 74, 80, 81, 83, 85, 93, 94, 96, 97, 98, 99, 100, 106, 107, 108, 109, 110, 112, 113, 114, 117, 118, 119, 120, 121, 122, 123, 124, 125, 126, 138, 139, 141, 145, 146, 148, 157, 158, 159, 160, 161, 162, 163, 167, 179, 184, 193, 197
Trump, Melania, 62
Turney, Edmund, 203
Twitter, 100, 221

U.S. Capitol, 21, 158
U.S. Constitution, 96, 97, 99, 130, 136, 160
U.S. Department of Justice, 86, 149
U.S. Marine Corps, 124
U.S. military, 113, 115, 150, 160
U.S. national security, 113
U.S. Supreme Court, 4, 5, 7, 11, 16, 21, 22, 45, 52, 53, 87, 88, 98, 100, 145, 158, 179, 206, 208, 218
Ukraine war, 112, 113, 114, 118

United Arab Emirates (UAE), 181, 182
United Auto Workers (UAW), 69, 165
United Nations Armed Trade Treaty, 88
United Nations General Assembly, 181
United Nations Security Council, 188, 191
USMCA, 69
utility workers, 165

Vance, James David "J.D.," 27-28, 63, 107, 120
Vietnam War, 53, 97
vigilantism, 137

Walz, Tim, 11, 18, 26, 32, 33, 37, 38, 39, 41, 42, 46, 47, 120, 124, 126
War on Drugs, 97

War on Terror, 97
Washington, George, 3, 157, 162, 163
wealth inequality, 120, 179
Weingarten, Randi, 152, 165
Wells, Ida B., 228
White, William Jefferson, 203
Williams, Brandon, 154
Williams, Talithia, 214
Williams, Tessie Prevost, 45
Winfrey, Oprah, 44
Witkoff, Steve, 82
women's rights, 7, 161
Wonder, Stevie, 230
World War III, 65, 84, 125

YouTube, 100, 111, 210, 213

Zelenskyy, Volodymyr, 113, 193, 195
Zuckerberg, Mark, 220